What Men Owe to Women

What Men Owe to Women

Men's Voices from World Religions

Edited by

John C. Raines
and
Daniel C. Maguire

STATE UNIVERSITY OF NEW YORK PRESS

Published by
State University of New York Press, Albany

For information, address State University of New York Press,
90 State Street, Suite 700, Albany, NY 12207

Production by Kristin Milavec
Marketing by Fran Keneston

Library of Congress Cataloging-in-Publication Data

What men owe to women : men's voices from world religions / edited by
John C. Raines and Daniel C. Maguire.
    p.   cm.
    Includes bibliographical references and index.
    ISBN 0-7914-4785-5 (alk. paper)—ISBN 0-7914-4786-3 (pbk. : alk. paper)
    1. Women and religion.   I. Raines, John C.   II. Maguire, Daniel C.

  BL458 .W47 2001
  291.1'78344—dc21   00-027494

10 9 8 7 6 5 4 3 2 1

To the memory of
Ze'ev Falk

Contents

Introduction

John C. Raines

GENDER PROVIDES A REVEALING entrance into the world's religious traditions. How gender is viewed reflects itself not simply in the moral practices of those traditions, but in their metaphysics. Gender shapes their worldview and ethos. In Taoism, for example, ultimate reality is feminine, and what is seen as truly powerful is what adapts and adjusts. Judaism, Christianity, and Islam privilege the masculine. For these religions, what counts for ultimacy is the power to control and command. Religions are gendered entities, although often presenting themselves as something simply natural or God-ordained, and therefore objective and universal. Viewing the various religions through the lens of gender, as we do in this volume, opens up a hidden landscape. It reveals what is usually veiled, puts voices into officially sanctioned silences, and makes more complex what we see and hear and learn from the past. It enriches our grasp upon the heritage of the sacred.

But the purpose of this volume reaches beyond intellectual enrichment. As authors, we intend to be advocates. We intend to pursue gender justice. And that task demands of us that we be critical but also constructive. Even as we unveil the patriarchal bias that so often embeds itself in the sacred, we seek to appropriate from that heritage more positive resources. Each of the religious traditions has a strong theory of social justice, and these resources can be harnessed to contemporary issues of gender. It is this constructive purpose that has persuaded us to focus our analysis upon the classical texts and thinkers of our religious traditions. We ask, how can our Scriptures, how can our founding Prophets, how can our ancestors be used today to further justice in relations between the genders?

It is a question that seems to us unavoidable. Like our personal genetic inheritance, we cannot simply walk away from our religious past. That past is alive and powerful within our various cultures, even those that seem quite secular. Two-thirds of the world's humans affiliate with one or another of the world religions. And the other third continues to live out cultural scripts whose deep roots reach back into religion. To pursue gender justice demands of us as authors that we engage actively in the struggle over interpretation, the struggle over the perceived meanings of the texts and teachings of our religious legacies. It is a contentious terrain precisely because it continues to deeply affect people in their daily lives. Yes, interpreting the sacred is a scholarly task, but it is also a highly political task, because interpreting the sacred shapes how power is used in society. To interpret the religious tradition is to enter a conflict and to make a choice. Our appropriation of our heritage is never neutral; it displays our intention and purpose for its use. It is taking up sides even if, or perhaps especially if it claims not to.

Taking sides means having your feet on the ground; it means knowing where you stand. And today, the ground upon which all humans stand is changing. The way of human life on this planet is being transformed more rapidly and more profoundly than ever before in history. Global capitalism, a set of economic and political institutions but also of pervasive cultural values, is everywhere more and more revolutionizing the on-the-ground conditions of human living. For example, for the first time in history the poor of the world (overwhelmingly women and their children) need money. In all of previous history subsistence living, day by day survival, was "in the hands" of the poor themselves. They could grow or gather food, sew garments, and build shelters out of indigenous natural materials.

Today the global market has drawn the everyday life of the poor into a worldwide money system. Everywhere in the world, survival involves the eternal struggle to make money. Rice, corn, and grain cost money. Tin and lumber and store-bought clothes cost money. Even clean water costs money! This is why the poor, in the most massive and sudden migration in all of history, are flocking to the cities. They need paid work to survive, and the cities mean money. Village life, life embedded in the extended family, with all of its oppressions but also its protection—its material but even more its moral resources for daily survival—is unraveling. In rural areas all around the world the young leave for the cities, looking for paid work. Poor women already living in the cities look for paid work, and their children look for paid work, even if it's only peddling cigarettes or water bottles to motorists on clogged city streets. Money, used in the past by the special few for purposes of ostentation or conquest, has today found its way into the intimacies of daily survival. Modern reality is pervasively monetized.

As modern interpreters of our religious traditions, we have had to take very seriously the fact that our religions were shaped in their classical period under circumstances of everyday life vastly different from the new world being born out of the global market. Today these religious traditions often seem uprooted, outdated, and cast aside, or they appear compulsively to hold onto a past that inevitably continues to slip away. Posing to ourselves the issue of gender justice requires of us a double mediation—not simply to interpret the sacred texts as to their original gender meanings, but as a mediation between the world within which those originating texts first took shape and our modern world, with its vastly transformed terrain of power and cultural values.

Moreover, in responding to the task of interpretation, we address very different audiences. Our strategies of interpreting the sacred texts must necessarily respond to the politics of local religious situations. If we wish to be heard, we must speak in a way that is deemed religiously acceptable. Nowhere is this more evident than in how, as authors, we differ in applying criticism to the most sacred texts and honored teachings of our traditions—those held to be revelation. Some of us privilege that revelation from direct criticism, claiming that the words and teachings of the founder or the Prophet, if properly interpreted, support gender justice. And they do this in debate with those in their indigenous cultures who use those same texts to define and confine women to subjugated social positions. For example, the orthodox rabbi Ze'ev W. Falk places himself in debate with other orthodox rabbis in Israel, and in that context makes "revolutionary" suggestions that will appear to the nonorthodox North American reader as extraordinarily modest. But in his own context, Falk confesses to having a hard time finding a publisher. Or a scholar of Islam, Asghar Ali Engineer of India, literally puts his life on the line (four attempts have been made on his life) by insisting that only the Qur'anic material is authoritative for Muslims and that everything else (the recorded sayings of the Prophet, the body of Islamic laws, etc.) is conditioned by its historical (which means patriarchal) context. Still another Muslim scholar, Farid Esack of South Africa, speaking out of a different cultural setting, deals critically with the Qur'an itself in a fashion that causes him to be accused of "no longer being a Muslim," in response to which he replies: "Am I seriously to believe that on the Day of Final Judgment God will ask, How did you deal with my text?!"

Or again, a scholar of Theravada Buddhism, Tavivat Puntarigvivat, uses his religious heritage to address the issue of justice for poor women in Thailand, particularly the tragedy of prostitution and AIDS in that country, in a way that may appear to many Western readers as simply quaint. But how in fact to improve the concrete lives of women is always a culturally specific and particularized task. For some, the chance to become a fully ordained nun, under the religious supervision of one's peers, may offer a surer path to freedom and dignity than access to a professional career. For other women, making the religiously sanctioned ways of divorce more difficult or revising the religiously sanctioned practices of burial rites may do more to improve their standing in society than expanding university enrollments (which should also be done). The language of human rights is becoming widely shared around the world, but those rights can be articulated only in the particularity of diverse cultural locations.

Exposed to this pluralism of critical strategies, the readers of this volume are invited to expand and to make more complex the vision of what gender justice requires. Each of us live in the parochialism of our own culture, which is most assuredly the case where this expresses itself by denying that it is parochial, by thinking of itself, for example, as "advanced and developed" in the face of other cultures viewed as backward. The discussion of gender justice places all of us, not just some of us, in unexpected territory, and that's the excitement that this volume invites you to enter.

Another issue needs examination here at the onset. It is an undeniable fact that we are a group of all-male scholars. How strange but not untypical, it could be said, to exclude the female voice from a discussion about "what men owe to women!" But sexism is a problem we men have. It becomes a problem for women only because men, almost everywhere and always, have had power over women, power we have used to advance our own positions. Our tasks as males and as scholars are not to discover what men should do for women, but how as men we can liberate ourselves from the intellectual and moral perversion of sexism. "What men owe to women" is not more paternalism but more honesty, and based upon that honesty active collaboration with women in culturally specific struggles for gender justice.

Moreover, the female voice was not, in fact, excluded from the production of this volume. Generous support from the Ford, John D. and Catherine T. MacArthur foundations allowed the authors, coming literally from around the world, to meet face-to-face, once before beginning our writing and again after reading each others' initial drafts. Not only were we sharply critical of each other, but in our second meeting we met with a panel of four, highly regarded women feminist scholars of religion. All of this produced many hours of heated debate, usually cordial but not always. The criticisms were vigorous. But we were also vigorous in our listening, in our learning to hear the inevitable diversity within which our shared goal of gender justice is culturally embedded. The resulting chapters are stronger, which is a process that can be partially traced in the accompanying footnotes. Still, in the end there was no consensus, and indeed could not have been, either among the men or between the men and women. What we could do and did do was learn from our diversities rather than deplore them. There is no single path or uniform way to pursue gender justice given the heterogeneity of human life in culture. But that does not mean we have nothing to say to each other. We need to be self-critical, and that needs the critique of our own criticism by others outside our culture. That is a process we believe we have begun in this volume, but only begun. We invite you as our readers to pick a fight with us. That is what we've done with each other. A good argument is a rare accomplishment and is the only thing that can knock us off balance and make us take the next step.

Summarizing to this point:

1. Gender offers a powerful entrance into the world religions because religion both reflects how gender is constructed in society and then assigns social privilege and disprivilege on the basis of that reflection.

2. Interpretation of our religious tradition is always a political act, demanding that we choose sides regarding how power works in society.

3. The diversity of audiences intended to be influenced by these chapters necessarily shapes how differing authors deploy their critical analysis; effective arguments must be culturally specific, and no culture holds a privileged position.

4. The plurality of the world's cultures requires a plurality of strategies to pursue gender justice within those cultures; proposals that work must be culturally specific.

These are four of the larger issues that can help orient the reader to this volume. But they need to be supplemented by more specific introductions. Who are we as a group? Who are we as individual scholars?

We are a group of ten scholars of world religions drawn together by the Religious Consultation on Population, Reproductive Health, and Ethics. Under the guidance of its president, Professor Daniel C. Maguire of Marquette University in Milwaukee, the Consultation has undertaken a series of initiatives to bring religion and the well-being of women around the world into a more friendly and productive relationship. As Maguire has written: "The Religious Consultation's overall goal is to promote internationally the voices of progressive religious scholars on the issues of population, ecology, reproductive health and the empowerment of women."

Regarding the individual scholars of *What Men Owe to Women*, several of the women feminist critics responding to our first drafts remarked upon the importance of "fully contexturalizing" the authors. Only in this way, they argued, could we dispel the notion that we speak from an impartial or abstractly scholarly position. We are not only men, they noted, but very particular men located socially, culturally, religiously, and historically in very particular ways. Because we are highly educated, for example, we enjoy class privileges within our cultures of origin. Speaking out of our religious traditions on behalf of gender justice, we realize that the vast majority of women in the twenty-first century in Third-World countries will live and die in poverty. Their personal life stories as poor women, daughters, wives, and mothers struggling to survive, are and will remain sharply different from our own. And it is our voices, not their's, which you will hear. That is why we owe you readers an introduction, however brief, to our personal stories, so that you can put our voices in context. The stories are presented in the order in which the authors appear in the text.

Liu Xiaogan was born in 1947, two years before the People's Republic of China was established. His parents were both members of the People's Liberation Army, and he spent the first two years of his life dragged from one battlefield to the next. After that, Liu was raised in Beijing and in Tianjin, two of China's largest cities. Because his parents did not join the Communist Party, the family was consigned to a marginalized position in society. He remembers that during the early 1960s in what is officially remembered as "the three difficult years," when food was in short supply, a chicken their family used for eggs suddenly died. Without telling anyone, his mother, who suspected the chicken died of disease, nevertheless cooked it and tasted it. Only the next day, when she had not fallen ill did she tell the family that the chicken was their's to eat. To this day, Liu remembers how his mother risked her life to feed her family.

In 1968, during the Great Cultural Revolution, Liu and his sister were sent to Inner Mongolia to do farm work as "pupils" of the local peasants. There Liu learned firsthand what it meant to live, as he put it, "at the bottom of the country." In 1973 he entered college; and in 1978, having scored first on an entry exam, he started the process of becoming one of the first batch of Ph.D. holders bestowed by the Chinese government. His field was Chinese philosophy, and he graduated in 1985 from Beijing University. During the tragedy at Tian'anmen Square in 1989 he was a visiting scholar at the Harvard-Yenching Institute. He decided not to return to his position at Beijing University and now teaches at the National University of Singapore. He specializes in Taoist studies and has published widely in Chinese, English, and Korean. About his research he says:

> My studies in Taoism give me the general idea that the weak may finally overcome the strong, and the soft may change the hard. I admire my mother, grandmother, and my wife, not because they

are women sacrificing for men, but because they are representatives of the spirit and power of the weaker part of the world, which is usually underestimated. . . . I think not only women, but also men, should apply the principle of femininity to realize gender justice and harmony, in addition to remedying the mistakes and disaster caused by global capitalism, which is in a sense the representative of masculine force.

Fleeing in the face of the Japanese invasion, Tavivat Puntarigvivat's parents left southern China and settled in Bangkok, where Tavivat was born in 1950. Influenced by both Thai and Chinese Buddhist cultures, he was at first drawn to studies in economics and graduated from Thammasat University in Bangkok in 1972. But he became dissatisfied with that field and felt powerfully drawn into comparative religious studies. A Rockefeller Scholarship led to an M.A. in philosophy—from the East and West Institute of the University of Hawaii in 1975. Later in 1984–1986 a Japanese Ministry of Education Scholarship allowed him to pursue further studies in Zen Buddhism at Kyoto University.

According to Tavivat, what changed his life was the time he spent in 1980 as a *bhikkhu* (a Buddhist monk) in poverty-stricken northeast Thailand, where he received his daily food as a gift from poor villagers who barely had enough to eat for themselves. This experience allowed him to combine religious studies with social activism. A year later, he took a sabbatical leave from his teaching post at Mahidol University in Bangkok and returned to a remote Buddhist monastery in order to write a book on the history of religion in China and Japan. As before, although now he was lay, "the poor villagers provided daily food to me as they did to the monks!" He became determined to do whatever he could to improve the well-being of these poor villagers, and especially the young girls sent off to the city as prostitutes.

Tavivat was drawn to the religious and social teachings of the Thai Buddhist monk and activist, Bhikkhu Buddhadasa. He wrote his doctoral dissertation at Temple University using Latin American liberation theology to critique the "Dhammic socialism" of Buddhadasa as lacking in a systematic or structural analysis of global political economy. Today, Tavivat is the chairperson of the Comparative Religion Graduate Program at Mahidol University in Bangkok. He has published six books in the Thai language, three of which have been translated into English and writes a weekly column for the *Bangkok Business News*.

Rabbi Ze'ev W. Falk was rector of the Seminary of Judaic Studies in Jerusalem. After a brief but severe illness he died on September 19, 1998. Unfortunately we were not able to get from him before he died personal stories of his life. At the time of his death he was working on

"A Commentary on the Pentateuch" and on a book on "The Theology of Torah." He previously published several volumes in Hebrew, English, and German on ethical issues facing contemporary Judaism. Since we lack his own words, I turn to the comments by Dr. Laurie Zoloth-Dorfman, one of our four women feminist respondents and the chairperson of Social Ethics and Jewish Studies at San Francisco State University, who had known Ze'ev for nearly fifteen years. In a letter to Daniel Maguire she wrote: "It is very hard to imagine Judaism without him! We will miss him very, very much, as a leader, teacher, rabbi, legal scholar, and friend." She wrote about the last night she saw him, in 1998 in Philadelphia:

> It is the end of Shabbat, and we had spent the day walking, and joking and seriously talking of family and work, and had a wonderful meal, and now the fireflies are out, and the men have gone back to talk about their book. It is a warm July night, and the dark lawn is wet, and the shadows of small creatures move across it. The woods are lit with fireflies, and I think they are like stars, or like havdalah candles in the dark world at the end of Shabbat, flickering for a moment, and then gone, barely imagined—is there light? Is it real?

> There is another light in the otherwise dark world. It is the circle of light over the table in the room where the men are meeting. I walk by; they do not see me. I watch them for a long moment, me in the dark air, they circled around each other, bent over the texts and papers. Ze'ev has his hand in the air, his face lit up by a question. So? he is asking, and bending his head to hear the response. I had thought to write to Ze'ev and tell him of the hopefulness it creates for me to know that such rooms are lit in the world.

> Please, in your book, be sure to tell those who may not know, how rare a man this one was, how daring, how much a mensch, and an elegant and kind one.

This, then, was Ze'ev W. Falk. All of the members of the *What Men Owe to Women* team agreed that this collection should be dedicated to his memory.

Farid Esack was abandoned by his father when he was three weeks old. He and his five older brothers were raised by a single mother who rose before dawn to work in a factory and returned after dark. Working like that, day after day and year after year, she would "under the burden" die an early death. Of those years he remembers: "long periods passed during which we had no shoes and I recall running barefoot across the frost-covered fields to school." But the hardship he endured resulted from more than personal misfortune.

Consigned by apartheid to live on the poorest and most barren of land set aside for "non-whites," Farid remembers that "on our Christian [Black] neighbors we depended for a cup of sugar, a rand until Friday, and a shoulder to cry on."

Shared oppression led young Farid to reject notions of religious exclusivity, even as he began to develop a more intense interest in Islam. "I was strangely and deeply religious as a child," he said, "with a deep concern for the suffering which I experienced and witnessed all around me . . . and an indomitable belief that for God to be God, God had to be just and on the side of the marginalized." Farid was still in high school when he was first detained by the security police of South Africa.

After that, he spent eight years on a scholarship in Pakistan studying Islamic theology. It was "a frightfully conservative institute" and deeply suspicious of other religions. But his experience of being a Muslim and a minority in South Africa made him alert to the religious persecution aimed at Christians and Hindus in Pakistan. Moreover, he became aware "of the many similarities between the oppression of women in Muslim society and that of Blacks in apartheid."

Once back in South Africa, Farid joined the resistance. He helped found the "Call of Islam"— affiliated with the interreligious United Democratic Front—the major liberation movement still operating inside that country in the 1980s. After years of resistance, of strengthening interreligious alliances and, yes, of further detentions, and joining their efforts with the outlawed African National Congress, they would defeat apartheid.

Today, Farid is a senior researcher at the Institute of Religion, Identity, and Culture at the University of the Western Cape. He is a commissioner of gender equality for South Africa and is widely published on gender, liberation theology, interfaith relations, and Qur'anic hermeneutics. He writes regularly for the Muslim press, both locally and around the world. Of his strange journey, he once wrote: "The religious act is always both a faithfulness to a tradition, and a restatement and a rupture, a novelty in relation to a personal history. The act of believing is a decision that finds real meaning based on a tradition, yet drawing away from it with a view to re-creation." The author continues this journey into disruption and re-creation in this volume.

It is not just that Asghar Ali Engineer argues on behalf of the rights of Muslim women. In the turmoil of poverty and greed that is the social reality of modern India, religion has become radically politicized. For many Muslims, as for many Hindus, strict adherence to conservative beliefs is the only sure sign of fidelity to one's own kind. And Asghar argues that only the Qur'an is authoritative, not the sayings of the Prophet or the Shari'ah, the body of traditional laws. Concerning the latter two, Asghar holds powerful reservations as to the degree to which they are infected by the particularity of their original historical and social contexts. He uses the Qur'an to criticize their legitimation of the patriarchal oppression of women.

How did he come to a position that is considered so dangerous by many of his fellow believers in India? He was, after all, born into a most pious and traditional Muslim home. In his own words: "I was born into a family of a Bohra Muslim priest and raised in an intensely religious atmosphere." From early childhood he studied not only the Qur'an, but also *tafsir* (commentary), *hadith* (the Prophet's sayings), Islamic jurisprudence, and *aqa'id* (dogmatics). Although Asghar's mother tongue was Gujrati, he studied and became fluent in Arabic, Persian, and Urdu. He also studied European languages and "developed a keen interest in philosophy and wrote articles in leading Urdu journals on Spinoza, Kant, Hegel, Bertrand Russell, Sartre, and Marx."

But it was not his interest in European philosophy that got him in trouble. "I went to college and graduated in civil engineering and this contributed to my secular and rational outlook, though I remained intensely religious in my orientation." He became convinced by his studies of the Qur'an "that the Qur'an is very open to other religions, advocates pluralism and gender justice. Thus I began to write on women's rights in Islam." Asghar also became a public critic of the Bohra Muslim priesthood because "it was highly authoritarian and did not permit any freedom of thought or reinterpretation of the Qur'an and Shari'ah." In response: "I was assaulted nearly fatally four times—thrice in India and once in Egypt inside the mosque." Concerning his own beliefs he maintains: "I am no less committed to Islam than any other Muslim, but my views and understanding differ from the fundamentalists."

When you read Asghar's arguments remember that these are arguments for the rights of Muslim women based upon the Qur'an for which the writer lives in India today under constant threat of death.

There was no culturally sanctioned reason why Mutombo Nkulu-N'Sengha's father took only one wife. Neither he nor his wife were Christian. They were the son and daughter of chiefs in the ancient Luba empire region in what was in 1959 called the "Belgian Congo," and polygamy was a common practice among the Baluba. But today, Mutombo remembers his father's decision as the first lesson he learned in "what men owe to women." The instruction contradicted other practices he saw around him as a young boy. "The beating of wives was pretty much part of daily life. Some uncles practiced polygamy and one divorced because his wife had only girls."

In the thirty-nine years between then and now, Mutombo has become fluent in six Bantu languages (Kiluba, Swahili, Lingala, Kizeela,

Kisanga, and Kihemba) and three European languages (French, Italian, and English) with a passing knowledge of Spanish, Latin, Greek, biblical Hebrew, hieroglyphics, and Coptic. But he remembers that the Jesuits who were his first teachers "advised the Belgian colonial regime that it was not good to create universities because Congolese people were not mature enough for such learning."

Another of his early instructors was our country's CIA, who arranged for the assassination of the Marxist-leaning but democratically appointed first prime minister of the Congo, Patrice Lumumba. As Mutombo says: "having lived under the dictatorship of Mobutu [who then came into power] since 1965, the issues of social justice became a focal concern of my life and my thought." About these early years he says: "I grew up in a world marked by both traditional religion and Christianity. However, everybody spoke African languages and the daily life was marked by the traditional worldview."

Eventually, Mutombo would train to become a Jesuit priest, first in the local seminary at Lubumbashi, Zaire, then at the Gregorian in Rome. He gained certificates in Egyptology and political science, and received a B.A. in theology and an M.A. in philosophy—all from the Gregorian—and, after deciding against ordination, came to the Department of Religion at Temple University where he is currently finishing his doctorate. About his education Mutombo says: "my initiation in traditional culture and education allows me to look critically at both tradition and modernity, both African and Western cultures."

As a scholar teaching at Dartmouth College, Christopher Ronwanièn:te Jocks situates himself among his own Iroquois relatives in the Kanien'keha':ka (or Mohawk) Territory, near Montreal. From that standpoint, Chris reminds us of a still living but intensely marginalized space called "North American First Nations," where "global structures of male hegemony have long attempted the same lethal eradication of alternatives posed by indigenous societies, as they have of alternatives posed by women within their own." About this space Chris claims: "in fact some have created, built, and maintained societies that are seen as models of mutual respect and shared power between genders. Among these are the communities of the Longhouse People, the Iroquois, from whom I descend, and among whom most of my relatives are counted." Chris remembers that "my Mohawk grandmother and aunts never had to convince anyone among their male relatives to take their advice, their opinions, their contributions, seriously."

But that is a memory that had to be recovered, because Chris did not in fact grow up among these relatives. And it is due to this fact that he credits his second source of concern for "what men owe to women." "My (Iroquois) father served for twenty-three years in the military, and from age seven until I left for college I grew up in a working-class neighborhood in southern California." It was there that Chris first learned from that severe but powerful teacher called "grief." "There I witnessed two processes that I would always see as related, symbolically if not directly: the degradation of the natural environment around me and my (Irish American) mother's journey into deep depression." He speaks of her quitting college for marriage and motherhood, of her struggle "because of her strong ideals, her strong activist temperament, her illness, and her isolated life as a housewife." The culture of southern California in the 1970s had little place for the sacred, either the sacredness of the land or the sacredness of human community. Our human connectedness to land, to each other, and to what Chris calls the "relationships between human and Other-than-human species"—these forgotten and abused dimensions of life, the feminine—Chris saw everywhere around him giving way to the male preoccupation with control, exploitation, and success.

He wrote to Dan Maguire, our convener, about his concern for presenting indigenous religious traditions, whose insights and power are not preserved in grand texts and written commentaries but rather in the fragile face-to-face of storytelling, poetry, and community ritual. Dan wrote back: "I believe that even in the text-heavy traditions the main messages are delivered in ways not unlike the native traditions. My ritually and poetically rich mother was more influential on me than Thomas Aquinas." In his classes at Dartmouth, Chris insists that his students consider "First Nations religious thought and action not as a curiosity, not as something romantic or inspiring but exotic and essentially impractical. Rather, I insist that they use their limited understanding of these traditions to question and critique the ideas, the definitions, the structures of relationship that inform and claim to determine the scope of their own lives."

Seeing the religious other not as an object of exotic appreciation but as a perspective of critical distance upon one's own, always parochial perspective—this is the task each chapter in this volume pursues and invites you, our readers, to pursue.

Gerard S. Sloyan was born into a Roman Catholic family in New York City. Out of that family of origin, three would enter into the religious vocation. Gerry became a parish priest and a Catholic educator. About all this he writes: "my interest in the place of women in the Catholic church began, I think, with twelve years of quality education at the hands of religious Sisters. Two of my sisters entered that life, and were educated at the doctoral level by the church." One would become the president of the college where she began as a teacher of mathematics. The other became a specialist on the liturgy. The reform of the public worship of the church was also an early concern of Gerry, and as a leading member of a national Liturgical Conference he helped "bring on what became the reform of all the sacramental rites" by the Second Vatican Council.

It was only after the council (1965), and especially after the revision of church law in response to that council (1983) that Gerry, in his own words: "began to see that women remained voiceless in the Catholic church in matters touching their own sexuality and their capacity for leadership." He speculates about the reason for that. "Although I have been an ordained priest for fifty-five years, it dawned on me slowly— academic clerical life being different in many respects—that clericalism is the problem. Catholic women tend to think that the celibate life is at its root. But identical patterns of dominance by married clergy has made me think otherwise. I see the problem as one of male inadequacy bolstered by cultures worldwide that have ceded authority in the home, in the polis, and in all the religions to men."

Gerry became a specialist in New Testament Studies and in the early Fathers of the church. From that perspective he argues there can be no doubt. From apostolic times it has been the conviction of the church that "coming to birth renders all humans equal. Religiously, this equality is intensified by the initiatory rite into the church of baptism." But he admits: "Christians have been slow learners about the implications of their faith. There is retrograde thinking and acting, even in our day." Nevertheless, Gerry concludes that "in the Catholic church it becomes increasingly clear on all the continents and islands, that the male hegemony is over, as the Christian Scriptures demand."

Marvin M. Ellison is a professor of Christian Ethics at Bangor Seminary in Maine. He tells much of his personal story about how he came to issues of "what men owe to women" in his chapter, so this introduction can be more brief. Marvin was born and grew up as a relatively privileged white male in the old South, under the strict segregationist practices of Jim Crow. Early he learned how the white church was complicit with this iniquitous "peculiar institution." But he also witnessed in the civil rights movement of the 1960s church, mostly black but also white, which became a center first of resistance and then of successful rebellion. About that he says: "I prize my Southern roots and the heritage of a faith tradition that places justice-making at the center of spirituality." As a "scholar-activist," he speaks of himself today as "a social mystic who believes that the power and presence of God are most real for me in my connections with others. Broken, unjust, and alienated relationships frustrate and impede our God connection as well as our experience of community." Marvin coauthored the 1992 Presbyterian Church study of sexuality entitled *Keeping Body and Soul Together*. He is a single (and sole-surviving) parent of a teenage daughter and has been active in gay rights, as well as in prochoice and antiviolence work. About institutionalized religion he says: "I stay with the church, despite all its many shortcomings, because this community has an explicit mandate to seek justice and compassion for all the world, . . . although it often fails to fully honor this commitment." Still, at its best, "the church offers a kind of free zone to experiment with freedom and try on this radical call to inclusivity and mutual well-being for all."

Anantanand Rambachan was born in Trinidad. His great-grandparents had migrated to that Caribbean island during a time of famine in North India. Both of his grandfathers "served the Hindu community as priests, performing domestic rituals and sacraments in homes, celebrating festivals in temples, and reading and expounding sacred texts." Although of the Brahmin caste, Anantanand's own mother suffered from the gender bias of their tradition. Anantanand writes about it this way.

> My own mother was married at the age of twelve, after just three years of primary school education. In the living room of our family home in Trinidad, there is a framed original of her last school report card. Her grades and class rank reveal her to have been among the brightest in her class. She still speaks with sadness about the fact that her education was abruptly ended and that many of her male classmates went on to successful professional careers. Women of my mother's generation had limited choices.

Choice became a burning issue for Anantanand at the University of the West Indies. It was the late 1960s and early 1970s and "Black consciousness" was challenging "the Europocentric curriculum with its demeaning and prejudicial assumptions about the significance of African and Indian history and culture." Later, when studying under the late Swami Chinmayananda, Anantanand got another lesson in choice. His swami "provoked the ire of orthodox authorities in India by his willingness to allow women and students of all castes to study the sacred texts of Hinduism." About his own study Anantanand claims that "the Upanishads convinced me that Hinduism expounded an uncompromising doctrine of the spiritual equality of all human beings that contradicted and challenged its social structure of caste and gender inequality."

Anantanand completed his doctorate at the University of Leeds in the United Kingdom. It was there that he found students from other traditions who shared his views.

> The religious life, I grew to see more clearly, is not only about one's relationship to the absolute, but also about the quality of one's relationship with one's fellow beings. The concern for social and eco-

nomic justice which I saw in my Asian Christian and African friends resonated sympathetically in my own heart, and I sought and found similar values in Hinduism. The doctrine of nonviolence, for example, while traditionally interpreted in very narrow ways, implies justice and liberation from oppression.

Today, Anantanand teaches at St. Olaf College in Minnesota, where the female students "have made me much more aware of the patriarchal biases in the Hindu tradition and of the ways in which the voices and concerns of women have been silenced in sacred texts." Also, in 1987 his first child and daughter, Ishanaa, was born. Anantanand concludes: "I owe it to her as a father and as a scholar to question and challenge structures of inequality and to ensure that the tradition to which we belong helps her in freedom and responsibility to realize her wonderful gifts and potential in the service of all beings."

As stated earlier, we male authors gained critical distance upon our own standpoints by criticizing each other's early drafts. This was a vigorous process and, at the final stage of revision, made even more vigorous by the added voices of four women feminist scholars. I list their names here not because they in any sense endorse these final products of our (male) efforts. Rather, they were an important part of the process and deserve recognition. They are: Christine Gudorf, Riffat Hassan, Eva Neumaier-Dargyay, and Laurie Zoloth-Dorfman. Dr. Gudorf teaches in the Department of Religious Studies at Florida International University and is a leading Catholic ethicist. Some of her publications are *Catholic Social Teaching on Liberation Themes; Women's Consciousness, Women's Conscience: A Reader in Feminist Ethics;* and *Body, Sex and Pleasure: Reconstructing Christian Sexual Ethics.* Dr. Hassan is one of the world's leading feminist Muslim scholars. She is the chairperson of the Department of Religion at the University of Louisville. She is widely published on issues of gender justice in Islam and has just completed a research project in Pakistan and India called "Muslim Women's Empowerment and Self-Actualization." Dr. Neumaier-Dargyay is a specialist in Buddhism and is the chairperson of the East Asian Studies Department at the University of Alberta in Edmonton, Canada. Her publications include *The Rise of Esoteric Buddhism in Tibet,* and *The Sovereign All-Creating Mind: The Motherly Buddha, A Translation of the Kun-byed rgyal po'i mdo.* Her current work involves a feminist reappraisal of the Buddhist tradition. Dr. Zoloth-Dorfman is the chairperson of Social Ethics and Jewish Studies at San Francisco State University. Her most recent book is *The Ethics of Encounter: A Jewish Conversation on Health Care and Social Justice.*

It is time to conclude this introduction. To conclude is to begin. And where we began is by recognizing the fact that in defining gender and

appropriate gender relations religions have in fact gendered themselves. They are not unbiased or neutral in this; they take sides. That is
why authors who seek to side with gender justice, as we do, find ourselves having to stand against much that has been held to be authoritative in our faith communities. But authority is not sacred. It is human
and changing, and in terms of justice in gender relations it needs changing. As authors, we display our loyalty to our several traditions of the
sacred precisely by holding them accountable to the standard of gender
justice. That standard bears very different implications depending upon
the particular cultural and social conditions within which it must be
practiced. Moreover, as authors we acknowledge our own, very particular social and cultural locations. That is why throughout this writing
process we entered necessarily into debate, both with each other and
with our women feminist critics. Now you, our readers, are invited to
join us in that debate.

I

A Hindu Perspective

Anantanand Rambachan

Introduction

I N ANY DISCUSSION OF ATTITUDES toward women and the treatment of women in Hindu society, one must be attentive to the fact of diversity. "Hinduism" is more appropriately thought of as a family name that encompasses an astounding variety of philosophical viewpoints, religious doctrine, and practice. Although from an orthodox standpoint the Vedas are held to be the supreme source in matters pertaining to religious belief and observance, Hindus, in practice, look to an array of written and oral sources for guiding their lives. Regional customs and traditions differ and there is no central institution or figure speaking authoritatively for all Hindus in matters of doctrine and practice. The tradition has not insisted on uniformity in the religious life. In this regard, it is at a considerable remove from the Abrahamic religions, Judaism, Christianity, and Islam.

It should not surprise us, therefore, to discover significant differences in the status and roles ascribed to women in Hindu society. Although these differences must be readily acknowledged, it is still possible to make certain meaningful generalizations and to discern prevalent attitudes toward women. Although my discussion draws significantly from classical Sanskrit texts that are explicitly Brahmanic and masculine in their orientation, these texts have and continue to enjoy great prestige within the broad Hindu tradition. Although there is increasing evidence to suggest that the non-Brahmanic traditions have accorded greater value and recognition to women, it is also true that caste groups (*jātis*) seek to

ascend the ladder of the caste hierarchy by adopting the values and behavior of those at the top. This is the process known as "Sanskritization"
or "Brahmanization," which looks to the Hindu tradition presented in the
classical Sanskrit texts as normative.[1]

In her recent study on women in Hinduism, Katherine K. Young
draws attention to the disturbing trend in India where the economic
growth in the rural areas has resulted in more conservative attitudes toward women and toward their withdrawal from the work force. Young
associates this trend with the continuing process of Sanskritization or the
imitation of Brahmanic values. This new trend toward closeting women
seems to involve both cultural and economic factors. It obviously keeps
women out of the competitive job market and it also harkens back to the
idea that the status of a family increases if the women in the family are
not educated and do not work outside the home.[2]

Such trends should not be surprising when influential teachers in
India continue to advocate the position that a woman's place is only in
the home. In a recent publication, a popular Hindu guru and writer offers a ludicrous argument for closing the workplace to women. It is typical of such male arguments to claim that the intention is the well-being
of the woman and to assume the prerogative of defining and speaking
for the other. In Hinduism, as in other religions included in this volume,
apparent compassion for women amounts to a demeaning definition of
their nature. Women are more prone to tears and less capable of toler-
ating pain and scolding; thus they are better off if they are kept in the
safe seclusion of the home, protected by men who are brave and able to
bear the cruelty of the outside world.[3]

The continuing prestige and influence of the classical Sanskrit traditions make it possible to speak in certain general terms about
women's issues in Hinduism. Once the process of Sanskritization continues and as long as the values of the classical Sanskrit texts are held to
be normative, these texts cannot be ignored and will have to be engaged
in critical dialogue.

Paradoxical Attitudes toward Women

Any survey of attitudes toward women in Hinduism reveals glaring
contrasts and ambiguities. One of the earliest examples of these ambiguities comes from the most famous work on Hindu law, the *Manusmṛti*
(ca. 200B.C.E.–100C.E.). The author of this work, Manu, comments on the
duties and obligations of women.

> By a girl, by a young woman, or even by an aged one, nothing must be done independently, even in her own house.

> In childhood a female must be subject to her father, in youth to her husband, when her lord is dead to her sons; a woman must never be independent.

> Though destitute of virtue, or seeking pleasure (elsewhere), or devoid of good qualities, (yet) a husband must be constantly worshiped as a god by a faithful wife.

> No sacrifice, no vow, no fast must be performed by women apart (from their husbands); if a wife obeys her husband, she will for that (reason alone) be exalted in heaven.

> A faithful wife, who desires to dwell (after death) with her husband, must never do anything that might displease him who took her hand, whether he be alive or dead.[4]

Manu also requests that women be treated with honor.

> Women must be honoured and adorned by their fathers, brothers, husbands, and brothers-in-law, who desire (their own) welfare.

> Where women are honoured, there the gods are pleased; but where they are not honoured, no sacred rite yields.

> Where the female relations live in grief, the family soon wholly perishes; but that family where they are not unhappy ever prospers.[5]

If Manu appears too ancient and remote, it is important to note that his prescriptions for women continue to be influential. In a recent article, Vasudha Narayanan cites extensively from a Tamil manual titled, *Dirgha Sumangali Bhava,* which was published in 1979. It is a manual for the married Hindu woman that echoes many of the traditional viewpoints articulated by Manu and preserves ancient stereotypes.[6]

If we turn to a relatively recent text, the *Rāmacaritamānasa,* of the sixteenth-century poet Tulasīdāsa, we encounter almost every negative stereotype for women in the Hindu tradition. Tulasīdāsa's work is a vernacular reworking of the ancient Sanskrit *Rāmāyaṇa* of Valmiki and has been extremely influential. Gandhi described it as the greatest book in the religious literature of the world and a scholar recently described it as the Hindu's favorite book.[7]

In Tulasīdāsa's work, Dasaratha, the king of Ayodhya, blames the banishment of his favorite son, Rama, on the fact that he (Dasaratha) trusted a woman.

> What a thing to happen at a time such as this! I am undone by putting trust in a woman like an ascetic who is ruined by ignorance when he is about to win the fruit of his austerities.[8]

In addition to the suggestion that women ought not to be trusted, Dasaratha's outburst is also revealing because of the comparison that he chooses to make. He likens his own plight to that of an ascetic who is destroyed by ignorance when his spiritual endeavors are just about to bear fruit. This is a significant analogy because of the fact that women are also held to be responsible for the spiritual fall of men. In a conversation between the sage Narada and Rama, in the same text, the former asks the latter to explain why he did not allow Narada to get married. Rama offers a lengthy denunciation of women as obstacles to all that is noble and worthy in the life of men.

> Lust, wrath, greed, pride and all other violent passions form the sturdy army of infatuation; but among them all the most formidable and calamitous is woman, illusion incarnate.

> Listen sage, the Puranas and Vedas and the saints declare that woman is the vernal season to the forest of infatuation; like the heat of summer she dries up all the ponds and lakes of prayer and penance and devotional exercises.[9]

Later in the *Ayodhyākāṇḍa*, Bharata, Rama's younger brother, also vents his anger against all women. The following words are addressed to his mother, whom he blames for the banishment of Rama.

> How could the king trust you? Surely God must have robbed him of his senses in his last hour! Not even God can fathom the ways of a woman's heart, the repository of all deceit, sin and vice.

> Being simple, amiable and pious, how could the king understand the nature of a woman? [10]

Bharata pronounces many of the prevalent stereotypes. Women are difficult to understand; they are deceitful, sinful, and they exploit the simplicity and good nature of men. One of the most troubling statements in the *Rāmacaritamānasa* about women occurs in the *Sundarakāṇḍa* when women are lumped together with drums, rustics, animals, and members of the lowest caste and all of these are described as objects that are fit to be beaten.

A passage like this may be read easily as a justification for violence and abuse toward women. Such views encourage complacency toward domestic violence and convince women that it is a deserved form of punishment. Swami Ramsukhdas offers the following advice to an abused woman about an appropriate response:

> Question: What should the wife do if her husband beats her and troubles her?
>
> Answer: The wife should think that she is paying her debt of her previous life and thus her sins are being destroyed and she is becoming pure. When her parents come to know this, they can take her to their own house because they have not given their daughter to face this sort of bad behaviour.
>
> Question: What should she do if her parents don't take her to their own house?
>
> Answer: Under such circumstances what can the helpless wife do? She should reap the fruit of her past actions. She should patiently bear the beatings of her husband with patience. By bearing them she will be free from her sins and it is possible that her husband may start loving her.[11]

WOMEN ARE SIGNIFICANT ONLY IN RELATION TO MEN

What emerges clearly from the classical texts is that women are accorded significance and status only in relation to men. They are regarded with the highest esteem in their roles as wives and mothers. For a woman, marriage and the service of her husband become the purpose of her life and the means to her salvation. She is to look upon her husband as her lord. Through the service of her husband, she accomplishes what an ascetic might attain after many years of arduous religious discipline.

Hindu texts are notoriously one-sided in emphasizing the obligations of women to men in marriage. In the following quotation from the *Rāmacaritamānasa,* Anasuya, wife of the sage, Atri, instructs Sita about the obligations of a Hindu wife:

> Listen, O princess; mother, father and brother are all friendly helpers to a limited degree; but a husband, Sita, is an unlimited blessing; and vile is the woman who refuses to serve him.

Fortitude, piety, a friend and a wife—these four are tested only in
time of adversity. Though her lord be old, sick, dull-headed, indi-
gent, blind, deaf, bad-tempered or utterly wretched,—yet if his wife
treats him with disrespect, she shall suffer all the torments of hell. To
be devoted in thought and word and deed to her husband's feet is
her only religious duty, her only guiding rule.[12]

The tragic consequence of perceiving the significance of women
only in relation to men is seen most clearly in Hindu attitudes toward
women. Widows, particularly those in the upper castes, were regarded
as inauspicious. The widow not only mourned the loss of her husband,
but also suffered the guilt of living longer than him. It was felt in some
circles that if she was pure and faithful, like Savitri, she could save her
husband from death itself.[13] She was required to shave her head and to
avoid all forms of personal adornment. With the death of her husband,
she had lost the most important reasons for living and was debarred
from the quest for the first three goals of Hindu life, *artha* (wealth), *kā
ma* (pleasure), and dharma (family religious ritual). From an early age,
girls are instructed to pray for the longevity of their husbands-to-be in
order to be spared the plight of widowhood. Boys, however, are not required to pray or fast for the longevity of their wives. A married
woman whose husband is alive enjoys an auspicious status *(sumangali)*. A widow is inauspicious *(amangali)* and unfit for participation in
festivals and ceremonies.[14]

While the status of the widow has been improving, the stigma of in-
auspiciousness continues to linger. Narayanan reports that while widows are no longer required to shave their heads, some South Indian
communities do not permit them to be present before religious leaders
and they are not allowed to have the *sathari* (a symbol of God's grace),
touch their heads.[15]

The continuing practice of giving and receiving dowries is another
custom that demeans women and makes a daughter less desirable than
a son in many families. According to A. S. Altekar, the dowry system is
based on the Hindu view of marriage as a *dāna* or "gift." In the Hindu
marriage ceremony, the girl *(kanyā)* is given as a sacred gift *(dāna)* by her
father to the groom. Since a religious gift is usually accompanied by a
gift of cash or gold, the bride is accompanied by a small gift of cash or
ornaments.[16]

Whatever may have been its historical roots, today the dowry is a
condition for the performance of a marriage and a tool for the exploitation and degradation of Hindu women. Although its practice
was outlawed in India in 1961, its popularity has not declined and ris-

ing consumerism feeds the flames of desire and demand. The bride is increasingly seen as the means to materialistic aspirations for conspicuous items such as cars, scooters, refrigerators, and TV-VCRs. The young bride is often put under unconscionable pain and pressure by her husband and in-laws to keep the supply of consumer items flowing. Her hopeless predicament sometimes drives her to suicide. Where greed is untempered by compassion, she may even be murdered by her husband or by his relatives. The preferred method is to set her on fire and to explain away her horrendous death as an accident in the kitchen. The bridegroom is now free to exploit another family. At least two women are killed each day, in this manner, in New Delhi.[17]

Statistics released by the government of India in 1987 show a steady rise in the numbers of dowry deaths. These rose from 999 in 1985 to 1,786 in 1987. In 1993, the figure was 5,582.[18] Although these figures are extremely disturbing, the reality may be much worse since cases of domestic violence are not usually reported. Male education has resulted in an increasing demand for dowries since a college diploma enhances one's economic potential and allows the parents of the bridegroom to make higher demands for dowries. While the dowry was much more prevalent among members of the upper castes, the desire of the lower castes to imitate the higher ones has resulted in its widespread and increased popularity.[19] The Dowry Prohibition law, passed in 1961, has been largely ineffective in dealing with this tragic matter.

In this tragic and unjust context, the preference for sons in Hindu families does not come as a surprise. The increasing demands of the dowry system make daughters unwanted economic liabilities and Hindus are not averse to employing the most sophisticated technology to prevent their births or to ensure that they never attain marriageable age. Abortion is legal in India and medical procedures such as amniocentesis and ultrasound are commonly used to determine the gender of the unborn child and, if the fetus is female, to request a termination of the pregnancy. Figures for one New Delhi clinic in 1992–1993 show that out of a total of 13,400 abortions performed, 13,998 were of female fetuses. One study done in the state of Maharashtra revealed that out of 8,000 fetuses aborted, 7,999 were female. The exception was a Jewish mother who desired a daughter.[20] The practice of female abortion and female infanticide has lowered the ratio of men to women in India. In 1991, the ratio was 927 women for 1,000 men.[21]

The preference for a son *(putra)* in Hindu families is also rooted in religious belief and practice. The eldest son in a Hindu family enjoys a special status because he has the privilege of offering the *piṇḍa* (rice-ball) each year when the rites, called *śrāddha,* are performed for the departed father. This ritual saves the father from suffering in the afterlife. In the words of Manu: "Because a son delivers his father from the hell called *put*, he was therefore called *put-tra* (a deliverer from *put*) by the Self-existent himself."[22]

The role of the son in the performance of postmortem rituals causes preferential regard for male offspring and families sometimes continue to have children until a son is born. S. Cromwell Crawford calls for a reassessment of the beliefs surrounding *śrāddha* rituals and argues that Hindu ethics would be better served by emphasizing the doctrine of karma that teaches personal responsibility for our destinies.

There may be a very pragmatic reason why sons were given the responsibility of making annual offerings on behalf of departed ancestors. Traditionally, the married male child remained a part of the joint household, while the daughter left her home and took on a new identity as part of her husband's home. Her obligations were all centered on her husband and his family. Today, with the growth of nuclear families, both males and females are leaving the ancestral home and establishing households of their own. A married daughter may be closer geographically and may be interested in the performance of family rituals. Due to this change in family structure and pattern it is an appropriate time to reconsider the eligibility of women to perform these rituals.

Hinduism also debars women from leadership and participation in religious rituals because of the belief that the female becomes polluted during two of the distinctive expressions of female sexuality, menstruation and childbirth.[23] Women are usually ranked in the lower orders of the caste system and are prohibited from the study and recitation of the Vedas.[24] In orthodox homes the menstruating woman is not allowed to cook or to participate in domestic religious rituals. Among the Havik Brahmans of Mysore, for example, women must take special precautions to ensure that they do not pollute others during the period of menstruation. A Havik woman does not serve food to her family or eat with them during this time.[25]

Here again, it is necessary that Hindus adopt an enlightened and rational view of normal female bodily functions rather than continue to hold onto the superstitious beliefs of an era when the nature of such biologic processes was not understood. The perception of uniquely female bodily processes as polluting is clearly a male-centered view that provides a further justification for the exclusion of women from male-controlled spheres.

One of the promising developments, in recent times, has been the initiative taken by certain Hindu movements to train women as priestesses. In 1975, Shri Shankarrao Thatte of Pune began the training of women in priestly roles. Since his death in 1987, his wife, Mrs. Pushpabai Thatte, has continued this work under an organization known as "Shankar Seva Samiti" and it has spread to all parts of Maharashtra. Although there has been opposition from orthodox circles, the initiation of priestesses "has been accepted by most educated people, (and) welcomed as a revolutionary step in Indian society."[26] In South Africa, the reformist Arya Samaj movement, founded by Swami Dayananda Saraswati in 1875, has been training priestesses and a branch of the movement in Trinidad recently initiated its first priestess. While the training appears to be almost entirely focused on liturgy and religious ceremonies, one hopes that it will develop an intellectual and scholarly dimension that will enable women to be creative interpreters and assessors of the Hindu heritage.

The previous passage by Swami Ramsukhdas points to a sinister interpretation and use of the Hindu doctrine of karma to condone resignation and fatalism on the part of women with regard to their abuse and subjection to men. I have personally heard many accounts of abused Hindu women who were sent back by their parents or advised to return to the homes of their husbands since the suffering inflicted upon them was a just reward for their actions in earlier lives. A woman who chooses to leave her husband also causes disgrace and embarrassment to her parents and elders.

The doctrine of karma, however, ought not to be perverted and misused to sanction oppression and injustice. While the teaching on karma underlines responsibility by emphasizing that human actions produce consequences for the doer, it does not propose that all experiences in life are the consequences of actions in past lives and it certainly does not require silent and passive submission to injustice. Men who abuse women are choosing to do so and the doctrine of karma must not ignore this fact by transferring blame and responsibility to the victim. Instead of advocating resignation to abuse, Hindu teachers ought to condemn gender injustice as a violation of fundamental Hindu values. If karma entrusts us with responsibility for the condition of our lives, Hindu leaders ought to be empowering women to be active agents of change rather than advising stoic acquiescence in suffering.

"WHAT MEN OWE TO WOMEN": THE INTRINSIC WORTH OF WOMEN

The major problems faced by women in the Hindu tradition arise because of patriarchal and androcentric views that affirm the value and significance of women only in relation to men. In view of this fact, a

major task for us, as men, is to articulate a value for women that is not
dependent on their subservient relationship to us. This would be a
value that comes from the very fact of her being. Are there any resources in the classical texts for constructing such a view? I think such
resources exist and they are to be found in the same texts that exclude
and demean women. As the other chapters in this volume indicate, all
religions sin in this way. They all contain the elements of a rich theory
of justice but they do not always apply that to women.

The classical texts and the major traditions of Hinduism are unanimous in the view that the human being embodies the real and infinite
divine spirit (*Brahman*). While the divine is present in everything, it is
uniquely expressed in the human being. The various traditions of Hinduism have characterized the relationship between the divine spirit and
the human self (*ātman*) in different ways, dependent on their philosophical standpoints. The nondualists speak of the ultimate identity of
the two, while the qualified nondualists describe the relationship as one
of inseparability but not identity. All of them agree, however, on the fact
that the divine exists equally and identically in all beings and things. As
the Bhagavadgītā puts it:

> He who sees the Supreme Lord,
> Existing alike in all beings,
> Not perishing when they perish,
> Truly sees.[27]

While the social implications of this truth are not consistently and
clearly drawn out in the classical texts, all of them articulate it in one
way or the other. When the implications for human relationships are
enunciated, they are done in terms of a vision of equality and there is
no good reason why this equality should also be construed in terms of
gender.

> In a *brāhman* endowed with wisdom and cultivation,
> In a cow, in an elephant,
> And even in dog or in a dog-cooker,
> The pandits see the same (*ātman*).
> Even here on earth, rebirth is conquered
> By those whose mind is established in impartiality.
> Brahman is guiltless and impartial;
> Therefore they are established in Brahman.[28]

The Śvetāśvatara Upaniṣad specifically identifies the divine with
women (*strī*) and unmarried girls (*kumārī*) as well as with men and boys.

> *You are a woman; you are a man; you are a boy or also a girl. As an old man,*
> *you totter along with a walking-stick. As you are born, you turn your face*
> *in all directions.*
> *You are the dark blue bird, the green one with red eyes, the rain-cloud, the sea-*
> *sons, and the oceans. You live as one without a beginning because of your*
> *pervasiveness, you, from whom all beings are born.*[29]

Although this teaching about the sameness of the divine in all beings has been clearly enunciated in the classical texts such as the Upaniṣads and the Bhagavadgītā, it has usually remained as a spiritual ideal and has not always been used as a reforming norm to question and critique social structures and unjust gender relationships. One reason is that it is usually sought by the celibate renunciant *(samnyāsi)* who is ritually freed from social ties and obligations and who may not be interested in harmonizing the spiritual ideal and social reality. A spiritual ideal, however, which is disconnected from social reality and from the life of the community quickly becomes irrelevant. The doctrine of divine equality, so deeply rooted in Hinduism, must become a powerful searchlight in order to illuminate and heal the exploitative and oppressive structures of Hindu society.

In the Hindu tradition, the divine is identified with that which is true or real *(sat)* and the real is not subject to change. As that which is absolutely real, the divine is understood to have the greatest value. Things that are subject to change do not lack value, but are not viewed as having ultimate value. The human form, though finite and perishable, is precious because it is the abode of the imperishable and it is the instrument for attaining liberation *(mokṣa)*. If the human form derives its value from divine immanence, then it must be a symptom of ignorance to despise and oppress the female forms which, like the male forms, embody divinity. The forms that express that which we consider to be of ultimate value must also command our respect and reverence.

Women have value and significance, not primarily because of their instrumental roles and relationships to us as wives and mothers, but because, like us, they equally embody the divine. Their worth is an intrinsic one and does not come indirectly through males. The great South Indian teacher, Ramana Maharshi (1879–1950) affirmed this truth in a firm stand that he took after the death of his mother. His mother spent the last years of her life at his *āśrama* and became his disciple. Upon her death, Ramana was convinced that she had attained liberation and was not subject to rebirth. It is customary for the body of a liberated person to be buried rather than cremated. Some disciples expressed doubt about whether the body of a liberated woman should be treated like that of a liberated man. Ramana's answer was unequivocal. "Since *Jñāna* (Knowledge) and *Mukti* (Deliverance) do not differ with the difference of sex, the body of a woman Saint also need not be burnt. Her body is also the abode of God."[30]

AHIMSĀ: ITS SIGNIFICANCE FOR WOMEN

The Hindu belief in the unity of existence through the divine and in the sacredness of all life that expresses the divine, is the foundation of its cardinal ethical principle, *ahimsā* (nonviolence). Belief in divine immanence requires us to demonstrate reverence and consideration for life in all its forms and to avoid injury or suffering to others. Divine immanence is so central to the Hindu understanding of God, that even a text like the *Rāmacaritamānasa* of Tulasīdāsa, full of misogynistic verses, cannot avoid its implications. In often-recited verses from the *Bālakāṇḍa*, he reiterates the doctrine of divine pervasiveness and expresses his reverence for all beings and for the entire creation.

> *Knowing that the whole universe, whether animate or inanimate, is pervaded by the spirit of Rama, I ever adore the feet of all with folded hands.*
> *Eight million four hundred thousand species of living beings, classified under four broad divisions, inhabit land, water and the air. Realizing the whole world to be pervaded by Sita and Rama, I make obeisance with folded hands.*[31]

The central ethical implication of divine immanence, which is nonviolence *(ahimsā)*, is also echoed by Tulasīdāsa. In the *Uttarakāṇḍa*, Rama speaks about it to his brother, Bharata.

> *Brother, there is no religious duty like benevolence and no sin like oppressing others. I have declared to you, dear brother, the verdict of all the Vedas and the Puranas, and the learned also know it.*[32]

If the teaching about divine equality is to be saved from being an abstract and insignificant ideal, then the meaning of its central ethic, which is *ahimsā*, must be enlarged and used to challenge gender inequities. Contemporary Hindu ethics, on the whole, must become more cognizant of the ways in which social structures affect peoples' lives and not limit its application to the sphere of individual relationships. The systemic nature of gender inequality has to be understood and addressed with earnestness.

Ahimsā is violated and women are oppressed when they are forced because of social values to abort fetuses merely because the fetus is female. They are tortured when the cruel custom of dowry strains the precious economic resources of the families into which they are born and makes them feel guilty for being women. They are demeaned by the practice of dowry that signifies that the value of a woman is so low that she becomes acceptable to another only when her family is able to satisfy his greed for the latest gadgets of materialistic fancy. Her suffering continues in the home of her in-laws when she is resented because of dissatisfaction with the dowry and when she is subject to verbal and physical abuse in order to extort more from her poor family. Her life is often in danger and she sometimes chooses to save her family by ending it herself. Women are not honored in a society that inflicts suffering on her in so many ways.

AHIMSĀ AND JUSTICE FOR WOMEN

In his understanding and interpretation of the meaning of *ahimsā*, Gandhi explained that in its negative form it means abstention from injury to living beings physically or mentally. In its positive form, *ahimsā* means love and compassion for all. For Gandhi, *ahimsā* also means justice toward everyone and abstention from exploitation in any form. "No man," claimed Gandhi, "could be actively non-violent and not rise against social injustice no matter where it occurred."[33] From this perspective, we owe women, not only the value, dignity, and respect that stems from their embodiment of the divine, but also justice. Justice for women, in the context of Hinduism, requires that we ensure them the same educational opportunities as men so that they realize the fullness of their human potential.

There are numerous studies that show that the status of women increases with access to education and that the latter also leads to lower population growth and higher standards of living.[34] The Indian state of Kerala has achieved 100-percent literacy among girls and a birthrate of two per family.[35] Kerala is one of the few states in India where women outnumber men and where the life expectancy of women exceeds that of men. Indian census figures for 1991 revealed 1,040 women for every 1,000 men. The national figure is 929 women for every 1,000 men. The birthrate in Kerala is eighteen per thousand and falling. Kerala's impressive literacy rate (higher than that of the United States), stands in sad contrast to the national literacy level in India that is around 52 percent. A disproportionate percentage of the illiterate in India are

women. One writer recently commented on the national consequences
of this fact.

> More attention to improving the lot of Indian women in general,
> empowering them to make decisions about such matters as repro-
> duction and family expenditure, and improving their access to
> health care, would undoubtedly have benefitted Indian society as
> a whole, notably by reducing the country's population. But not
> just that: freeing India's ordinary women from millennia of subju-
> gation would have liberated for the country the productive talents
> of half the population, which for millennia have been left to lan-
> guish exploited, abused, and taken for granted, but all too rarely
> fulfilled.[36]

There are many ancient traditions that can be creatively appropriated to support the education of women. The Bṛhadāraṇyaka Upaniṣad,
for instance, recommends a ritual to a householder to ensure the birth of
a scholarly daughter (4.4.18).[37] There are also Vedic hymns that are attributed to women. Early "forest universities" in India were coeduca-
tional and girls were entitled to commence the study of the Vedas after
the *upanayana* or "sacred thread ceremony." One class of female students
were the *brahmavādinīs* who committed themselves to a lifelong study of
liturgical and ritual texts and engaged in religious debates.[38]

Hindu classical texts, as was noted earlier, offer a one-sided emphasis on the obligations of women to men and are glaringly silent on
the obligations of men to women. Justice requires that this imbalance
be redressed and that mutual obligations be emphasized. There are
many ancient traditions that could be drawn upon to support gender
equality and mutuality. The Ṛg Veda, the earliest of the Vedic texts
stipulates that the wife must be present at all domestic religious rituals. Young argues that this presence was not just a silent one since, in
the absence of the men, the deities could not be left unattended and
the wife would have had to assume primary responsibility for making
offerings.[39]

While there has been a certain imbalance in the emphasis on female obligations and duties, the language of obligations and the significance that these have received in Hinduism are laudable and
instructive. The contemporary emphasis on human rights often leads
to an exaggerated individualism, and needs to be balanced by a stress
on human responsibilities and obligations. Freedom without a deep
sense of responsibility does little to foster and nurture human communities. The value for the language of obligations in Hinduism
arises out of its understanding of the unity and interrelatedness of all

existence. Whether we recognize it or not, from a Hindu viewpoint, our lives are inextricably intertwined with, and dependent on, the universe as a whole, which includes such life forms as the divine, nature, and humans. The wheel of the universe revolves only if we recognize and fulfill our duties to the whole in response to its continuous sustenance of our individual lives. One who enjoys the gifts of the universe without offering anything in return is considered in the Bhagavadgītā (3:12) a thief. The Hindu understanding of the source and necessity of obligations is a rich resource for promoting gender equity. A doctrine of human rights in Hinduism will be correctly inseparable from one of responsibility and obligations.

In asking that the Hindu tradition emphasize mutual obligations between men and women, I wish to clarify that this is not an argument for exclusive and complementary roles. This argument is often used to relegate women to the domestic sphere and to deny them the freedom to participate in all spheres of the human community. The justice that we owe to women implies freedom, and we must be aware of the many insidious arguments that are proffered to define her place. The following is one of many examples:

> Question: In these days women demand equal rights like men. Is it proper?
>
> Answer: No. It is not proper. In fact a woman has not the right of equality with man but she has a privilege. The reason is that she comes to her husband's house having renounced her parents etc. She is called the mistress and the queen of the house. It is her husband who has a privilege outside the house. As a chariot moves with two wheels which are kept apart, so do the household affairs run smoothly with their separate rights. If the two wheels of the chariot are joined together, it can't be driven smoothly. If both of them have equal rights, how will a man like a woman conceive? Therefore right of equality in fact means separate rights of the two, and this is real freedom for both of them.[40]

Even Gandhi, who advanced the cause of women's freedom by drawing them into the struggle for national independence, argued conservatively for separate and complementary roles. While he argued for spiritual equality, he also claimed that the vocations of the two were different and that the woman's place was in the home. "The duty of motherhood," wrote Gandhi, "which the vast majority of women will always undertake, requires qualities which men need not possess. She is passive, he is active. She is essentially the mistress of the house. He is the bread-winner. She is the keeper and distributor of the bread."[41]

Nontraditional Roles for Women

To counteract such role stereotyping and exclusivity, we need to high-light the many women in the history of Hinduism who liberated them-selves from traditional roles and made their own destinies. They can become inspiring role models for women. Most of them come from the devotional traditions of Hinduism that emphasize the centrality of love in the divine-human relationship and that dispense with the role of priestly intermediaries. These movements have also employed vernac-ular languages of India as their mode of religious expression.

Prominent among these women are Andal (sixth century c.e.) and Mirabai (fourteenth century c.e.).[42] Andal was the daughter of Vishnu-chitta, a temple priest at Srivilliputtur in South India. Growing up in the shadow of the temple, Andal cultivated a deep love for God that resembled the intense and passionate relationship between Krishna and his *gopis* (milkmaid devotees). She turned down the option of marriage and, according to traditional accounts, disappeared into the image of Vishnu. The devotional compositions of Andal are recited daily in Hindu temples. Mirabai was a childhood devotee of Krishna. After her marriage to Bhojraj, the prince of Chitor, her passion for Kr-ishna became a source of embarrassment to her in-laws. Fleeing perse-cution in her husband's home, Mira fled to Vrindaban, the sacred city of Krishna. Here, she poured out her heart in poetic songs and, like Andal, was mystically united with the image of her beloved.[43]

In more recent times, we continue to see women circumventing traditional roles and assuming leadership roles as spiritual teachers. Prominent among these are the Bengali mystic, Anandamayi Ma (1896–1982), and Swami Jnanananda (b.1931).[44] While some excep-tional women have left deep imprints on the Hindu tradition by fol-lowing their profound religious leanings, my purpose in citing their examples is not to suggest that this ought to be the only alternative for women who may not wish to follow conventional roles. What is nec-essary today, in the Hindu world, is the creation of opportunities and a climate of attitudes in which women enjoy the freedom and right to self-development and are not constrained into roles that are demar-cated for them by a patriarchal and androcentric culture. We owe it to women to become partners with them in the liberation of both genders from the constraints of patriarchy.

The doctrine of divine immanence and the sanctity and worth of the human person that follows from it must become the foundation of a Hindu challenge and critique of all attitudes, values, and actions that demean and trivialize women and reduce them to sexual objects. Hinduism must resist and respond to the challenges of a materialistic- and consumer-oriented culture in which people determine their own value and the value of others by the worth of the commodities that they own. In a materialistic culture, human value varies with the worth of our possessions and rises and falls with the upward or downward movements of the market. A tradition that affirms unequivocally that the significance of the human being is to be found in the fact that human nature embodies the divine cannot condone the commercialization of human existence. It must champion the dignity of all human beings and attitudes of respect and reverence for all human life.

FEMININE IMAGES OF GOD

One of the great contributions of feminist theology has been to demonstrate the relationship between patriarchy and male images of God. These images are predominant in male-dominated societies and reinforce, in turn, male authority roles and figures.[45] The images of God in any religious tradition are significant since they affect social structure and human consciousness. The Hindu tradition, however, cautions us about positing any necessary relationship between the presence of feminine images and forms of God in a religion and the status of women. Even though the Mother Goddesses dominated some regions in India, this fact did not translate into greater status for women.

It must be of some significance, however, that the Hindu tradition has not hesitated to use a variety of feminine symbols and appellations for the sacred, and there are no philosophical problems in Hinduism with imaging the divine as feminine. Although many of the goddesses in Hinduism are subordinate to the god-figures and mirror the subordination of women to men, there are figures like Kali that embody all of the traditional features of God. A popular image represents the divine as *ardhanārīśvara* and shows God as the perfect integration of male and female characteristics. One-half of the image is male and the other half is female. What is especially noteworthy about this icon is that the integration of the male and female is complete and equal.

The fact that the tradition uses both male and female metaphors for God underlines the truth that God is neither male nor female. The challenge before us here, once more, is to see the implications of religious insight for social reality and to question the contradictions that result from isolating both. The feminine images of God in Hinduism are a

rich source to be retrieved and interpreted by advocates of gender justice, equality, and rights.

The Hindu tradition, as already noted, accords value and respect to
women primarily in their roles as wives and mothers (of sons). In her
role as mother, the woman is even more venerated than the father or the
teacher. Her role as an educator and spiritual teacher of her children is
clearly recognized.[46] In so many other ways, however, she is devalued
and debased. The challenge for Hinduism is not to strip the mother of
the sanctity and dignity it has traditionally reserved for her, but to help
create the conditions under which women can freely choose their paths
to self-development and to ensure that they are treated justly and with
honor in nontraditional and traditional roles.

SCRIPTURAL RESOURCES FOR CHANGE

Hinduism has traditionally distinguished between *śruti* and *smṛti*
texts. *Śruti* literally means, "that which is heard," and designates those
Scriptures that are considered to be revealed and that enjoy supreme
authority. The term is regularly employed as a synonym for the Vedas.
Smṛti, on the other hand, means, "that which is remembered," and
refers to sacred texts that have a human origin. The *Dharma-śāstras* or
law books of Hinduism, such as the *Manusmṛti*, are classified as *smṛti*.
These texts are secondary in authority to the *śruti* and, more importantly, deal with those aspects of the tradition that are contextual and
limited to specific time periods and social conditions. Julius Lipner lu-
cidly discusses the relationship between *śruti* and *smṛti*.

> In so far as *smṛti* is humanly authored, it is generally fallible and li-
> able to change. It is also liable to criticism. As such, it is a selective
> term. Sometimes, what is *smṛti* for you may not be recognized as
> such by me; or rather, though it may be necessary for both of us to
> recognize the authority of a particular slice of *smṛti*, we may weigh
> this authority differently according to the particular traditions out
> of which we come or the exigencies of the situation. *Smṛti* is the
> medium through which we hear the voice of *śruti*; it is interpreta-
> tive, selective, collaborative, flexible.[47]

Although the *śruti* texts are acknowledged to be revelation, the
sphere of their authority is carefully defined and limited. The purpose
of the *śruti* is to reveal only those things that cannot be known through
any of our ordinary means of knowledge and its revelations should not

contradict what we learn about the world through other sources of knowledge. For the Vedānta schools of the Hindu tradition, the primary purpose of revelation is to inform us of the nature of absolute reality *(Brahman)* and the relationship between specific ritual actions and their results.[48]

The distinction between *śruti* and *smṛti* and the limits placed on the authority of the former are valuable and creative resources that can be utilized by Hindu interpreters for meaningfully addressing contemporary issues, including those of gender injustice. The problem here, however, is that androcentric views, although predominant, are not limited to those works that are regarded as *smṛti*. Young notes this fact.

> That Hindu reformers from the nineteenth century on have looked to the Vedas as the "Golden Age" for Hindu women may be based, consequently, not only on an appreciation of the values of this early society, but also on an early apologetic already structured into the texts. What the reformers often overlooked, however, was how the Vedic Age, especially the periods for the Brahmanas and the Upanisads—also gave rise to many of the features of classical and medieval Hinduism that would eventually be criticized.[49]

Androcentric views in the *smṛti* texts must be dealt with by showing how they reflect specific social structures, beliefs, and patterns of authority. Such texts must be replaced by new *smṛtis* that express the aspirations of women for justice. The explicit recognition that the *smṛtis* are contextual works grants us the liberty to undertake this task. The challenge is greater, but not insurmountable, where androcentric views are expressed in the *śruti*. In dealing with such views, our approach may be twofold. We must affirm that the specific purpose of revelation is to inform us of those things that cannot be known through other available sources. The purpose of revelation, as we have already seen, is to tell us of the nature of the absolute *(Brahman)*. We must infer and apply the implications of this revelation for gender relationships. The Hindu tradition, as already discussed, posits that the absolute exists equally in all beings and this must translate into a social order characterized by relationships of justice and mutual respect. This view of the purpose of revelation also gives us the freedom to see that there are *smṛti* (namely, contextual) texts within the *śruti* and these do not have to be granted the same degree of authority. "A hundred *śrutis*," says Sankara, "may declare that fire is cold or that it is dark; still they possess no authority in the matter."[50]

CONCLUSION: AVIDYĀ (IGNORANCE) AND PATRIARCHY

The Hindu tradition broadly describes the fundamental human problem to be one of *avidyā*, or "ignorance." Human conflict and the suffering that it causes are rooted in a fundamental misunderstanding of the
true nature of reality. Hinduism, on the whole, is optimistic about human nature that is not considered to be fundamentally flawed or defec-
tive. Ignorance can be overcome and, when it is and when we are
awakened to the true nature of reality, there will be a corresponding
transformation in the quality of our relationships and greater social harmony. In the Bhagavadgītā, knowledge of the highest kind is described
as "that knowledge by which one sees One imperishable being in all beings, undivided in the divided" (18:20). Inferior to this way of knowing
is "that knowledge which knows as separate different beings of various
kinds among all beings" (18:21).[51] The imperishable that exists in all beings is identified in the Bhagavadgītā with the *ātman* or the "deepest
level of the human self." It is here that true human fullness and happiness is discovered and that one learns to see oneself in all others.

Every human being, in the view of Hinduism, yearns for a fullness
and freedom from want. This fullness, however, is already inherent in
one's nature at the level of one's true self where one is inseparable from
the imperishable absolute. Ignorant of this, and driven by a sense of in-
completeness we seek to become full beings through the multiplication
of our possessions and through power. Men seek self-gratification by
treating women as objects of possession and by exercising power and
control over them. Since the value of wealth or power comes from the
fact that these are exclusive and unequally distributed, the one who
seeks his happiness through these means lives in continuous anxiety
and insecurity. He is diminished by the power and wealth of others.
"The spiritual problem with greed," as David Loy observes, "—both the
greed for profit and the greed to consume—is due not only to the consequent maldistribution of worldly goods (although a more equitable
distribution is, of course, essential), or to its effects on the biosphere, but
even more fundamentally because greed is based on a delusion: the
delusion that happiness is to be found this way."[52] Loy will probably
agree that his observation is also true of the greed to possess, dominate,
and control other human beings.

While the historical roots of patriarchy are complex, we must also
see that is an expression of *avidyā*, a fundamental misunderstanding of
the spiritual equality and unity of human beings and a false search for
fullness through human subjugation. Such an understanding helps us

to see clearly that the liberation of women to become full beings is a necessary condition of our own true liberation.

NOTES

1. The caste *(varna)* system is a hierarchical ordering of society into four occupational groups. At the apex of the social order are the *Brahmans* (priests and scholars), followed by the *ksatriyas* (rulers and warriors), *vaiśyas* (merchants and traders), and *śūdras* (laborers and servants of the first three groups). Those who did not belong to one of these four groups constituted the outcastes or untouchables. They are considered ritually impure and do not enjoy the rights and privileges of the higher castes. In practice the four main groups are divided into many subgroups that are referred to as *jātīs*.

2. Katherine K. Young, "Women in Hinduism," in *Today's Woman in World Religions*, Arvind Sharma, ed. (Albany: State University of New York Press, 1994), 115.

3. Swami Ramsukhdas, *How to Lead a Household Life* (Gorakhhpur, India: Gita Press, 1994), 56.

4. G. Buhler, trans., *The Laws of Manu* (London: Oxford University Press, 1886), 5:147–149; 154–156.

5. *Laws of Manu*, 3:55–57.

6. See Vasudha Narayanan, "Hindu Perceptions of Auspiciousness and Sexuality," in *Women, Religion and Sexuality* (Philadelphia: Trinity Press International, 1991), 64–92.

7. Klaus K. Klostennaier, *A Survey of Hinduism* (Albany: State University of New York Press, 1994), 89.

8. *Rāmacaritamānasa*, R. C. Prasad, trans. (Delhi: Motilal Banarsidass, 1991), *Ayodhyākāṇḍa*, 270.

9. Ibid., 506.

10. Ibid., 354.

11. Ramsukhdas, *How to Lead a Household Life*, 50.

12. *Ayodhyākāṇḍa*, 468.

13. The story of Savitri is told in the *Mahābhārata*. Savitri decided to marry Satyavan although he was destined to live only one more year. On the day appointed for his death, she followed him to his place of work and stayed at his side. When the deity of death, Yama, came to claim Saytavan, Savitri refused to let her husband go alone and followed him to the realm of the departed. In order to dissuade Savitri, Yama offered to fulfill any of her wishes except the return of her husband to the world of the living. He quickly consented to her first

two wishes. Her third wish was for many sons. Yama readily granted it, but Savitri kept following him. When he told her to return, she reminded him that a widow could not remarry. Yama had no choice but to return Satyavan. For a retelling of this story see Sister Nivedita, *Cradle Tales of Hinduism* (Calcutta: Advaita Ashrama, 1975).

14. Sakuntala Narasimhan, "India: From Sati to Sex Determination Tests," in *Women and Violence*, Miranda Daves, ed. (London: Zed Books, 1994), 45–50.

15. Narayanan, "Hindu Perceptions of Auspiciousness and Sexuality," 85.

16. A. S. Altekar, *The Position of Women in Hindu Civilization* (Delhi: Motilal Banarsidass, 1938), 71.

17. S. Cromwell Crawford, *Dilemmas of Life and Death* (Albany: State University of New York Press, 1995), 35.

18. From "Global Dharma" in *Hinduism Today*, November, 1994.

19. See Elisabeth Bumiller, *May You Be the Mother of a Hundred Sons* (Delhi: Penguin Books, 1990), 48–49.

20. Narasimhan, "India," 51.

21. Narayanan, "One Tree Is Equal to Ten Sons: Hindu Responses to the Problems of Ecology, Population, and Consumption," *Journal of the American Academy of Religion* 65(2):314 (1997).

22. *Laws of Manu*, 9:138.

23. Narayanan, "Hindu Perceptions of Auspiciousness and Sexuality," 85–88.

24. See *Laws of Manu*, 9:18.

25. See David R. Kinsley, *Hinduism: A Cultural Perspective* (Englewood Cliffs, NJ: Prentice-Hall, 1993), 164.

26. From V. L. Manjul in *Hinduism Today*, January, 1997.

27. The Bhagavadgītā, Winthrop Sargeant, trans. (Albany: State University of New York Press, 1984). The Hindu view of God is not a simple polytheism that affirms a multiplicity of independent deities. Hinduism affirms the oneness of God while maintaining a multiplicity of God-forms and figures, both male and female. Hindus enjoy the freedom to choose a particular God-form as the focus of their religious life. Ultimately the divine transcends any form and name attributed by human beings.

28. Bhagavadgītā 5:18-19. See also Īśa Upaniṣad, 6–7.

29. The Upaniṣads, Patrick Olivelle, trans. (New York: Oxford University Press, 1996), 259.

30. Arthur Osborne, *Ramana Maharshi and the Path of Self Knowledge* (York Beach, Maine: Samuel Weiser, 1970), 79.

31. Prasad, *Rāmacaritamānasa*, 8–9.

32. Ibid., 719.

33. Mahatma Gandhi, *All Men Are Brothers* (New York: Columbia University Press, 1958), 89.

34. For some statistics in the Indian context see Narayanan, "One Tree Is Equal to Ten Sons," 312–316.

35. From "Global Dharma" in *Hinduism Today,* November, 1994.

36. Shashi Tharoor, *India: From Midnight to Millennium* (New York: Arcade Publishing, 1997), 296.

37. See Altekar, *The Position of Women in Hindu Civilization,* 3.

38. See Ellison Banks Findly, "Gārgī at the King's Court: Women and Philosophic Innovation in Ancient India," in *Women, Religion, and Social Change,* Yvonne Yazbeck Haddad and Ellison Banks Findly, eds. (Albany: State University of New York Press, 1985), 37–58.

39. Young, "Women in Hinduism," 62.

40. Ramsukhdas, *How to Lead a Household Life,* 55.

41. Gandhi, *All Men Are Brothers,* 161.

42. For brief discussions see David Kinsley, *Hinduism: A Cultural Perspective* (Englewood Cliffs, NJ: Prentice-Hall, 1993), chap. 7.

43. For more detailed biographical accounts see Swami Ghanananda and John Stewart-Wallace, eds., *Women Saints: East and West* (Hollywood, CA: Vedanta Press, 1946).

44. For Anandamayi Ma see A. Lipski, *Life and Teachings of Sri Anandamayi Ma* (Delhi: Motilal Banarsidass, 1977). For Swami Jnanananda see Charles S. J. White, "Mother Jnanananda of Madras, India," in *Unspoken Worlds: Women's Religious Lives in Non-Western Cultures,* Nancy Auer Falk and Rita M. Gross, eds. (San Francisco: Harper, 1980), 22–37.

45. See Mary Daly, *Beyond God the Father* (Boston: Beacon Press, 1973).

46. See *Laws of Manu,* 2:145.

47. Julius Lipner, *Hindus: Their Religious Beliefs and Practices* (London: Routledge, 1994), 75.

48. See Anantanand Rambachan, *Accomplishing the Accomplished: The Vedas as a Source of Valid Knowledge in Sakara* (Honolulu: University of Hawaii Press, 1991), chap. 2.

49. Young, "Women in Hinduism," 71–72.

50. *The Bhagavadgītā with the commentary of Sri Sankaracharya,* A. Mahadeva Sastry, trans. (Madras, India: Samata Books, 1977), 18:66.

51. *The Bhagavadgītā,* Winthrop Sargeant, trans. (Albany: State University of New York Press, 1984).

52. David Loy, "The Religion of the Market," *Journal of the American Academy of Religion* 65(2):286 (1997).

2

A Protestant Christian Perspective

Marvin M. Ellison

THE FEMINIST AUTHOR GLORIA STEINEM observes that many women respond to the idea of a men's movement with a mixture of skepticism and hope. "We both want to believe in male change," she writes, "and have little reason to do so" (Steinem 1992, vii). Other feminists echo her sentiments. Some express apprehension that a "men's movement will do what men have always done, at least since the advent of patriarchy: blame women for their problems and defend their own privileges" (Starhawk 1992, 28). Others are puzzled, perhaps even amused, at the announcement of a men's movement. The feminist poet of color Hattie Gossett ponders all the commotion and pointedly asks: "What? a mins movement? what you mean a mins movement? aint they still runnin the world? what they need a movement for?" (Gossett 1992, 20).

Gossett's questions are well worth pondering. Why do men need a movement, and furthermore, who is likely to benefit? In my judgment, if a men's movement is to be good news for women and not "for men only," it will encourage a shift in men's loyalties, away from defending male privilege and toward embracing a comprehensive justice for women and men alike. It will call for men's moral-spiritual conversion and fortify them for a radical break with oppression structured on the basis of race, class, gender, and sexuality. It will challenge the use of religion to legitimate social dominance and the exploitation of the earth. It will scrutinize every truth claim and hold religious authorities accountable for how their theologies affect people in their everyday struggles. Moreover, because it will be a movement for spiritual renewal as well as for social transformation, it will be invested in soul-craft as well as community rebuilding.

The purpose of this chapter is not to survey Protestant Christian attitudes toward women or to analyze particular Protestant responses to gender oppression. My scholarly interest is not to mount an apologetic defense of Protestant Christianity or to catalog the many positive (or negative) things Protestantism has had to say about women. Male theological discourse that continues to objectify women, even in affirmative tones, can hardly exonerate Protestantism in light of its feminist critics. The project I envision here is liberationist rather than reformist in character. I am interested in exploring men's justice work and how Protestantism might contribute to a men's movement for gender and for other kinds of justice.

Liberation theological discourse begins in a feminist mode with women's global eruption as the subjects of their own lives, with their breaking silence and speaking their own truth, including their spiritual truth, in their own voices. This global uprising has ample room for men who are willing to listen to and learn from women (rather than speak at women or render them invisible) and who celebrate women's empowerment. Men as well as women are needed in this struggle to humanize the globe and to care for the earth. Therefore, rather than insulating my religious heritage from feminist and other liberation theological critiques, I welcome such criticism and its transformative impact because patriarchal Christianity, in its Protestant as well as in its Catholic and orthodox forms, has persistently legitimated women's oppression while also sacralizing male power. At the start of the millennium, the spiritual vitality of Protestant Christianity (and every religious tradition) depends on its investment in advancing women as well as men's well-being and on its contribution to the survival of the earth itself. A revitalized Protestantism will be chastened by its encounter with feminist and other liberation movements but also renewed by its adoption of radically inclusive egalitarian values and commitments.

Apologetics will keep faith communities stuck in cultural reaction and also siphon energy away from the urgent business of justice-making as personal and communal restoration. Plunging into justice work requires a never-ending search for creative ways to resist injustice and to create new forms of solidarity across barriers of social difference. In response to patriarchal oppression, men must continue to explore with women how they, as men, can become trustworthy allies in women's struggles for justice, especially women who are the poorest of the poor. However, men must also engage with other men across differences of race, class, and sexuality and specifically inquire how a faith tradition transformed by feminism might energize and guide men's own struggles for gender and for other forms of justice. This chapter focuses on men's change agenda and on resources for justice-making to be reclaimed from some streams of Protestantism.

As a Protestant liberation ethicist, I start with three questions reflective of the methodological wisdom of diverse liberation theologies. First, Who is the theologian speaking, and what is (in this instance) his community of accountability? Second, What is the social-cultural, as well as religious, context that frames the theological conversation and to which it responds? Third, What is the political character of the theological project? As the feminist theologians Susan Brooks Thistlethwaite and Mary Potter Engel stress, liberation theology from the start recognized the fact that social location matters. There is no theology that is not contextually limited and shaped (Thistlethwaite and Engel 1990, 2–3).

Social Location, Context, and Religious Project

As I write, I am mindful of some of my limits, as well as of the limits of the power of social conditioning. North American, white, middle-strata men such as myself have social power within a highly stratified social order because of our privileged race, class, and gender identities. Education and professional credentials further enhance male power by increasing access to goods and resources.

I was raised a Protestant Christian in the southern United States, educated at elite universities, ordained as a minister within the Presbyterian Church, and for nearly twenty years have taught Christian ethics at a Protestant seminary in northern New England. These and other contours of my social location have restricted and perhaps even impaired my perceptions of the world. However, I am also mindful that our viewpoints are also shaped by the moral commitments we sustain. As an educator-activist for justice in church and society, I am well aware of the fact that my own outlook on the world and, more specifically, my scholarship as a Christian theologian are being shaped and continually revised because of my involvement in several human rights projects. For five years, I have cochaired a statewide organization in Maine, the Religious Coalition Against Discrimination, which seeks to secure civil rights protections for homosexuals. More recently, I have helped to found and currently chair the Maine Interfaith Council on Reproductive Choices, a statewide network of religious leaders working to protect women's moral and legal rights to reproductive self-determination. I also work with local battered women's projects to educate clergy and congregations about ending male violence against women and children.

From the vantage point of these concrete practices, I have gained a heightened awareness that Christian theology always stands against human oppression. I have also learned that, at its best, Christian theological reflection is a communal task shared with many others as together we engage in, and critically reflect on, justice-making as central to the practice of faith. The call to justice and compassion is the animating heart of the Christian life. Justice means the ongoing, never-ending project to extend the community by strengthening relationships, setting wrongs right, and establishing the conditions for the well-being of all men and women. Compassion means the capacity, literally, to feel with and make common cause with others, to value others as our coequals, and not to lose sight of our common humanity as well as of our particularities, including diversities of age, race, gender, sexuality, culture, and religious tradition. [1]

At its best, the Christian tradition sparks the moral imagination and impels us to fall more deeply in love with life, with one another, and with God, the mysterious source of life and possibility. Loving God with passion, intelligence, and devotion also means loving, protecting, and delighting in life gloriously conjoined with others. These loves are intertwined, something the Jesus tradition has long emphasized by identifying love of God and love of neighbor as one indivisible activity (Mark 12:28–34). For this reason, the Protestant theologian H. Richard Niebuhr has spoken of the "danger of speaking of God without reference to the being [God] loves and that loves [God]; of speaking about religion or love of God as distinct from ethics or the love of neighbor." As Niebuhr points out: "there is no love of God where God's cause is not loved," namely, the sustenance and renewal of all creation (Niebuhr 1956, 34, 35–36).

As a person of faith, my life passion is to work alongside others for my liberation and theirs, helping to create a world (and church) in which gender, racial, class, sexual, and other oppressions will be seriously reduced if not eliminated altogether. The faith struggle is not to abandon hope that all people are created for—and called to—mutually respectful, peaceful relationships with each other. In light of the fact that this passion for justice is both a gift and a task, the Episcopal priest and lesbian-feminist theologian Carter Heyward has written of the urgency of recovering an energizing "religion of passion," one that is spilling over with careful caring and appropriate indignation (Heyward 1984, 21–22).

A religiously rooted passion for justice has nurtured me from an early age and has also radicalized me to be persistent and not to bail out from an open-ended process of self- and world-discovery. Time and again, in a process at once educational and redemptive, my peace has been disturbed. I have come to appreciate, sometimes slowly and often times reluctantly, that hope lies precisely in such unsettling. Troubled waters are often a sign of the movement of God's Spirit, an unsettling situation that intensifies whenever a faith community awakens to injustice, confronts and names moral evil, analyzes its contours, and grapples with how to dismantle it. Throughout justice struggles, being graced means surviving with integrity, holding onto one's sanity, sustaining an abiding gratitude for God's endless goodness, and never giving up.

Globally, injustice is the fundamental problematic of our day. In theological language, we speak of social sin or structural evil. Oppression in myriad forms divides and alienates, and dehumanizes and terrorizes. Justice-making bursts forth as protest and resistance. It begins with hearing the cries of human affliction, including our own, and with rightly naming the multiple causes of distress. Redressing institutionalized patterns of unequal social power is also required. Entrenched power inequities, most especially economic inequities, deny meaningful life for many and for others life itself. At the same time, others accumulate wealth, take unearned privileges for granted, and presume entitlement to dominance. [2] Given this context, taking a stand against injustice requires an honest sorting out of where we stand in the midst of intersecting injustices and examining how we are involved, consciously or not, in perpetuating injustices.

Resistance to injustice is the core virtue of Christian faithfulness in our time. Confronting oppression presses faith communities to envision alternative possibilities ("Your sons and your daughters shall prophesy, your old shall dream dreams, and your young shall see visions"[Joel 2:28; also Acts 2:17]). In addition to moral imagination, people need to nurture a stubborn willfulness that insists, against the odds, on the possibility of both personal and social reconstruction (Brock 1995, 71–84). Undergirding such commitment is the radicalizing belief that injustice is not divinely sanctioned but humanly constructed and, therefore, historically contingent. A liberating spirituality, the theologian Robert McAfee Brown notes, begins with the conviction that "the world should not be the way it is" (Brown 1988, 125).

Immersion in social justice movements has allowed many people of faith, myself included, to gain fresh moral insight; for example, during the U.S. civil rights movement in the 1950s and 1960s, I gained some initial awareness as a white person of the meaning (and limits) of whiteness in a racially segregated South. Confronting more directly the entrenched violence of white racism has required, among other things, facing white Christianity's complicity in racial injustice. Soon after, the Vietnam War taught a generation of young men (and women) not only about imperialism and state-sanctioned violence, but also about class privilege and how the U.S. government makes soldiers out of a disproportionate number of poor and disenfranchised young men (boys really) from working-class and minority communities. My own exemption from military duty was a function not only of my pacifist convictions, but also of my class and white racial privilege. This was a lesson I was able to grasp only after discerning that the "enemy" was not the enlisted soldier fighting in Southeast Asia but the neocolonial war system itself.

About this time, during the early 1970s, many women (and some men) active in the antiwar, labor, and civil rights movements joined the second wave of feminism. Feminism is a multidimensional project of sociocultural change, not only critiquing institutional structures and cultural patterns but also hitting closer to home. Inequities of power and status require correction among intimates, as well as throughout the social order. Doing right necessitates personal as well as social change, from men and women alike.

More recently, the gay liberation movement has offered additional learning opportunities. This social justice movement from "the underside of the underside" both protests against heterosexism and calls for reconstructing Christianity's long-standing sex-negativity. As a gay man standing within this movement, I am learning anew that justice-making not only requires something *of* me, but also offers something *for* me. Claiming my self-respect on a daily basis encourages me, even in a hostile culture, not to become lost in fear but to join openly with other gay, bisexual, and transgendered persons, as well as with nongay allies, to assert the moral integrity of our lives. Our passion for justice allows us to claim unapologetically our right to love and to be loved, as persons created fully in the divine image.

Moral awakenings about racism, classism, sexism, heterosexism, and ecological destruction have taught lessons about faith and moral vision, about the tenacity of injustice, and about the joys of seeking justice by plunging headfirst, along with many others, into the struggle for right-relatedness and communal well-being. Among lessons gained is that justice-making is not a "doing for" others, but rather a "being for" and an "acting with" that honors our mutual, interdependent good. In a crisis-ridden world, this shared goodness is far from fully actualized, but faith allows it to be imagined and desired deep down. Religion serves us well when it sparks this desire for a radically different world and keeps us in touch with the unsettling, liberating power of the sacred grounded in and among us. In sharing a commitment to an inclusive, comprehensive justice, we can begin the slow, often painful, but also exhilarating process of meeting across socially constructed differences and together creating a remarkable solidarity in which all parties are transformed as our connections are enlarged and strengthened.

Theological discourse is shaped by context in addition to social location. Any theology worth the effort today must critically assess the contemporary cultural crisis, a protracted and disruptive process of structural change precipitated largely by the global consolidation of a capitalist market economy. Capitalism is more than an economic system. It is also a cultural system of values and loyalties which, in its global expansion, is reordering power and meaning at every level. Massive political upheaval, for example, is taking place across the globe, including the literal remapping of Eastern Europe and much of Africa and Asia. In addition, the global cultural crisis is evident in family life, especially in the disruption of traditional patterns of human sexuality. However, the widespread crisis in the family is not a discrete, independent crisis, but rather one component of this larger, highly conflictual restructuring process. The cultural transformation of sexuality and gender is being further propelled by a grass roots feminist movement across the globe.

Feminism: The Longest Revolution

Feminism aims to break the hold of patriarchal social patterns and cultural norms, including patriarchal religions, and to reorder power between men and women, inside the family and beyond. By patriarchy I mean something similar to Adrienne Rich's definition. It is a male-controlled social force that uses ritual, tradition, law, and language, as well as customs, etiquette, education, and the prescribed division of labor to ensure that the female remains subsumed under the male (Rich 1976, 56).

Patriarchy is a dual system of institutionalized male power, a social structure and belief system that legitimatizes the power that men as a group exercise over women as a group, but also the power that some men (white, affluent, able-bodied, heterosexual, Christian) exercise over other men (black, poor, disabled, gay, and non-Christian). Sexism is intertwined with other oppressions, including racism, ableism, and classism. In racist patriarchy, all social differences are ranked hierarchically. The social superior is entitled to control the life (and life plan) of the less powerful, and the social inferior-dependent is obligated (or coerced) to acquiesce to the dominant order.

In relation to social dominants, social inferiors are naturalized, feminized, and typically sexualized as the nonnormative Other. This pattern has been sacralized by the dominant Christian tradition. Patriarchal Christianity blesses powerful males as ordained to rule and ascribes to women, the ruled over, the roles of helper, servant, and especially the "good woman," the obedient wife and devoted mother who suffers silently. As Mary Daly points out, Christianity has idealized for all—but especially for women—the qualities of a victim, glorifying weakness and the passive acceptance of suffering (Daly 1973, 77). Patriarchal Christianity sanctifies women's powerlessness and subordination as morally good.

Male gender supremacy is a moral evil that patriarchal Christianity has helped to perpetuate by legitimating male control as divinely sanctioned, supposedly beneficial for all parties. My interest as a liberation ethicist is in dismantling this system and, in particular, in challenging the religious underpinnings that hold Western white patriarchal cultural norms in place. However, I am cautious about making claims about Protestant Christianity's resourcefulness for (or interest in) unraveling gender oppression. I agree with the warning that the feminist ethicist Beverly Wildung Harrison gives, that the Christian church has yet to fully experience, much less work through, the painful encounter it must have with the full force of feminist critique. "We have very far to go," she asserts, "before Christianity acknowledges adequately its complicity in breeding and perpetuating the hatred and fear of the real, full, lived-world power of female persons" (Harrison 1985, 4–5).

Christian feminists insist that patriarchal Christianity's denial of women's humanity, its disrespect for their human rights, and its idealizing of women's powerlessness is far from accidental. This system of male control naturalizes dominant-subordinate relationships for the purpose of legitimating male supremacy. Its continuation depends, to a great extent, on the compliance of women and men to its norms and ideological assumptions about gender. When gender conformity and compliance to racist patriarchal norms break down, patriarchy turns violent, especially when women display autonomous self-direction and "when we women live and act as full and adequate persons in our own right." As Harrison explains: "It is never the mere presence of a woman, nor the image of women, nor fear of 'femininity,' that is the heart of misogyny. The core of misogyny, which has yet to be broken or even touched, is the reaction that occurs when women's concrete power is manifest" (5). The Catholic feminist theologian Rosemary Radford

Ruether observes similarly that "Misogyny is male-dominance engaged in self-defense of its right to define and control women and all other reality" (Ruether 1985, 705).

In patriarchal Christian theology, the male is the presumed center, the defining norm, and the exclusive representative of the human. He alone bears fully the divine image. The female, defined as secondary and subordinate, occupies an auxiliary place in relation to (and in service to) the male, but she never occupies the center or represents humanity in her own right. Although this cultural pattern that differentiates "man's world" from "woman's place" is characteristic of gender oppression, the content and boundaries of "his" world and "her" place shift historically (Janeway 1971). What remains constant is patriarchal Christianity's subjection of women to male definition and approval. Real women are rendered silent and invisible. For this reason, actual women are largely absent from an androcentric, male-defined Christian tradition. Furthermore, women's concerns are discredited and not taken seriously as part of the dominant theological agenda.

Whenever concerns related to justice for women are pressed, they are met either with derision as trivializing the "great" (male) tradition or with panic as subverting the prevailing social (male supremacist) order. This response holds whether the concerns are sexual and domestic violence, masculinist (as well as racist and classist) language and theological imagery, reproductive freedom and sexual difference, or women's authority and leadership roles. Patriarchy's fear is that women will collectively break silence and speak out, step out of patriarchally defined space, and assert their humanity as coequals with men. When women become powerful, androcentrism that is often unconscious typically gives way to overt misogyny. When patriarchal Christianity's interests are threatened, reactions to women's self-definition are often angry and defensive and may become harshly punitive because a patriarchalized faith tradition, Ruether notes, is "defined not only without the participation of women, but to exclude the participation of women" (Ruether 1985, 703).

As a broad-based grass roots social change movement, feminism is greatly admired and feared for the same reason. It aims at transforming the world (and church) by dismantling patriarchy and by debunking the ideological supports that legitimate male supremacy and female subordination. Because of the tenacity of patriarchy, feminism has been called "the longest revolution." It marks the struggle, always personal and political, to establish equality and mutual respect among persons, regardless of gender. However, feminism at its best goes beyond gender concerns ("gender feminism") and embraces a more encompassing change agenda ("justice feminism") by seeking to undo not only sexism, but all forms of oppression and their interstructuring, including racism, colonialism, classism, able-bodyism, and heterosexism.

Given feminism's far-reaching change agenda, this social and cultural revolution intends to be radical, aiming to reorder social relations at their root. As a politics of resistance to oppression, feminism seeks to offset the *patriarchal bias against* women by insisting upon an *egalitarian bias for* women. This corrective bias may be temporary or prolonged, depending on what is required to put sustainable conditions of genuine mutuality in place (Farley 1994). Both justice feminism and the more narrowly circumscribed gender feminism make women's well-being a priority, and both take women's diverse experiences and life struggles into account. However, justice feminism operates with a decisive difference. It proceeds with an explicitly political and theological-ethical accountability to those women who are doubly and triply marginalized, including women of color, poor women, women with disabilities including mental illness and HIV/AIDS, and lesbians. When a theological ethic takes into account economically and socially marginalized women and places them at the center of the discourse, then their voices, their interpretations, and their needs receive primary moral weight in the moral analysis. Feminist accountability, in its justice frame, is explicitly to those on the margins, and as bell hooks has pointed out, marginality is more than a site of deprivation. More importantly, it is a place to practice freedom and to gain moral vision. For this reason, the margin is not a place from which to exit too quickly (hooks 1990).

In a Christian perspective, what the biblical scholar Elisabeth Schussler Fiorenza calls a "discipleship of equals" (Fiorenza 1997, 2) perhaps best describes a normative feminist vision for gender and for other social relations in church and society. In this discipleship, women and men who both image the divine would both have equal status and rights, and would enjoy equal access to the multifarious gifts of the Spirit. This would amount to a radical democratic vision and reality that would be an alternative to the current kyrarchal structures of domination.

Backlash has been fierce within Protestant Christianity against feminism's visionary "discipleship of equals" and women's collective empowerment. This backlash is illustrated by the near hysterical furor over the Re-Imaging Conference, held in Minneapolis during the fall of 1993.[3] This theological conference, attended by 2,200 women and some 85 men, was explicitly feminist, multiracial, and multicultural. Its agenda was to explore the reimaging of the Christian faith so that women's authority and women's contributions could become central to the ongoing reformation of the tradition. As Elizabeth Dodson Gray suggests: "The conference embodied the reality of women finally stand-ing up in the Christian tradition as equal participants in 'the naming game'" (Gray 1994, 1).

The "naming game" refers to how socially powerful men, including religious elites, have reserved for themselves the right to interpret real-ity and to shape the patterned ways of perceiving and negotiating the world. Those who control cultural power are able to promote their own interests and to enforce their social and religious constructions as nor-mative. The feminist movement within the Christian tradition, as else-where, is challenging elite male monopoly of cultural, as well as political and economic, control, including the authority to name reality, especially the sacred. Women in every religious tradition are asserting their right to be "doers" rather than the "done-to." They are critiquing male supremacist definitions of women, no matter whether women are defined as the inferior, evil, unclean, and grotesque Other, or as the de-rivative and secondary Other, or as the morally superior and "more spiritual" Other.

Christian feminism insists that women are fully human, neither more nor less human than men. Both women and men are bestowed with a comparable range of strengths and weaknesses. Both are morally accountable for their moral choices. Gender justice aims at achieving two intersecting goals, a fair redistribution of social goods and re-sources and also cultural recognition of women's humanity and full au-thority as moral subjects (Fraser 1997). Although the economics of injustice should never be slighted, Gray argues that the conflict that the Re-Imagining Conference surfaced was, at its core, a cultural conflict about respect for women and control of the myth-making system. "It is a fight," she writes, "about who is to keep watch over the boundaries of orthodoxy and heresy, and who has the 'naming' right to define those boundaries and make those definitions authoritative" (Gray 1994, 1). The question is, will Christianity remain a patriarchal tradition, or will it be transformed from a male-centered, male-defined, and female-denigrating religion into a faith in which men will share with women the cultural power to name, including the power to name, invoke, and represent the sacred?

PROTESTANTISM AT A TURNING POINT

Historically, Protestant Christianity is poised at a turning point. Subju-gated peoples across the globe are rising up and claiming, first of all, their right to exist. In addition, the marginalized and disenfranchised are naming their right to a fair share of social resources, to a legitimate say in decision making that affects their communities, and to the respect due all persons as persons. The question not yet answered is how those in relatively privileged, protected positions, ourselves included, will respond to these global-yet-localized movements toward justice. In this volume, we are asking specifically about men's work in ending patriarchal oppression and in renewing religious traditions so that they become safe and hospitable sacred spaces for women. What, then, is men's work in advocating justice for women, and what might Protestant Christianity offer as justice-enabling resources?

Protestant Christianity is not a single tradition but rather multiple traditions, often in conflict. Denominational diversity and the absence of a centralized teaching authority make it difficult to identify a single, unified Protestant voice on gender justice or on other issues. However, within the diversity of Protestantism, a liberationist stance understands that the theological task is never simply to preserve and transmit the Christian tradition as received, but rather to evaluate the received wisdom and to offer critique and moral transformation as needed. What the biblical scholar Walter Brueggemann says about the Bible applies more generally to the pluriform Christian tradition. "The popular mind," he suggests, "regards the Bible as a seamless cloth with a unified teaching." However, the truth is that "the Bible present[s] powerful theological views in deep tension with each other, if not in contradiction to each other. Responsible use of the Bible requires the effort to notice the differences and to sort them out" (Brueggemann 1989, 57). Scripture and tradition are pluralistic. The task is not to accept or reject them as a whole, but rather to identify appropriate criteria for sorting out the differences. How do we identify what is revelatory? How do we distinguish theologically what is authoritative from what is not?

From a feminist liberation perspective, a justice hermeneutics is needed for critical discernment about gender and about the Christian tradition. The tradition, and the praxis it has generated, is approached with suspicion in terms of how Christian communities have reinforced sexist exclusion and violence against women, children, and less powerful men. Such suspicion is warranted because Protestant Christians have been far too self-congratulatory about how their faith tradition has "elevated" (white, middle-class) women. The historical record shows at best a mixed picture, including ongoing ambivalence about women as autonomous subjects of their own lives, an ambivalence starkly illustrated by the deep-seated conflict over women's exercise of reproductive choice with respect to childbirth and childrearing. The judgment offered by the Catholic feminist scholar Barbara Andolsen could easily be echoed by her Protestant counterparts. She experienced the "official" tradition of the Roman Catholic Church as profoundly alienating. Women were seen through the eyes of men, often celibate men, who were distrustful of women. These men, who were sometimes ambivalent about their own erotic feelings, could project their sexual passion on women, characterizing them as wanton and seductive. The tradition simply did not include the "self-understanding" of women (Andolsen 1992, 57, 59).

Feminist theologians have also documented a persistent ambivalence in Protestant tradition about nature and materiality. As Catherine Keller sums up the issue: "Protestantism has not yet as a public mass or an intellectual tradition outgrown its ambivalence toward 'nature'" (Keller 1997, 361, 363). The paradox of Protestant rationality is that while this tradition fosters a "worldly asceticism" that embraces the world as the arena for Christian vocation, its indifference to nature makes the way clear for the rationalized control and exploitation of nature. As Keller argues: "Without this religious base it is impossible to grasp the peculiar North American dynamic of cheerful capitalist optimism spliced with messianic righteousness, on the one hand, and, on the other, a blithely apocalyptic willingness to destroy the material matrix of life itself" (361, 363).

Negative Christian attitudes toward nature and the ambivalence Keller describes about materiality are also reflected in long-standing, highly negative Christian teachings about the human body (and especially about women's bodies), sensuality, sexual intimacy, and the right ordering of sexual and gender relations. For the most part, the watchwords in Christian moral discourse about sexuality have been *suspicion, avoidance,* and *restriction.* From Augustine on, characteristic motifs have been repeated in Christian responses to sex. In the popular mind, sex is an alien and dangerous force to be contained. Sin is defined essentially in sexual terms, above all as loss of control over the body and capitulation to sexual desire. Because women are associated with the body, emotionality, and "lower" nature, they must be supervised and kept under control for men's safety as well as "for their own good." Sex itself is morally suspect and redeemable only if it serves a higher purpose outside itself, namely, procreation. And (male) homosexuality is condemned, in part, because it is nonprocreative and, in part, because in the sexual act one partner is supposedly passive (the female) and the other active (the male), and it is demeaning for a man to act womanish or to be treated as a subordinate.

This solemn and joyless moral legacy is both fear-based and exceedingly wary of sex, women, and sexual difference. In the patriarchal

Christian perspective, sex is perennially cast as a problem, typically as precipitated by the female or gay Other. The fear response to otherness is couched in terms of reasserting control and punishing nonconformity to (patriarchal) Christian norms of celibacy and heterosexual procreative monogamy. Guilt, shame, and repressive control mark the dominant Christian tradition's moral response to sexuality.

The Catholic moral theologian Daniel C. Maguire speaks of a regrettable turn in the history of the church, beginning with the Constantinian establishment, toward "pelvic theology" and its obsession with sexual control. In the third and fourth centuries C.E., as the church shifted from prophetic to establishment status, it no longer defined its identity in terms of resistance to the imperial state and to its cult. Increasingly, the hierarchy asserted power by controlling the sexual behavior of believers and by creating a heightened clerical image for itself. Citing Samuel Laeuchli's historical investigation of the Council of Elvira (309 C.E.), Maguire observes that the church turned increasingly to sex in order to define both orthodoxy and clerical authority. This "Elvira syndrome" continues to operate today whenever church elites project a narrowly clerical image of the church and rely upon sexual control as a primary tool for that project. As Maguire conjectures: "Contrary to popular myth, Constantine did not convert to Christianity. Christianity converted to Constantine, and Elvira signals the first symptoms of this perversion" (Maguire 1989, 38–39).

Three assumptions are characteristic of this imperial approach to Christian sexual morals. First, moral truth is located in the past, in a tradition defined by patriarchal authority. Second, theological discourse about sexuality proceeds in a highly abstract, ahistorical, and largely deductive manner. Third, there is deep suspicion of advocates speaking out of their particular moral struggles, especially those appearing self-interested in making ethical claims. Religious elites proceed on an assumption that they are offering a disinterested, "pure" ethic above the rancor of social divisions and untainted by particular biases or interests.

In contrast, a liberating sexual ethic operates with quite different assumptions born out of a participatory, communal mode of ethical inquiry. First, moral truth is found in the past, but also grasped anew as communities of conscientious people encounter new circumstances and inquire whether and how the past offers insight and direction. Second, reappropriation of the past is never a simple matter of applying past truths to present issues, but rather a creative, dynamic process of engaging (and being engaged by) a living, pluriform tradition involved in its own continual change and adaptation. Third, although a liberating ethic is aware of the fact that the past makes claims on the present, the present also makes claims on the past. Insight from the past is dependent upon and filtered through, always through, the interests and limitations of present communities as they recognize and value the past. Therefore, we may engage the past freely and critically, claiming our responsibilities as authoritative interpreters and shapers of the Christian tradition in company with many others, some of whom we will agree with and others we will not.

The patriarchal Christian tradition has obscured the central place of justice in biblical faith, as well as downplayed how justice-making restores the vitality of communities. Marginal communities among women, gays, and the poor have rediscovered that the biblical God's passion is for justice shared across the earth. In an open-ended process of reinterpreting and appropriating the tradition, those on the margins today claim their right to evaluate and to transform the tradition in light of their experience of God as a God of liberation, not of oppression. A liberation ethic assumes that no source for ethical insight, past or present, is exempt from moral scrutiny. All tradition must be tested in terms of how the lives of women and marginalized men of all colors are impacted. Rather than asking abstractly what a male-centrist and misogynistic tradition says *about* women, feminist women and profeminist men must not only critically examine the tradition, but also, as needed, reconstruct it if it is to become genuinely inclusive, life-giving, and morally accountable—that is, concretely answerable—to women and especially to women further marginalized by racism, colonialism, poverty, and so forth.

A justice hermeneutics recognizes the moral authority of those voices from a tradition that embraces the dignity and moral agency of women, calls men into mutuality with women, and strengthens the community to resist evil and to celebrate life before and with God. Otherwise stated, life-giving spiritual power is found in tradition, Scripture, and contemporary faith experience that expresses a loving and caring justice *as defined by a justice-bearing, explicitly feminist faith community accountable to women.* A Christian theology, ethic, or model of ministry that lacks an unshakable commitment to gender, race, and economic justice as communal right-relatedness is no longer worth the bother (Ellison 1996, 59–75).

Given our conflicted cultural situation, where do we find moral wisdom? The critical impulse toward transformation, including spiritual renewal, is found largely at the margins of church and society, among disenfranchised groups and their allies who are seeking to rebuild the community as a place inclusive and respectful of human diversity. Along these lines, the Protestant ethicist Larry Rasmussen

argues: "More and more, Christianity [is becoming] a faith of struggling peoples who are recasting it amidst those struggles." Globally,
Christianity is shifting "from [being] the religion of the rich to [becom-
ing a] faith of the poor." This means, among other things, that "the vitality of Christian faith has passed from the European and North
American world to peoples in Africa, Latin America, and Asia, to the
women's movement most everywhere, and to the communities in our
own midst who are most in touch with these" (Rasmussen 1988, 178).

Several faith claims stand out from those Protestant traditions that
nurture movement toward a comprehensive justice. One central conviction is that hope, as well as moral insight, emerges from social justice movements and from their resistance to moral evil. The call to
resistance is enhanced by a faithful insistence on the radical regenera-
tion of the world toward fairness and mutuality among peoples. A radicalizing faith tradition also identifies with a divine passion for justice
and compassion that lies at the heart of the universe. Faithfulness to
this justice-loving God is demonstrated by the community's own re-
sponsiveness to the vulnerable, to the outcast, and to the powerless.
Biblically speaking, testing the relative fairness of a situation is
straightforward. First, it is necessary to ask how the least powerful and
well positioned are faring; then to ask if we are willing to trade places
with them. Hesitation on the part of the protected and privileged indicates that all is not rightly ordered.

MEN'S JUSTICE WORK AS SPIRITUAL RENEWAL

In *The Soul of Politics* Jim Wallis, a progressive evangelical Protestant,
offers a guiding principle for restoring a community that is particularly applicable to restoring men's moral integrity. "Those who benefit from [an injustice]," Wallis suggests, "are responsible for
dismantling it" (Wallis 1994, 97). The feminist Christian ethicist Karen
Lebacqz argues similarly in *Justice in an Unjust World* that justice requires something different from the powerless than from the powerful. On the one hand, God's response to injustice invites the oppressed
to cry out, protest, and resist. On the other hand: "for the oppressor,
God's response to injustice takes the form of rebuke and requisition.
Both require redress—the setting right of things gone wrong"
(Lebacqz 1987, 149). As members of the dominant gender class, men
are called, first and foremost, to repent and to make amends. Therefore, men's work includes not only respecting women's rights and
changing unfair social conditions, but also recognizing our complicity

in injustice, repenting of that wrongdoing, and taking concrete steps to make restitution.

Men's work is not to take charge of the feminist movement or even to "help the ladies," but rather to do our own justice-making, especially with other men, by transforming the norms and established patterns of male culture. In the meantime, we need to keep our feet off women's necks and, instead, collaborate with them to alter the social practices and ideological underpinnings of male dominance and male violence, in the multiple forms of battering, rape, sexual harassment, and clergy abuse of power, including sexual abuse.

Although a men's justice agenda cannot be adequately mapped out by any single individual, a preliminary outline is possible of "what men owe to women." Justice for women requires at least the following of men: telling the truth; making confession; exposing dominative power and seeking an alternative; becoming newly responsible; and entering into solidarity with women—and facing our fears.

Telling the Truth

Justice-making begins with men's candid acknowledgment that male gender supremacy is a pervasive form of social oppression that has corrupted Protestant and other faith traditions. Often men dominate "in good conscience" by means of a religious ideology that downplays or erases women's reality. When men no longer feel obligated to listen to real women as peers and companions, then it becomes more likely that they will take their own social constructions of reality for granted as really real. Male moral myopia is perhaps illustrated most dramatically by rapists who believe that women welcome coerced sex. Such men not only inflict harm, but also remain insensitive to their impact on others, all the while justifying their misconduct as "something she asked for" and even deserved (Scully 1990, 97–135).

Men have an obligation to start telling the truth about male power, about male gender and white racial supremacy, and about how their lives have been constructed not on the basis of reciprocity and mutual respect with others, but on the basis of hierarchy, competition, and fear. "As men," the profeminist activist John Stoltenberg writes, "we know more than we've ever really disclosed about how men keep women down, how men use race hate and sex hate to feel superior, how men despise 'faggots' in order to feel masculine" (Stoltenberg 1991, 8). Sharing this knowledge may, and probably will, cause men discomfort, embarrassment, even shame, but men should not shy away too soon from these feelings. Shame and feelings of remorse are essential moral resources that communicate to us that our actions have been wrong, disrespectful, harmful, and in need of correction. However, the first step in reconstructing our lives is to have our settled ways of knowing disrupted. Then, while holding onto our worth as persons, we may confront how we have caused pain in the world.

Making Confession

Justice-making requires that we acknowledge how we have participated in, and benefited from, the gender system of injustice. Here the specific challenge is to reframe the moral problem as one that involves all men, not simply a particular segment of men.

Because men as a group benefit from unequal social power over women, men are the ones primarily responsible for restructuring social relations, as well as religious traditions, toward greater justice for women, as well as with other men. Becoming responsible as men requires, in particular, giving up our innocence about male power and its effects on others. We must become *politicized*—publicly aware and accountable—as to how even good-hearted, compassionate men of faith participate in, and benefit from, systems that dehumanize, degrade, and inflict suffering on women and on marginalized men.

Paul Kivel, an educator at an Oakland, California, community project that works with men on ending male violence against women, speaks of this shift in self-understanding. "When confronted with the impact of male violence on women's lives, I originally wanted to say, 'It wasn't me,' 'I respect women,' 'I wouldn't hurt anyone.'. . . Yet as I learned more about male violence it became all to clear that I participated in perpetuating the system of violence that engulfs and imprisons us. Sometimes it was through my actions; other times it was through my denial or complacency. I could no longer claim innocence or feign ignorance" (Kivel 1992, xiii–xiv). We do ourselves a disservice by presuming that an absolute dichotomy exists between batterers (and rapists) and all other men. This dichotomizing among men discourages us from examining how as members of the dominant gender class, we participate in and, to varying degrees, contribute to a social and religious environment that promotes inequality. Candid self-reflection about male gender, white racial, and class privilege is a necessary component of our work as men of character.

While it is true that all men are not batterers or rapists and, therefore, not all men are morally culpable for doing women direct harm, that point should not be overemphasized to allow us to evade recognizing that all men share responsibility, as members of the male gender class, for the social and cultural norms that legitimate men's violence and control of women. Men of faith bear particular responsibility for transforming androcentric religion into more fully humanizing, and egalitarian, faith traditions.

Exposing Dominative Power and Seeking an Alternative

Although men are powerful as a social group, most individual men do not consider themselves powerful. The power given men is hierarchical power that defends and upholds the system of male, as well as class and race, privilege. An alternative kind of power, one that enables critique and transformation, comes from another source entirely, namely, from the willingness to join with others to seek another way, constructed on mutual respect and care. Specifically, this alternative involves transforming the model of manliness into the capacity to embrace others as equals, including the gendered, raced, and classed other.

Any system of injustice is maintained not by external controls alone, but by becoming internalized into people's character structures. Masculinity is the culturally constructed character ideal promoted for men, which invests men's lives in gaining superiority over and distance from others. However, the justice-bearing, largely marginalized traditions within Christianity carry subversive knowledge of a possible character transformation through which persons gain new lives. New life in the Spirit is possible, as early Christians gave witness, by renouncing and revoking old patterns and entering into intentional community as coequals and interdependents with others, including the outcast and dispossessed. A revitalized religious tradition is needed to empower men to engage in radical experimentation with alternative, culturally subversive models of masculinity. The manliness we need to instill is not based on conquest and on distancing ourselves from others, but on combining power with compassion and strength with fairness and respect for others.

Becoming Newly Responsible

Instead of feeling guilty, ashamed, or defensive about ourselves as men, we need to gain critical understanding of our place in the male supremacist order and become newly responsible for using our relative privilege and social power to promote justice rather than masculinist interests. Social change arises out of two sources, shared outrage over injustice and a shared vision of possibility. At its best, Christianity sparks the heart's desire for a new thing, for genuine mutuality of respect and care between men and women, men and men, and women and women.

Provocative theologies of desire are needed to stimulate in us a deeply felt desire for justice. However, such desire will only take place as Christians embrace the body and bodily existence as the realm of the sacred. The dominant Protestant tradition has focused almost exclusively on duty as a moral guide and approached pleasure with strong suspicion, but a liberating Christian spirituality must reclaim a morally principled pleasure that energizes men and women alike to claim mutual delight and enjoyment as coequals.

Entering Into Solidarity with Women—and Facing Our Fears

Men owe solidarity with women, not based on charity but rather on a respectful identification with women and on a willingness to take personal risks to advance the cause of promoting a women-friendly culture, including women-friendly faith traditions. To become women-identified men means running the risk that we, too, may become targets of male violence and be repudiated and rejected by other men as unmanly and as no longer "one of the boys." Such rejection is often a man's greatest fear.

At the same time, we must recognize the fact that many men find it difficult to admit that they lack power because it is not manly for men to admit powerlessness. Therefore, it is often harder for men than women to critique the status quo and to assess how exactly they as men have been harmed by present social and cultural arrangements. Yet it is precisely this damage—the lack of individual power for most men in a culture that demands that men exert power—that lies at the root of their desire to abuse and control women, children, and other, less powerful men. A liberating Christian faith must provide an alternative framework so that men can gain new vision and come to recognize that their own prospects for safety, well-being, and integrity are intimately bound up with the safety, well-being, and integrity of others, especially of women.

The spiritual calling for men is to enter into relationships with women as coequals without losing our identity or taking over the other. Otherwise said, men's moral obligation is to become dissidents from the dominant gender order. Troublemaking is a spiritual practice for the sake of our own humanity, as well as for the sake of the women we love and respect.

CREATIVE TROUBLEMAKING:
DEFENDING WOMEN'S REPRODUCTIVE RIGHTS

Justice-making often takes the form of repenting past mistakes and setting out on a different, more constructive course. In fact, Edmond N. Cahn describes justice as the active process of rectifying injustice or "of remedying or preventing what would arouse the sense of injustice" (Cahn 1949, 13–14). As one example of how men can engage in justice work that benefits women, I want to outline a profeminist male liberation response to women's reproductive health and self-determination. Because of historical patterns of male sexual exploitation and control of women's lives and bodies, including their procreative power, men owe women a radically different response to pregnancy, childbirth, and childrearing. A constructive response will focus men on increasing their responsibility for family planning, reproductive health (including protection from disease), and the care of children. Men will also need to promote women's sexual health and well-being, as well as to honor women's primary decision-making authority. Solidarity with women is further grounded in two moral principles: the principle of minimizing coercion (no woman should be made to act against her own free will) and on the principle of maximizing respect for women as moral authorities who have also historically carried the greater weight of the care of children.

Defending women's moral authority and legal right to make informed decisions about pregnancy and childbirth threatens patriarchy at its core and, therefore, has generated severe social conflict in the United States and elsewhere, especially because of the organized assault by the Christian right to reassert male control of women's lives and to return women to their traditional place of social and domestic subordination. A Protestant profeminist stance must encourage all men, but especially sexually active heterosexual men, to take responsibility for their behavior, to take steps to avoid unintended pregnancy and transmission of disease, and to speak out in support of women's reproductive freedom.

In the Protestant reformed theological tradition in which I stand, a profound shift has taken place within the last twenty-five years, from regarding abortion as taboo to viewing abortion as a responsible moral choice. Although the discovery of a pregnancy is often an occasion for joy, bringing new life into the world is not always a blessing. Assuming our freedom as moral agents requires that we bear the responsibility, at times burdensome and at times exhilarating, to make the most reasoned decisions we can. Being human also means acknowledging our finitude and accepting real limits, including our personal limits but also social and economic limitations. Because birthing a child is not always opportune or necessarily the most responsible moral decision, a woman-friendly, liberating religious ethic will honor birthing and parenting but refuse to turn either into an idol or an unqualified good.

The decisive question, in Christian moral perspective, is not when life begins but rather the question of whether, in a particular case, the woman (and her partner) are willing to care for a child and to be able to assume the responsibilities of parenthood. (Inability to care for children should not be viewed narrowly as a personal failing, but contextually as a socially created problem compounded by poverty and by other social ills.) Birth by choice, always preferable to birth by coercion or necessity, is a moral good that strengthens the well-being of women and enhances the common good. Elective birthing recognizes that the pregnant woman has the moral responsibility to judge her situation and to make a decision whether or not to intervene in the pregnancy.

At its best, the reformed Protestant theological tradition has celebrated the fact that new times bring forth new questions and often new duties. In an age in which the feminist movement has raised critical awareness of women's full humanity and their authority as decision makers, we are no longer in a credible position to question whether women have the right (or competence) to make these decisions. Misogyny is at work, in law and tradition, whenever women's capacity to make responsible decisions is denied and whenever others, including clergy, judges, and doctors, are turned to as the experts better qualified to decide about pregnancy and childbirth. Furthermore, we are living in a time when, because of advances in scientific knowledge, we have finally gained the power to create human life purposefully. Therefore, for the first time in history, we possess the means to guarantee that every child is welcomed and cared for. Because of these two historic developments, the world has changed, and we no longer have the right to create life unintentionally, against a woman's will, or simply willy-nilly.

In most pregnancies the question of abortion will never arise, but when it does, it should be recognized as an effort to exercise responsibility and to make a decision based on the woman's freely formed conscience and her religious convictions. We should applaud, not condemn or second-guess, the moral courage of women as they proceed, in company with those they trust, to consider the best course of action. Moreover, when a pregnancy is terminated, the appropriate moral response is not guilt or shame, but perhaps regret (that it was not possible to birth a child at this time), relief (that pregnancy did not obligate the woman to bear a child not wanted), and affirmation (that she has exercised her moral freedom with courage and dispatch).

The question now before Protestant (and other) churches is how they can support women, recognize and honor their moral courage, and help them integrate the decision to have an abortion with a view of themselves as responsible and faithful persons. In the past, the church has either condemned or silenced women about these matters. It is now overdue for us to acknowledge that women have struggled long and hard, against incredible odds, to exercise their procreative powers wisely. Often they have had to take great risks, including risking their own lives and health, to avoid unwanted or problematic pregnancies. Too often, in the midst of these struggles, we have allowed them to stand alone without support, guidance, or our abiding respect.

It has been the church's moral failing not to recognize and support women's reproductive freedom. Women—including our grandmothers, mothers, sisters, wives, and daughters—have not been the sinner, but the sinned against. To repair this moral damage, the church—and its majority male leadership—must now publicly declare its resolve to defend women's right to birth by choice and also to fearlessly advocate public policy that reflects this commitment.

WHICH MEN'S MOVEMENT? WHICH SPIRITUALITY?

Which men's movement will be most welcome by feminist women inside the church and outside?

In North America the news from the Christian right is bleak. The Promise Keepers movement, urging men to reassert leadership in the family, is thinly disguised patriarchal Christianity: men should control "their" women, homosexuality is sinful, and gender complementarity (dominant male, dependent female) is the Christian norm for family and society. Again, *control of women* is the operative watchword. Promise Keepers say almost nothing about male violence against women, but celebrate male bonding across racial differences as proof of a long-awaited reassertion of (patriarchal) manhood in each and every social stratum.

What would be a progressive, profeminist alternative to the Promise Keepers, and where might that movement emerge? A justice-based men's movement would delight in the empowerment of women, promote women's safety and bodily integrity as moral goods, and hold both men and women accountable for how their power affects others. Such a men's movement would create a climate of intolerance for gender, race, and class injustice and also protest male violence against women, children, and less powerful men. It would also appreciate the difference between women's oppression and men's spiritual malaise. Both are painful, but not equivalent. One feminist theorist draws the distinction by saying: "Oppression is what the slaves suffer; malaise is what happens to the slave owners whose personalities are warped and whose essential humanity is necessarily undermined by their position." Recouping the humanity of the masters depends on the liberation of the slaves. Otherwise stated: "the necessary first step in the cure for what ails the slave owner is to free the slaves" (Starhawk 1992, 29).

For most men, the first step toward justice for women (and themselves) is to start listening to women's voices and actually hearing what is being said. Taking women seriously requires learning how to keep company, respectfully, with those different from ourselves, including women (and men) from other classes, races, and religious traditions. Entering into and sustaining alliances is life-giving, transformative work, as the feminist ethicist Eleanor H. Haney eloquently describes in *The Great Commandment: A Theology of Resistance and Transformation* (1998). Men's alliance-building with women will require us to renounce male gender privilege (as well as race and class privilege), to actively listen to and learn from women, and to join in solidarity with women to dismantle racist patriarchy. When sufficient numbers of men daily practice these moral gestures, the cultural system of male gender supremacy will have been defeated, at least spiritually.

This justice work will be difficult as well as exhilarating, among other reasons because it requires men, in keeping company with women as coequals, to face our fear that we will be perceived as being "like women," as "no better than women," and therefore as unmanly. Homophobia, including men's fear of being feminized and losing male status, is a major impediment to forming a progressive men's movement because it prevents men from confronting how heterosexism keeps men in fear and competition with other men. Heterosexism, the institutionalization of gay oppression, is the linchpin that keeps sexism in place by punishing gender nonconformity—that is, "stepping out of line"—as sinful, criminal, and perverted. Patriarchy (and its religious cohort, patriarchal Christianity) makes intimacy between and among men taboo, and yet, without men's principled self-love and audacious love for other men (and for women as equals), a profeminist men's movement is, to say the least, unlikely. If men are in the movement only for women's sake and not for our own, we are likely to bail out when the going gets tough. Because of the close affinity between sexism and heterosexism, it is doubtful that men will be able to repair their alienation with women unless and until they also repair their alienation from themselves and from other men. No oppression stands alone; none falls alone. That is true of sexism, racism, and heterosexism.

The faith wager of a liberating Protestant spirituality is that men can live more principled lives when we reject the belief—and the social practice—that men are more important than women. Our lives become better, more fulfilling when we refuse to take advantage of women. We become more worthy of respect when we speak up and protest sexism and other oppression. Our spiritual vitality as men of faith increases when we no longer grasp for control but enthusiastically embrace others as our coequals. Our integrity increases when we acknowledge that most men, as most women, fear men's violence and that we often strategize to protect ourselves by allowing women to be the primary targets of men's rage and abuse.

On that glorious day when men stand up in protest against patriarchal religiosity, when men break with the dominant cultural system that legitimates male and other social privilege, there will be strong reason to rejoice about a genuinely earth-shattering new thing: that manhood in Protestant Christian culture will no longer be associated with woman-hate or coercive power, but rather with moral character and with the courage to resist injustice. That day cannot come too soon, for women and men alike.

Notes

1. The New Testament scholar Marcus Borg in *Meeting Jesus Again for the First Time* (San Francisco: HarperCollins, 1994) argues that the Christian moral life is an *imitatio dei* that "joins together an image of God and an ethos for the community" (50). He speaks of the Jesus tradition as modeling a politics of compassion in which compassion is not only an individual virtue, but also a sociopolitical commitment to break down social barriers and to reshape the community as respectful, caring relationships among coequals.

2. Peggy McIntosh observes that people with class, race, and other privileges are taught not to see their privileges as unearned advantages, and when they become aware, they are also challenged to become newly responsible. See her "White Privilege and Male Privilege: A Personal Account of Coming to See Correspondences Through Work in the Women's Movement," Center for Research on Women, Working Paper 189, Wellesley College (Wellesley, MA, 1988).

3. A second Re-Imaging Conference was held in 1998, again in Minneapolis, but without the furor generated by the first conference.

References

Andolsen, Barbara. 1992. "Whose Sexuality? Whose Tradition? Women, Experience, and Roman Catholic Sexual Ethics." In *Religion and Sexual Health,* Ronald M. Green, ed. Boston: Kluwer Academic Publishers, 55–77.

Brock, Rita Nakashima. 1995. "Ending Innocence and Nurturing Willfulness." In *Violence Against Women and Children: A Christian Theological Sourcebook,* Carol J. Adams and Marie M. Fortune, eds. New York: Continuum, 71–84.

Brown, Robert McAfee. 1988. *Spirituality and Liberation: Overcoming the Great Fallacy.* Philadelphia: Westminster Press.

Brueggemann, Walter. 1989. "Textuality in the Church." In *Tensions Between Citizenship and Discipleship,* Nelle G. Slater, ed. New York: Pilgrim Press, 48–68.

Cahn, Edmond N. 1949. *The Sense of Injustice: An Anthropocentric View of Law.* New York: New York University Press.

Daly, Mary. 1973. *Beyond God the Father.* Boston: Beacon.

Ellison, Marvin M. 1996. *Erotic Justice: A Liberating Ethic of Sexuality.* Louisville: Westminster John Knox Press.

Farley, Margaret A. 1994. "Feminist Theology and Bioethics." In *Feminist Theological Ethics: A Reader,* Lois K. Daly, ed. Louisville: Westminster John Knox Press, 191–212.

Fiorenza, Elisabeth Schussler. 1997. "Discipleship of Equals: Reality and Vision." In *In Search of a Round Table: Gender, Theology and Church Leadership,* Musimbi R. A. Kanyoro, ed. Geneva: World Council of Churches Publications, 1–11.

Fraser, Nancy. 1997. *Justice Interruptus: Critical Reflections on the "Postsocialist" Condition.* New York: Routledge.

Gossett, Hattie. 1992. "Mins Movement? A Page Drama." In *Women Respond to the Men's Movement,* Kay Leigh Hagan, ed. San Francisco: HarperCollins, 19–25.

Gray, Elizabeth Dodson. 1994. "Interpreting the Furor Over the Reimagining Conference." Unpublished article.

Haney, Eleanor H. 1998. *The Great Commandment: A Theology of Resistance and Transformation.* Cleveland: Pilgrim Press.

Harrison, Beverly Wildung. 1985. *Making the Connections: Essays in Feminist Social Ethics,* Carol S. Robb, ed. Boston: Beacon.

Heyward, Carter. 1984. *Our Passion for Justice: Images of Power, Sexuality, and Liberation.* New York: Pilgrim Press.

hooks, bell. 1990. *Yearning: Race, Gender, and Cultural Politics.* Boston: South End Press.

Janeway, Elizabeth. 1971. *Man's World, Woman's Place: A Study in Social Mythology.* New York: Dell Publishing Company.

Keller, Catherine. 1997. "The Lost Fragrance: Protestantism and the Nature of What Matters." *Journal of the American Academy of Religion* 65 (Summer): 355–370.

Kivel, Paul. 1992. *Men's Work: How to Stop the Violence that Tears Our Lives Apart.* New York: Ballantine Books.

Lebacqz, Karen. 1987. *Justice in an Unjust World: Foundations for a Christian Approach to Justice.* Minneapolis: Augsburg.

Maguire, Daniel C. 1989. "The Shadow Side of the Homosexuality Debate." In *Homosexuality in the Priesthood and the Religious Life,* Jeannine Gramick, ed. New York: Crossroad, 36–55.

Niebuhr, H. Richard. 1956. *The Purpose of the Church and Its Ministry: Reflections on the Aims of Theological Education.* New York: Harper & Row.

Rasmussen, Larry. 1988. "New Dynamics in Theology: Politically Active and Culturally Significant." *Christianity and Crisis* (May 16, 1988): 178–183.

Rich, Adrienne. 1976. *Of Woman Born: Motherhood as Experience and Institution.* New York: Norton.

Ruether, Rosemary Radford. 1985. "The Future of Feminist Theology in the Academy." *Journal of the American Academy of Religion* 53 (December): 703–713.

Scully, Diana. 1990. *Understanding Sexual Violence: A Study of Convicted Rapists.* Boston: Unwin Hyman.

Starhawk. 1992. "A Men's Movement I Can Trust." In *Women Respond to the Men's Movement,* Kay Leigh Hagan, ed. San Francisco: HarperCollins, 27–37.

Steinem, Gloria. 1992. "Foreword." In *Women Respond to the Men's Movement,* Kay Leigh Hagan, ed. San Francisco: HarperCollins, v–ix.

Stoltenberg, John. 1991. "A Coupla Things I've Been Meaning to Say about Really Confronting Male Power." *Changing Men* 22 (Winter-Spring): 8–10.

Thistlethwaite, Susan Brooks and Mary Potter Engel, eds. 1990. *Lift Every Voice: Constructing Christian Theologies from the Underside.* San Francisco: HarperCollins.

Wallis, Jim. 1994. *The Soul of Politics: A Practical and Prophetic Vision for Change.* Maryknoll, NY: Orbis Books and the New Press.

3

Bumuntu Paradigm
and Gender Justice

Sexist and Antisexist Trends in
African Traditional Religions

Mutombo Nkulu-N'Sengha

Rationale of the Study

MY AIM IS TO OFFER A REFLECTION on the dialectic between the feminine and the masculine in the African concept of *Bumuntu* (Personhood).[1] In so doing, I intend to interrogate the whys and wherefores of African traditions in matters pertaining to the welfare of women. More specifically, this study discusses "what do men owe to women"[2] from the perspective of African traditional religion and from a Third World standpoint. It is well-known that religion permeates all aspects of African life and institutions,[3] and that traditional religion has a preponderant influence on the various forms of African Christianity[4] and Islam. In 1970, during the symposium of Cotonou (a meeting of theologies), for example, African intellectuals declared African traditional religions "the main source" of the values of African civilization.[5] In 1977, the Ecumenical Association of African Theologians, newly created in Ghana, defined African traditional religions as one of the five important sources for the articulation of African Christian theology.[6] Though practitioners of indigenous religions represent about 31 percent of the African population, the values of those religions and their worldview continue to strongly influence the

69

Moslem (41 percent) and Christian (28 percent) populations.[7] The crisis of identity generated by the encounter with modernity and Western culture, has led Africans to seek in their ancestral customs, specifically traditional religion, the antidote to the current social malaise. An understanding of African traditional religions is therefore crucial to the issue of sexism in the African context. Comparative studies have shown that these religions exhibit common features[8] that impact African attitudes toward women in various regions of the continent. Grown in cultures rooted in oral tradition, these religions do not refer to a compendium of written sacred texts. However, the doctrine transmitted orally has been written down by various scholars.[9] This doctrine is found mainly in myths of creation, proverbs, art, prayers, ethical codes, and also in various religious teachings underlying rites of passage. This body of religious wisdom stands at the core of African traditions and of the perception of the nature and role of women in African societies.

When it comes to women, African societies are no exception to the "global evil" of sexism.[10] In Africa, as elsewhere, ancient and current history is replete with instances of open or subtle exploitation where women have been and continue to be treated with contempt and callousness. The security and dignity of women is often imperiled by the ambivalence of cultures that revere mothers, queens, and goddesses, while at the same time maintaining the "Eve-and-Evil"[11] syndrome that ostracizes women as witches, polluters, or minors to be controlled and disciplined by men. With regard to the dignity and the role of women in society, African traditions remain paradoxical. Traditional societies opened the door to female rulers, priestesses, and even army commanders. However, a close scrutiny of African history reveals that the African tradition—as the authoritative source of legitimization—has often functioned negatively regarding women's self-determination. In a world where the "gods act as policemen,"[12] tradition has often served as a mechanism of social control to protect male privileges. Given that, very often, patriarchy draws its imagined potency from the symbolic power of religious discourse,[13] it is necessary to engage in an "archaeology of religious rhetoric and practices" in order to get behind the mask of the sacred and unveil the process by which men create God in their own image and manipulate the *Kishila-kya-Bankambo* (the will of the ancestors) to preserve their social privileges and power. In this context, the anguish of African women becomes an important hermeneutical device for questioning the meaning of African native religious traditions. This necessitates a revisiting of tradition, and even reinventing new ones in light of the ontological category of *Bumuntu*, which, as the embodiment of African conception of the authentic mode of being, is the fundamental criterion of both manhood and womanhood. Therefore, I shall investigate the place and perception of women in traditional African culture in order to identify positive sources for their empowerment. Realistically, this also implies the authentic empowerment of men, insofar as gender harmony is indispensable for the well-being of both genders. Moreover, I propose to relocate the debate over sexism by placing it within the cultural and economic context of the emerging global market. Since life is not lived in a vacuum but in a concrete world of political and economic structures, I find it exhilarating to grapple with the special problems created by the multinational corporations and their might.[14] Situating the discussion here shows clearly that sexism in Africa is a multifaceted reality, and should not be studied only from the perspective of traditional customs and gender interactions. A more comprehensive approach is needed. The global market generates new forms of sexism, while provoking a cultural backlash. The inability of traditional cultures to cope with social transformations creates a radicalization and absolutizing of tradition that has nothing to do with the actual will of the ancestors. Thus I have introduced the theme of "underdevelopment" and global capitalism to prevent the antisexism, profeminist discourse from being taken hostage by the game of realpolitik. This threat of global capitalism makes it clear that conflict between men and women in Africa today can only foster the weakness of our continent to resist the new macrostructures of global domination. Gender justice is paramount to the building of a Pax Africana, which is a *sine qua non* for the future of African people in the global village. By linking tradition and global capitalism, I intend to drive the debate of sexism out of a conflict of ideas into the realm of praxis. I seek a genuine humanism that avoids turning "women's liberation" into a "strategy of containment" of Third World rebellion against exploitation. As John S. Mbiti so rightly pointed out, Africa is going through tremendous changes.[15] But African tradition is not going to be replaced by Western culture. The fact that Africans wear jeans, use cellular phones, and drink Coca-Cola does not mean that the African traditional worldview is dead. The African tradition is not a fossil, a thing of the past. It is a living reality, which reacts, mobilizes, and creates antibodies to resist aggression from without. However as F. Eboussi Boulaga warns, in the actual situation of Western global hegemony, naive exaltations concerning African religion, culture, and traditions come under suspicion of being either ideologies of mystification or diverting entertainment.[16] It is an illusion to think that global capitalism and the hegemony of Western cultures can be resisted simply by some African folkloric or religious practices, with trance and dance and songs and divination. Given that

global capitalism presents a serious cultural challenge to the very survival of African traditions, it is crucial to discuss issues of birth control,
ecological disaster, and wealth disparities when addressing issues of
sexism.

LOCUS AND PERSPECTIVE OF THE DISCOURSE

This study does not pretend to elaborate an African feminist theology.
Only women can truly elaborate such a theology. As a Luba (African)
proverb puts it, *Munda mwamukwenu kemwelwa kuboko nansha mulele bu-
tanda bumo* (Even if you share the same bed, you can never put your
hand in another person's heart). My discourse is therefore an examination of conscience, a dialogue, primarily with my fellow men. It is also
a way of honoring my mother who gave me life and taught me to respect women.

Let me stress from the start that I do not pretend to speak for all
African men, nor for the totality of African cultures and religions. I have
chosen as the locus of my discourse that region of Africa known in
Western popular imagination as the "Heart of Darkness," which is Central Africa, specifically the Congo Basin region. But for the sake of a
meaningful "theoretical discourse on Africa" I shall use a comparative
approach between Luba religion and traditional religions of selected
other regions, for instance, South Africa and West Africa. This will shed
light on some core values in African cultures beneath the variety of
modes of expression. I also draw from my own experience as an African
child born and raised in African villages, who had the opportunity to
live and study in Europe and America, and thus to confront different
worldviews of motherhood and womanhood embodied in different
philosophies, religions, cultures, family values, and lifestyles. I know
that I grew up in a patriarchal ethnic group where parents preferred to
provide more for the studies of their sons than for the education of their
daughters. With that experience in mind, let me highlight an important
methodological issue.

For a fair and productive reflection, it would be particularly important to guard against the sort of apologetic that became prevalent during the rise of the Negritude movement and African nationalism in the
1950s: the tendency to claim that sexism is a Western invention, since
the African traditions produced queens, valued women, and indeed
promoted human rights. In this reaction against the West, and in the
name of African identity, some Africans adopted another tactic. They

granted, grudgingly, that in the tradition of the ancestors women were treated "differently" from men. But they then insisted either that this did not mean women were thereby any less valued or that, in any case, it was "better" that they be "differently" treated for the harmony of the family and for the stability of the society. Here polygamy, genital excision, and other practices are defended in the name of the autonomy of the African tradition, the claim being that Africa has its own vision of moral values and its own version of women's liberation and should be protected against the hegemony of Western arrogance. In this context the struggle against colonial alienation is captured by a problematic postmodernism which, by denying a decent universality of common human values, promotes a narrow relativism that tends to sanctify all aspects of local culture. Meanwhile, and not at all incidentally, such a move preserves men's privileges. The main question to be raised then is, What is African tradition? A careful study of African history shows that tradition has never been monolithic. The permanent dynamism of African traditional cultures suggests that the symphony of traditional ethical voices has always been a polyphonic polysemy, where female voices were spoken and heard in spite of us men.

Finally, my notion of "African traditional religion" relies both on my personal experience and on the new scholarship of the last three decades. These studies allow us to gain a pretty fair picture of African traditional religion. Suffice it to note that this religion has a body of doctrine (albeit oral), a vision of God, and a set of moral rules, which must be taken into account for a fair and accurate understanding of the African vision of womanhood.

THE CRY OF AFRICAN WOMEN

According to Anne Nasimiyu-Wasike, a survey conducted in Nigeria among men and women that asked: "If you could be born again, would you choose to be a man or a woman?" revealed that 48 percent of the girls wanted to be born as boys, whereas only 6 percent of the boys wanted to be born as girls.[17] The cry of African women reveals the existence of sexism and the need for a change. This cry has been analyzed by male authors such as Wole Soyinka, Sembene Ousmane, Cheikh Anta Diop, and Joseph Ki-Zerbo, to name but a few.[18, 19] However the best anatomy of the cry of African women is found in the writings of women novelists and theologians who have pointed out how the African tradition, both religious and cultural, has been used as a tool of oppression.[20] In Africa, as elsewhere, it is not an exaggeration to argue that the concept of taboos introduced *fear* as an important component of religion. In the common African worldview, there is a belief that people suffer the consequences of their evil deeds in the present world. The universe is conceived of as a unified organism where every act has an impact on its author and on his or her relatives. The world is a dynamic play of different forces that influence each other. In this context each evil action diminishes the vital force of its author and the members of his or her family, and empties their humanness. The result is a series of bad luck events in life. In this context any disagreement with religious taboos turns immediately into a curse for oneself and for one's entourage. To break a taboo is to introduce death into one's own house. "If a woman does such and such, her husband or brother will be impotent, her child will die, her father or mother will die, and so forth." This looming menace of the ancestor's curse explains the oppressive logic of tradition as a powerful mechanism of social control.

In Africa, sexism can be perceived at the level of the common practical behavior of people, as well as at the level of religious principles. These principles embody traditional wisdom, for instance, myths of creation, proverbs, customary law, penal code, and taboos. When careful attention is paid to the life conditions of women in Africa, the first thing that comes to mind is the paradox of African traditional wisdom and the contradiction of actual African lifestyles. On the one hand, one finds traditions of matriarchy and a long history of women's leadership in political and religious spheres. On the other hand, one is faced with taboos and rituals that often burden women far more than men. In African tradition we are told that speech is female, and yet everywhere we witness the deafening silence and glaring absence of women from the public sphere.[21] Myths of creation and proverbs seem to have been largely produced by men, who use them to spread a negative image of women.[22] Oftentimes, men have found in this very traditional "wisdom" justification for keeping women "in their place." Among obvious examples of sexism in Africa are the practice of polygamy and "female genital mutilation." We also find the assumption that husbands are entitled to discipline their wives and that women without children deserve bad treatment; there is also an "ethical double standard" in the punishment of wrongdoings. There is also the widespread view that kitchen and domestic work are the natural duty of women. And often, men rejoice in the birth of a son more than in that of a daughter. In ancient times dead kings were buried with some of their living wives. Also women more than men are often accused of—and punished for—witchcraft.

The wisdom coming from African proverbs sends some ambiguous messages by suggesting that women ruin men and possess bad characters; for instance, young boys are taught that "To marry is to put a snake in one's handbag." This negative view of female nature is reinforced by a general perception of female genitals as death-radiating, or as a source of bad luck;[23] for instance, it is assumed that if a woman climbs a tree, the tree will die or become unproductive. Tradition teaches that a man preparing to travel, to go fishing or hunting, or to undertake other important missions should abstain from any sexual relationship; otherwise he will have an accident or fail in his endeavor. The bad luck and the danger are even greater if the partner is a menstruating woman. All over Africa women are considered unclean and a source of bad luck during their period of menstruation.[24] They are even forbidden to cook for their husbands and are kept far away, spending their nights in a different hut.

In the field of taboos, marriage rituals, and sanctions for misconduct, the ethical double standard shows clearly how tradition can be an enormous burden for women in Africa. As M. A. Oduyoye pointed out so poetically, the tragedy of ethics in a polygamous setting is the injustice inherent in the unspoken assumption that the female is to be a "monotheist" while the male can act as a "polytheist"—arrogating to himself the freedom to worship the bodies of several women.[25] This double standard is flagrant in many cases. In many ethnic groups, to be a virgin at marriage is still considered the ideal, and a girl who is not a virgin cannot marry with honor.[26] However this requirement is not applied to men. And sanctions for adultery are more tragic for women than for men. Where the taboo of incest is extended to in-laws, as among the Baluba of Katanga, two sisters sleeping with the same man are called with contempt *mbwa* (dogs), and sometimes forced to eat dog's meat in a ritual of purification. Prostitutes are also called "dogs." The same judgment is applied to women who share the same man with their daughters. However men involved in these situations are never called "dogs." In Kinshasa, men exchange proudly the expression *Kudia nsusu kudia maki* (to eat the chick and the eggs) to show their prowess in the "art of hunting women."

Finally, men often evoke the traditions to exclude women from the public sphere. The most explicit illustration of this can be found in the Hausa proverb: *Kworria tagari tana ragaya* (A good woman stays home).[27] On the eve of the third millennium, the cry of African women involves a refusal to stay at home. And this rebellion is nurtured by the very nature of African tradition that has always been dynamic and open to new metamorphoses.

Why Men Do Not Listen

On the one hand, men who see their sisters beaten by their husbands, or their fathers beating their own mothers will agree that sexism is a serious problem. However, when it comes to analyzing their own behavior toward women, few men confess that they are sexist. This is why it is difficult to convince men to get genuinely involved in the struggle for women's equality. Drawing from experience, from what as a man I hear from other men, I would summarize men's unwillingness to change into four points: invisibility of patriarchal privileges, fear of social judgment, identity crisis due to the burden of a falsely constructed malehood, and selfishness.

By invisibility of privileges I mean the fact that many men do not see themselves as holding power and privileges at the expense of women. In Africa, as elsewhere, gender is to a certain extent a social construct. A young boy learns that men do not cry, that men must be tough, build a house, hunt, and protect the family. Young girls are expected to play different roles that culminate in childbearing and child-caring. The kitchen is their prerogative. Mothers and grandmothers tell young girls: "If you do not cook you will not get a husband." In such a context it will not occur to an African man to think that it is unjust to play a role specific to women. He may even cook in some circumstances, but will surely not view that issue in terms of domination, oppression, and injustice. Instead, men feel the burden of fulfilling their own roles as defined by the society. This burden leads men to identity crises, in a society where women despise men who by their standards, lack ambition, do not have a house or a job, in one word men with whom "there is no future." Women, so say the men's club, love heroes and despise weak men. These men struggling with their own "manhood identity" view the whole notion of patriarchy as a figment of women's imagination. Moreover a man playing the role of a woman, for instance, cooking and baby-sitting, will be mocked not only by other men but also by women and by his own sisters. His mother will be ashamed of him as somebody who "is colonized by his wife" or made obedient to her. This fear of losing one's "manhood" is an important obstacle to gender equity. In many urban centers, it is common for middle-class women to hire men for domestic work. But the same man who cooks for women as part of his profession, will not cook at home for his own wife. The reason is that a man is not allowed by custom to intrude in a role specific to his wife. Thus, several stories are told about women who abandon their husbands because of such interference in the division of labor. In such a situation, it is said the wife is unhappy thinking that the husband cooks to send a message that she is good-for-nothing. Moreover, men tend to think that "the more you help your wife in domestic work, the more she gets lazy, expecting you to do everything." And in Africa, a lazy woman is of course a "curse" for the husband. Men also believe that it is not "wise" for a man to reveal his income to his wife, because of the supposedly "women's tendency to spend money" buying nonsense. Man's control of the domestic budget is understood as necessary in order to control the wife through discipline. Some men say that women enjoy being beaten because it shows a lack of indifference; in other words the man who gets angry shows that he cares for what his wife does. In some cases, beating as an expression of jealousy for a woman returning late at home, is seen as a positive manifestation of love. According to many men, if you do not beat your wife, she will think that you have mistresses. Therefore she will create conflicts constantly until you beat her. This type of reasoning stems from a long tradition of so-called wisdom regarding female psychology. Men already in crisis with their own identity face another crisis in their incapacity to comprehend women's behavior. In this context, men see themselves as victims of "women's impossible characters." Sexism appears to them not as an issue of power and dominion over women, but as a necessary authority and as a normal response to women's unreliable and irresponsible behavior. At close scrutiny all this, of course, is nothing else than the expression of selfishness and the rationalization of sexism. Indeed, it is a self-serving defection of moral courage, a somewhat calculated refusal to face the problem.

Tradition as a Source for Gender Equity and Equality

From what has just been said, it may seem contradictory to think that the African tradition can be a source of liberation for women. The large body of literature produced by Africanist scholars and by their disciples has propagated the myth of a primitive society, static, fragmented into microscopic clans and tribes, practicing cannibalism, fetishism, witchcraft, and polygamy. Recently this picture has started to evaporate under the scrutiny of "enlightened scholars" such as Kajsa Ekholm Friedman. We know today, Friedman argues, that many of the societies that anthropology used to think were traditional (meaning original) were in fact later phenomena, created through transformative contact with an expanding Europe.[28] They were products of a global historical process that for their part meant gradual disintegration, peripheralization and, in some cases, even complete elimination. The so-called primitive societies were frozen only insofar as the expanding civilization handicapped their natural growth, and they were seen as primitive and backward because of the position they were forced to occupy within the global system. By presenting these societies, exploited and in crisis, as the real "traditional Africa" anthropologists have introduced distortions not only for foreigners trying to understand Africa, but also for Africans themselves. As Bénézet Bujo rightly pointed out, the main trouble of Africa, is that, after the tornado of slave trade and colonialism, many Africans, today, have lost contact with the best of truly African traditions.[29] In many cases, what is meant by African tradition is the miserable picture spread by the colonial library, produced to justify the "civilizing" mission, and some new practices invented by people in despair, attempting to challenge the overwhelming impact of Western conquest and exploitation. As Takyi-waa Munah pointed out, when Western scholars interested in women's rights depict African women as powerless and oppressed by various systems of customary law, they forget that in many cases these customs are new constructions and that they create a situation that is neither customary nor legal.[30] Precolonial African societies manifested a variety of attitudes and practices toward women, with women possessing political, religious, and social power in some systems and having little or no formal power in others.[31]

A careful study of African traditional languages and customs suggests that there is more in African tradition than polygamy and excision, tools of oppression in the hand of patriarchal authority; they also contain nevertheless positive elements that may result in the construction of new and empowering traditions. I will limit my analysis to the African notion of personhood (*Muntu* and *Bumuntu*), God (*Leza*), ethics (*Mucima Muyampe*), and the place of women in the hierarchy of traditional religion. A specific emphasis will be put on the particular genius of African languages and the role that names of people play in the African worldview.

The Concept of *Bumuntu* and Its Divine Origin

Paramount to African traditional understanding of personhood is the concept of *Bumuntu*, which emphasizes the intrinsic equality between men and women. The element of utmost importance in African traditional religion was neither rituals nor sacrifices, but the concept of personhood, known as *Bumuntu* in Central Africa, *Ubuntu* in South Africa, and *Eniyan* or *Iwapele* in West Africa. The full meaning of *Bumuntu* is rooted in the concept of creation, which points to the "transcendent origin of human existence" and to the notion of free will. The belief in the individual power of self-cultivation, the capacity to improve one's own character, and the ability to grow morally as a good human being, was part and parcel of traditional worldviews.

African traditions start by stressing the sacredness of life *(Bumi)* in general and the sacredness of every individual, male or female, in particular. This sacredness does not derive from gender attributes but from the transcendent source of life. According to an Akan proverb from Ghana, *Nnipa nyinaa ye Onyame mma obi nnye asase ba* (All human beings are children of God; no one is a child of the earth).[32] For the Baluba people, as for the Akan, all human beings, men and women, are *Bantu ba Leza* (God's people), *Bana be Vidye Mukulu* (children of the Great Spirit), and God is the supreme judge of human behavior. In other words, a woman is not the property of her husband or her parents. She has her own value as an individual. Kings, parents, and husbands are not "owners" of anything or anybody, but simply custodians of God's property.

That every individual is divine is more explicit in the Yoruba religion. According to the Ifa creation myth, *Eniyan* (human being) is made up of *Ara* (body), *Opolo* (brain), *Okan* (heart), *Emi* (spirit), and most importantly *Ori* (destiny controlled by inner spiritual head). The creation of such a being is the result of the work of *Olodumare*, the supreme being, and some of his subordinate spirits (Orisa-nla and Ajala). First, *Ara* (the body) is constructed by *Orisa-nla*, the arch-divinity, the crafter of the body. Second, *Olodumare* supplies *Emi* (spirit) that activates the lifeless body. After the *Emi* has been put in place, the newly created human being proceeds to the next stage—the house of *Ajála* (potter of heads) for the choice of an *Ori*. Each being picks up her preferred case without knowing what is stored there. But whatever is stored therein will determine the life-course of the individual in the world. That is the destiny and therefore the personality of the individual. The concepts of *Emi* and *Ori* are crucial for our understanding of the African concept of womanhood and for the notion of equality between men and women. According to Yoruba theological anthropology, once *Ara* (body) is supplied with *émi* through the action of *Olodumare, ara* (body) now has *éémi* (breath) and begins to *mi* (breathe).[33] Thus *emi* is part of the divine breath. It is the active principle of life, the presence of the divine within every human being. *Emi* is the temple of *Olodumare* within every being. Everybody is a child of *Olodumare*, despite his physical condition or character. As a Yoruba proverb, specifies: *a ki I fi omo buruku fun ekun pa je* (We do not throw a child to the tiger just because he or she is bad).[34] The fact that *emi* is the same in all human beings ensures the equality and dignity of every human being. To mistreat somebody is to touch upon *Olodumare* who dwells in him. Reference to one as an *elemi* is an indirect warning against being mistreated.[35]

This notion of the divinity of human beings is reinforced by the concept of *Ori* and the subsequent doctrine of self-worship. In the Yoruba religious view, *Ori* (the inner spiritual head), is elevated to the level of a divinity. It is a personal divinity[36] within every person, and plays the role of a guardian and protector. As such, he receives sacrifices and is called the "partner" or "double," and regarded as one of the 401 *Orisha* of the Yoruba pantheon.[37] Not only do the Yoruba believe in the *imago dei* doctrine, but they build shrines for each person to worship his or her own spirit! While the *emi* is the same for all *Eniyan* (a human deserving of respect), the *Ori,* as bearer of personal destiny is the principle of individuation and the foundation of individual character, which the Yoruba call *Iwapele.* If *Ori* determines the destiny and personality of the individual, the specific behavior stems from *Opolo* and *Okan.* A person who misbehaves is described as "having no *opolo*" (no brain) or whose *opolo* is malfunctioning. But it is mainly *Okan* (heart) that is considered the source of character. Among the activity of *Okan* we find willing, desiring, wishing, hoping, worrying, believing, intuitive thinking, and so forth. *Okan* is also identified as the basis of activities such as *ifé* (love), and *ikorira* (hate). *Okan* is the source of character, and for the Yoruba character is the criterion of true personhood. *Iwa* is for the Yoruba the most important moral concept. It is interesting to note that among the Yoruba, the word *Iwa* means both "existence" and "character." That is why a true being is a being with a good character *(Iwa rere)* or a gentle character *(Iwa pele).*

It is crucial to understand that for the Yoruba, each person is responsible for the growth of his or her moral character, as is stated in the following proverb: *Iwa rere l'éso eniyan* (Good character—good existence—is the adornment of a human being). The *Ifa* corpus is even more explicit. *Owo ara eni, Làafi I tunwa ara enii se* (Each individual must use his or her own hands to improve on his or her own character).[38] This concept of free will and personal responsibility finds an interesting echo in the Luba proverb: *Vidye wa kuha buya nobe wa mukwashako* (God gave you beauty and goodness but you must help him), meaning God will not do everything for you. This notion of personal responsibility shows that the traditional ethic was not about blindly following the customs. It also shows that the notion of God as the foundation of morality reinforces the moral need for self-improvement. It is on this basis that men's behavior toward women becomes a matter of the former's self-growth in humanity. A focus on the Luba concept of *Mucima muyampe* (good heart), and the dialectic *Muntu-Kintu* process, will help us clarify the essence of the African traditional ethic and its value for women's liberation.

Muntu versus *Kintu*: *Mucima Muyampe* as the Essence of *Bumuntu*

The analysis of the Yoruba concept of being truly human *(Eniyan)* has shown that according to African tradition a human being is not fully human by the simple fact of being born from human parents. This dialectic between *Eniyan* as the "ordinary meaning" of human being and *Eniyan* as the "normative quality" of a genuine human being is well expressed in the Baluba distinction between *Muntu* (a person with good character) and a *Kintu* (a thing). Bantu ontology is expressed through the concept of vital force, which means that the being is not static but fundamentally dynamic. A human being can increase or lose his or her humanness. The quality of a human being does not stem from his gender or from his ancestors, but rather from his personal behavior. It is not even enough to be created in the image of God! This brings us to the centrality of ethics in African tradition. It is interesting to note that from West Africa to South Africa we find the same focus on moral character expressed through the widespread belief that people of bad character are not truly human. The Yoruba say: *Ki I se eniyan* (He or she is not a person).[39] In South Africa we find the expression: *Ga se Motho* (He or she is not a human being)[40] and the Baluba people of Central Africa say: *Yao Ke Muntu* (He or she is not human) or *I mufu unanga* (He or she is a dead body walking). In its attempt to define manhood, Yoruba traditional wisdom explicitly states: "A man may be very, very handsome; handsome as a fish within the water. But if he has no character, he is no more than a wooden doll."[41]

Even though it is difficult to find in African languages an equivalent to the Western words for *ethics* and *virtues*, Africans have their own words and expressions for good character, and establish a clear distinction between good and evil, and praiseworthy behavior and bad conduct. For the Baluba, the *Bumuntu* (the essence of a genuine human being) is embodied in the *mucima muyampe* (good heart), which expresses itself in *Mwikadjilo muyampe* (good way of being) or *Mwendelo muyampe* (good way of walking on the road of life). The opposite of good character is expressed through *mucima mubi* (evil heart, evil thought, and evil sentiment), *diso dibi* (evil eye or threatening look), *ludimi lubi* (evil speech and verbal abuse), and *bilongwa bibi* (evil deeds), four main expressions of unethical conduct. In the Luba vision of ethics, the *Bumuntu* or "good character" is something each person has to cultivate constantly: *Vidye wa kuha buya nobe wa mukwashako* (God gave you goodness, but you must help him), meaning that you should continue to cultivate your talent. This proverb highlights the fact that the Luba ethic is based upon the notion of free will and personal responsibility, despite the strong emphasis put by the Baluba on the community. By using the same word *buya* for "goodness" and "beauty," the Baluba express an ontological relation between ethics and aesthetics in the sense that good conduct is not understood as a matter of blind obedience to external rules but rather as an expression and celebration of the ontological elegance of the character of a person who lives in harmony with other life forces in the universe.

The Luba ethic starts with the distinction between two modes of being, the *Mu* or category of *Muntu* (existence-of-intelligence and genuine-human-being) and the *Ki* or the category of *Kintu* (a thing or person without moral values). The *Bumuntu* (humanness) oscillates between the status of *Kintu* and the status of *Muntu*, so that when a human being behaves badly he or she falls into the category of *Ki-ntu* and people call him or her different names. As the figure shows :

The MU-NTU category:
   good morality and intelligence
	The KI-NTU category:
	   bad morality and stupidity

Muntu: (good,
   respectable person)
	Ki-ntu: (thing,
	   person without self-respect)

BUYA paradigm
   MUCIMA MUYAMPE (good heart)
	BUBI paradigm
	   MUCIMA MUBI (evil heart)

TATA (good father)	KI-TATA (bad father)
MULUME (good husband)	KI-LUME (abusive husband)
MULOPWE (good king)	KI-LOPWE (tyrant, violent king)

FIGURE 3.1   Modes of Being: "Mu" and "Ki"

The language of *Ki* means that a human being can empty out his dignity *(Buleme)* and his humanness by thinking, speaking, or acting in a wrong way. For the Baluba, "to be" means "to be ethical," to think, speak, or act ethically. Thus, very often people talk about somebody who behaves unworthily, saying: *Yao ke Muntu ho* (He is not a human being).

The core of Luba ethic is well summarized in the proverb *Bwino bonso ke bwino, bwino i kwikala biya ne Bantu* (The genuine art or knowledge is to know how to live harmoniously with our fellow human beings). As this proverb shows, for the Baluba, the perfect man or woman is *Muntu wa mucima muyampe* (the person with a good heart), who has learned the art of living and who promotes the essential harmonies of life. The concept of *Mucima muyampe* includes such virtues as *Lusa* (compassion), *Buswe* (love), *Buntu* (generosity), *Boloke* (righteousness, honesty, integrity, and fairness), *Bubine* (truth, honesty, and integrity), *Butundaile* (hospitality), *Butalale* (peace), *Buleme* (dignity, respect, and politeness), *Bukwashi* (helpfulness), and chastity before marriage and faithfulness during marriage. The catalog of *mucima mubi* (evil heart) points out several other immoral behaviors such as *Mushikwa* or *Nshikanyi* (hate), *Bwivi* (robbery), *Bunzazangi* (hypocrisy), *Bubela* (falsity), *Busekese* (sexual misconduct), *Makoji* (adultery), *Kibengo* (arrogance or insolence), and *Ntondo* (discrimination). Rape is also specifically condemned among the Baluba as well as among the Yoruba, the Akan, and many other ethnic groups. Among the Asante regulations governing sexual relations, several condemn rape.[42]

It is significant that the notion of *Bumi* (life) is an important hermeneutic principle of the Luba ethics. The concept of *Buya* (goodness) refers to any behavior that promotes human flourishing. Everything (word, thought, and action) that threatens, destroys, or belittles the *Bumi* and the *buleme* (human dignity) is evil, because for the Baluba, life is the supreme gift of the creator whose highest attributes are purity, goodness, and fairness: *Vidye kadi katonye* (God is stainless, spotless, unblemished, and a just judge), say the Baluba. It is interesting to notice that the Luba name for the supreme Being, Leza, was created from a Luba verb that means "to cherish."[43] Because Leza cherishes his creatures, to mistreat women is to act against the will of God and the will of the ancestors, which aim at the well-being of all humans. In traditional religion, God's attributes are the norm of proper ethical behavior. People are expected to act according to the norms of goodness as established by the creator. Talking about bad behaviors, the Baluba people always say: *Leza kaswele nenki* (God does not like that). This ethic exemplifies the core of the African tradition, the very will of the ancestors. In other words, it conforms to the will of the ancestors to ask whether the life of African women is respected and protected. When patriarchy is analyzed in the light of the cry of African women, the conclusion is clear: sexism is unethical. It is a betrayal of the will of the ancestors. Moreover the sexist loses his own *Bumuntu* in the process of oppressing a woman.

African Antisexist Tradition

The previous study shows that traditional ethics and the concept of *Bumuntu* are important sources for the empowerment of women. The fundamental equality between men and women, rooted in the concept of *Bumuntu*, was translated into actual practice in the public sphere. Thus traditional religion had priestesses. It is significant that in African tradition God and the ancestors overflow gender boundaries. God is translated in both female and male images.[44] Among the Yombe, and among many other ethnic groups, God is clearly called "Mother."[45] An ancestor, male or female, once dead could be born as a boy and girl in different families and appear to his family in different forms. This vision of the supernatural world suggests that gender roles are not static in Africa, and should not be kept static in the name of tradition.

The concepts of God and ancestors thus appear to be liberating paradigms because they render male dominion morally ungrounded and illegitimate. African myths of creation and the attributes of God shed an interesting light on the African antisexist tradition. By examining the issue of sexism from the very question of the origin of human beings, we realize that African traditional religion stipulates the radical equality between men and women. The concept of creation offers two important notions of personhood. First, men and women are equally created by God. Second, is the independence of the woman who is created directly by God, not through man. This notion is also reinforced by the fact that in some myths of the creation women were created first and men later. The relevant idea to the issue of sexism is that the woman was not created in the image of man. It is not surprising therefore that in marriage the wife does not take the name of her husband.

In more or less all regions of Africa, the creator is understood as the creator and master of all life. The source of all beings is beyond the nature of each being. God is not a *Muntu* (human being); he is not part of the category of *Ntu* (creatures). He is among us, but nobody can touch him. *Vidye kadikula umwite ukwitaba, umulonde bukwidila,* says the proverb (God is not far away; if you call him he will answer you and you will hear his voice, but if you take the road to walk toward him, you will never meet him). This concept of the creator as the unknown is found in many traditions in Africa. In Nigeria, for instance, God is called *Ama-Amasi* (The One known yet never fully known). And a Pygmy hymn states explicitly:

> *In the beginning was God,*
> *Today is God,*

> *Tomorrow will be God*
> *Who can make an image of God*
> *He has no body*
> *He is as a word which comes out of your mouth.*
> *That word! It is no more,*
> *It is past, and still it lives*
> *So is God.*[46]

The Baluba say that God is like *Malango* (the thought) or *Luvula* (the wind). *Kimpumpu* (tornado) is said to carry the ancestors, and sometimes God himself. The metaphor of the wind is powerful. Nobody sees the wind; nobody knows its origin; nobody can describe it perfectly. Like the wind, Leza is beyond men's word, beyond men's explanations of life, beyond men's conception of morality and power, beyond men's definition of the supernatural. Thus, men's sexist definitions of women are obsolete because only Leza can define his creatures. We find in the transcendence of God a very important source of legitimacy for the creation of new traditions, for God stands beyond all male-made traditions. All structures of oppression are relative, and should be submitted to the scrutiny of criticism.

The transcendence of Vidye Mukulu gives African women the right to challenge traditions and to articulate new ones that reflect more adequately *Buswe* (love). Since God is the "known-unknown," nobody can claim that his view of the tradition, of the will of God, of the will of the ancestors is the only true one. This notion of God is also crucial to the understanding of African ethics. It is not up to men to determine arbitrarily right conduct toward women. Instead fairness and equality among genders are a matter determined by a higher court, the source of all life. Thus, in matters of sexism, a man is not his own judge. He is judged by the creator on the basis of his attitude toward life in general and toward women's life in particular. The fact that according to the tradition, a woman does not belong to a man, is indeed an important step toward a tradition of empowerment for women. This tradition also finds roots in African languages and in names of individuals.

Nommo and the Value of African Names

Since Wittgenstein's *Tractatus Logico-Philosophicus* and the "language-game" philosophy of the *Philosophical Investigations*, contemporary Western philosophy has become more aware of the connection between language and reality. This notion of the performative nature of language finds an interesting ground in Bantu philosophy.

In African worldviews, there is an important connection between ontology and language. The word is not simply an expression of a being, but it also *creates* the world. This powerful creative word is called *Nommo* (by the Dogon people); it is also translated as *Nenno* (in Kiswahili language). As Ngugi wa Thiong'o pointed out: "From a word, a group of words, a sentence and even a name in any African language, one can glean the social norms, attitudes and values of a people."[47] Language shapes deeply the relationships between men and women. Through language the child learns how to perceive other human beings and the role ascribed to them in the society. Since the publication of Bantu philosophy in 1945, African philosophers and theologians have pointed out some unique qualities of Bantu languages, which generate a worldview where God and human beings are not determined by gender differences. The first point to note is the intrinsically inclusive nature of Bantu languages, which do not make a distinction between the pronoun he *(il)* and she *(elle)*, which is so prominent in Western languages.[48] Another characteristic of Bantu language is the quasi absence of the verb "to have" that is replaced by the use of the verb "to be with" (*Kwikala-ne* in Kiluba, *Kuwa na* in Swahili); for instance, in Kiluba, to say "I have a wife," people say "I am with a wife" *(Ndi ne mukaji)*. Critical here is the philosophy of *etre et avoir*, "being and having."

Bantu languages value the being over the reifying aspects of possession. The philosophy of *Kwikala-ne* (to be with) teaches that the other is not an object I can possess and manipulate at will, but rather a subject capable of enriching my own being, an equal partner in dialogue and interaction. Considering the struggle over "inclusive language" so central to feminist discourse in the West, one may say that Bantu languages represent an important source for the possibility of articulating a philosophy or theology of equality between men and women. Indeed philosophizing or theologizing in African languages produces a very different type of knowledge, whose beauty and value are often lost in the translation into Western languages.

This equality between men and women is also expressed in the fact that generally men and women share the same names in Africa. Moreover in African tradition women never took the names of their husbands. This practice protected the freedom and identity of women. And this is not an insignificant contribution to the empowerment of women!

"What Men Owe to Women" in African Tradition

In the context of African tradition this question finds its meaning in the relationship between Leza (the creator), the ancestors, and women. Mothers and all women in general are directly connected to the origin and the meaning of life itself. This spirit of African traditional religion was well captured and expressed in a famous poem titled "Souffle" (Spirit) by Birago Diop, a Senegambian poet writing in French:

> *Those who are dead are never gone,*
> *they are in the breast of the woman,*
> *they are in the child who is wailing*
> *and in the firebrand that flames.*
> *The dead are not under the earth:*
> *they are in the fire that is dying,*
> *they are in the grasses that weep,*
> *they are in the whimpering rocks,*
> *they are in the forest,*
> *they are in the house,*
> *the dead are not dead.*

It is interesting to note that the poem mentions women but not men. Women play the major role in the transmission of life, in the connection between the world of the dead and that of the living, between the source of life and men. This fundamental attitude toward women was well expressed in a poem published in 1954 by Camara Laye, a Guinean writer, as a preface to his novel *L'enfant noir* (The dark child). The importance of this poem is shown by the fact that, for several decades, it has been taught in several schools all over Africa, as a classic of African literature. The poem goes as follows:

To My Mother

> *Black woman, woman of Africa,*
> *O my mother, I am thinking of you . . .*

> *O Daman, O my mother,*
> *You who bore me upon your back,*
> *You who gave me suck,*
> *You who watched over my first faltering steps,*
> *You who were the first to open my eyes*
> *to the wonders of the earth,*

I am thinking of you . . .

Woman of the fields, woman of the rivers,
Woman of the great river-banks,
O you my mother, I am thinking of you . . .

O you, Daman, O my mother,
You who dried my tears,
You who filled my heart with laughter,
You who patiently bore with all my many moods,
How I should love to be beside you once again,
to be a little child beside you!

Woman of great simplicity, woman of great resignation,
O my mother, I am thinking of you . . .

O Daman, Daman,
you of the great family of blacksmiths and goldsmiths,
my thoughts are always turning toward you,
and your own thoughts accompany me at every step.

O, Daman, my mother,
how I should love to be surrounded by your loving warmth again,
to be a little child beside you . . .

Black woman, woman of Africa,
O my mother, Let me thank you;
Thank you for all that you have done for me, your son,
who, though so far away, is still so close to you!

Even though the poem deals with mothers and not with wives or other women, it is indicative of the attitude toward women in general; for in African tradition every woman is respected as a potential mother. The category of motherhood also works as a "psychological police officer" for men. According to the logic of traditional culture, any mischief against somebody is an attack against the parents, and specifically against the mother. Thus the concept of "mother" stands as the core referent, which conditions the positive attitude toward women. As the poem suggests, a woman must be respected because she is *mater et magistra* to a man, she provides life, love, and all the necessary means of existence, that is, nurturance and education. It is then clear that "what men owe to women" is first of all their very existence. But as the poem clarifies, men live well and grow through the generosity of women, who are often forced to live a life of simplicity and resignation. Here is the tragedy, which calls for gender justice. "What men owe to women" is thus gratitude, respect, love, and most importantly justice. It is not the will of the ancestors that boys flourish at the expense of their sisters, and husbands at the expense of their wives. That is why selfishness is considered a horrible evil in Africa. It is not uncommon to hear women demanding of an egoistic child: *Taluka usaka kumuna* (Get out; you want to enslave me), and *Ndala mobe munda?* (Can I sleep in your belly? meaning I need food too). In other words, the traditional view of life, harmony, and love commands that women have the right to enjoy a life of dignity and happiness and not a permanent cross of resignation. More concretely, that means that men should share with their wives, domestic work, and the care of children, among other things. This is a way of translating love, equality, and respect into concrete action. A rigid division of labor is not likely to enhance equality and respect, for it is common for people to despise those who perform duties considered as lowly by society.

"What Men Owe to Women" in Global Capitalism

A little over a century ago, Conrad wrote his great novella *Heart of Darkness* that shed light on the rise of global capitalism then taking shape at the height of the "scramble for Africa."[49] As Edward Said so rightly pointed out, Conrad's anatomy of imperialism highlighted the fact that in the 1890s the business of empire, once an adventurous and often individualistic enterprise, had become the empire of business.[50] In 2000, the old "scramble for Africa" is being replaced by a new one, more sophisticated, a high-tech economic conquest. At the same time, human rights have become the dominant weapon of international politics and financial institutions, such as the World Bank and the International Monetary Fund (IMF), with a strong emphasis on the rights of women. The question that ought to be raised is whether this new environment entails more possibility for gender justice. Today, most African states have a GNP less than the Harvard University endowment or the profits of a major multinational corporation.[51] According to the 1990 World Development Report of the World Bank, even by optimistic assumptions about growth in per capita incomes, the number of people living in poverty in sub-Saharan Africa will rise by 85 million to 265 million in the new millenium. In other words, Africa will then account for over 30 percent of the developing world's poor and impoverished compared to 16 percent in 1985.[52]

Debt interest rates play a significant role in this impoverishment process. By 1990, Africa's foreign debt had risen to $272 billion, almost double the level in 1980. This is equal to over 90 percent of the region's annual production. Sub-Saharan Africa's debt in particular was 112 percent of its GDP, a far higher level than any other region of the world. To service this debt, African countries have to pay over $20 million a year in interest. Half of this amount comes from sub-Saharan Africa.[53] Though the debt of some African countries has been rescheduled and even erased, the overall mechanism of the world economy is such that Africa continues to sink into debt and impoverishment. Moreover, beside the debt burden beyond its GNP, Africa is being turned into a "western rubbish dump."[54] In this context of poverty some thinkers have raised the question of the kind of solidarity that white men and Black men can have in their struggle against sexism. By the close of the nineteenth century, white men controlled the global flows of capital, and European men specifically owned and managed 85 percent of the earth's surface.[55] Today the situation has not improved. The absence of Black men from the list of the richest people in the world is just one symptom of this global and systematic exclusion of Africa from the world economy.

Sexism and African traditions should not be discussed in a vacuum nor in abstract terms. On the eve of the third millennium, African traditional religions and cultures are not lived anymore in a "pure traditional setting," but rather in a modern world deeply shaped by the Western-style market economy with its consumerist mania and by the growing phenomenon of urbanism. In contemporary Africa, men and women "live, love, laugh, lie, and cry" in a world deeply affected by global capitalism and by its ethics of money and material success. The peripheralization and marginalization of Africa in the world economy increases poverty and affects the relationships between men and women. It can be argued that for some women, global capitalism represents a tremendous opportunity for access to economic power and education, and subsequently offers a possibility of liberation. However for most other women global capitalism worsens the situation of oppression where traditional structures of protection are eliminated in a society based on money, whose acquisition requires skilled training and education.

Before examining this point, let us first look at the real situation of African life under the global market. Global capitalism is not an abstract concept. It means a concrete world wherein the North, with about one-fourth of the world's population, consumes 70 percent of the world's energy, 75 percent of its metals, 85 percent of its wood, 60 percent of its food;[56] and where "The average American baby represents 280 times more environmental damage than that of a Chadian (African) child, thirty-five times that of an Indian, and thirteen times that of a Brazilian."[57] In this world, the richest 20 percent of the world population receives 82.7 percent of the world income, while the poorest 20 percent receives only 1.4 percent.[58] More significant is the fact that through the present rules governing world markets the poor countries lose at least $500 billion to the rich countries annually, which is ten times as much as they receive in aid.[59] From 1985 to 1990, sub-Saharan Africa paid out more in interest and debt repayment to the IMF and to the World Bank combined than it received from them in the form of grants and loans.[60] The consequence of this situation is obviously low income for workers, growing unemployment, and the deterioration of social conditions with negative consequences for the relationships between men and women. Global capitalism affects not only society but also the environment in which women live and struggle.[61] The disproportion of income between the haves and the have-nots suggests that in terms of energy consumption, CO_2 emissions, the amount of waste produced, pollution and other environmental factors, the richest 20 percent of the world population is also responsible for at least 80 percent of the destruction of the planet.[62] And yet, the neo-Malthusian mythology of ecology blame the Third World population for the degradation of the environment.[63] The overpopulation thesis portrays the problem of resource depletion and nature's degradation as apolitical, and uses the metaphor of the Black Peril to cast the whole issue of overpopulation in binary opposition, the "Rest" against the "West." This convenient and insidious way of framing the problem deflects attention away from the question of economic justice, capitalistic overaccumulation, and consumption disparities.[64] Given that the majority of the poor are women and that African people are the poorest of the poor, the debate over sexism and its related issues of birth control and overpopulation appears under a different light in Africa than in the West. Africa is the second largest continent of the planet (with 22 percent of the earth's land surface), but it is much less densely populated, with less than one-quarter the population of other regions. Most importantly there are more people living in the small country of India (with one-tenth the land area) than on the whole continent of Africa.[65] Though Africa represents less than 12 percent of world population, Western scholars, the IMF, and the World Bank have focused on the so-called overpopulation of Africa as the main cause of underdevelopment and more money is given to programs of birth control than to education.[66]

All this suggests that seen from an African perspective, sexism is a very complex reality, which cannot be approached with simplistic and superficial humanism. I would like to illustrate this connection between capitalism and sexism with three points: global justice, hegemony, and neosexism. Globalization as a heuristic devise helps clarify the connection between gender justice and "global justice." It appears that sexism cannot be separated from classism and racism. The struggle for gender equity is intertwined with issues of the economic exploitation of Africa and its cultural alienation. This points to the issue of hegemony. Solidarity between men in the struggle for gender justice will be efficient insofar as Western men pay attention to the issue of economic exploitation of the Third World. Otherwise the campaign for gender equality may be perceived as the usual "divide and conquer" strategy. Finally, by "neosexism" I mean both modern and postmodern sexism, or more specifically colonial sexism[67] and postcolonial sexism. These are new forms of sexism generated by modernity and global capitalism.[68] Included in this category are the phenomena of "leisure industry" or "sexual tourism," "professional prostitution," "bureaugamie" (modern form of polygamy), and the tyranny of Western images of "feminine beauty" just to name a few. The recent spread of casinos and striptease clubs in African cities is another example of the intensification of the image of women as sex objects.[69] The fact that the conception of feminine beauty, which plays an important role in the exploitation of women, depends upon aesthetic models and products sold by the global market is just one element of the visibility of the collusion between capitalism, sexism, and racism. The fact that Western movies and capitalist advertisements impose around the world Western feminine beauty as the ideal to aspire to by all other women, may affect seriously the self-esteem of many African women in the future. One only needs to walk in African markets to discover lotions or soaps called *Mekako, ambi,* and the like used by women to lighten their skin. The business of these aesthetic products used to Europeanize African hair and skin color has been booming since the seventies. Here again, the complicity between African men and global capitalism is obvious. And cases of parents and men pushing women into prostitution to feed the family show again how global capitalism generates new forms of sexism.

"What men owe to women" in a global capitalism is first of all life. In many countries working people receive a monthly income inferior to the price of basic food. Women are generally overworked; they work hard to nourish their children and husbands. In this context gender justice means that men should help women in domestic duties, and accept a fair competition in the access to means of existence. Parents should start this fairness in their own homes, among their sons and daughters. The issue of equal opportunity for education, jobs, and leisure time is fundamental for gender justice in the world of global capitalism.

WHERE DO WE GO FROM HERE?

Sexism is neither a metaphor nor a metaphysical construct. It is a painful existential condition that many men do not want to see happen to their mothers, daughters, and sisters. It implies moral, spiritual, psychological, and physical suffering. Sexism is about the world that engenders and is engendered; the world that names human beings and through this naming process ascribes meaning to male and female identities and their respective roles in the society. In a world where the ancestors indiscriminately play female and male roles, where men and women share the same names, where language is essentially inclusive, where God is called "mother" and "father" at the same time, where traditions accepted female rulers and priestesses, gender identity seems dynamic. This study has shown that African traditions have enough resources for building new and positive relationships between men and women. I would like, in conclusion, to highlight the following salient elements that will help transform relationships between men and women in the African context. Beside the change of attitude regarding the obvious practice of polygamy, dowry and genital excision, the following points need to be taken into account.

An African Problem

As noted earlier, the first step toward gender equity is to realize that sexism is indeed an African problem. One can easily imagine the conflict when a Muluba who does not practice excision marries someone from an ethnic group where such practices are part of the tradition.[70] In Africa, people of various traditions live together and some practices are already put into question, and not only in the large cities. Although colonialism and global capitalism have disorganized traditional structures and introduced new forms of oppression, African societies have never been a paradise. In this context, we, African men, must free our minds from some nationalist ideologies, which distort history for obscure purposes. Healing starts when one acknowledges that one is sick. But to acknowledge sexism as an African problem also implies an imagination capable of bringing about African solutions. This does not exclude solidarity with other ways of thinking about and seeing the world. In other words, an African can freely learn from other traditions, in the same way that African traditional wisdom can be a precious source of inspiration for people of other cultures.

Women's Liberation as Men's Liberation

Men's metanoia (conversion from male-centeredness) can occur only when we realize that the struggle against sexism is not only about the liberation of women, but also a golden road to men's liberation from their own misery. Borrowing from the popular language, which frames the power relations between men and women in terms of the "colonizer-colonized" metaphor, I maintain that every behavior that humiliates another human being also dehumanizes its perpetrator. What Aimé Césaire[71] said about the dialectic between the colonizer and the colonized can be applied *mutatis mutandis* to sexism, which is a certain form of colonization and enslavement. Between a woman and a sexist man there is no human contact, but only relations of "thingification," domination, faint submission, contempt, mistrust, self-complacency, swinishness, psychological or physical brutality, and sadism; in one word: a caricature of love. The sexist like the colonial master or the slaveholder is not sure of being loved; therefore he is forced to transform himself into a prison guard, a slave driver. Struggling with his conscience, his need to be recognized as a fine human being, he is forced to hide his intentions, to lie, to live in a permanent state of inner contradiction. He becomes a schizophrenic, living in a Manichean dualism, "decivilized," alienated by his own deeds and thoughts. Sexism generates only an illusion of happiness and satisfaction for the crazy grandeur of a man driven by the irrational will to power and its ethical nihilism. It is only through a genuine antisexist behavior that such a man can be reconciled with himself and find the courage to admire his face in the mirror. As liberation of both men and women, gender justice is then an important step for the future of Africa as a whole.

Changing Our Mind-Set

Despite the prevailing notion of power and the constructs of male-hood, we should realize that being a good man does not imply any type of superiority complex. Without humility it is impossible to fight against sexism. One way of testing our commitment to gender justice is to pay attention to our inner voice when we are challenged by women. How do we react? Do we immediately scream, look at this bitch! Are we capable of bearing with an injustice from a woman without bringing out our "complex of superiority"? The road of humility is indeed challenging. The struggle against sexism requires a serious psychological, spiritual, and intellectual metanoia. What is really at stake here, is being "born again"! The struggle against sexism is not an academic exercise. It is an existential commitment that implies a deeper meaning of life and a transformation of ways of being and of seeing the world. It can be said that one who has not yet experienced any pain is not really on the road of the struggle against sexism. The involvement in the struggle for gender equity requires moral courage to face the problem. It is crucial that men stop rationalizing sexism by presenting themselves as victims of women's expectations, or as equally oppressed by traditional customs. The fact that a large number of girls envy the status of their brothers and wish to have been born men shows that it would be preposterous to equate the burden of women to that of men under African tradition. We need to have the courage to face the reality of our male privilege and our complicity in a system that undermines the dignity and freedom of women.

A Mea Culpa

The transformation of men's attitude toward women starts with an act of confession and contrition for all the injustices that men of the past and the present have committed against women. As men, we are born in a world dominated by men. In this world we all benefit directly or indirectly from structures of injustice, which have marginalized women and used their energy for the well-being of men. In this world men and women do not, for instance, experience fear, anxiety, and insecurity in the same way. This awareness must lead to a commitment to do something to change the ongoing situation of injustice.

Looking for Information

Since injustice and structures of injustice are not always quite visible, men committed to fight sexism need to seek information regarding the situation of women. Beside publications by the United Nations and by various feminist organizations, a good way of gathering crucial information is through contact with women who have experienced abuses. In Africa, where the majority of the people still live in villages, it would be interesting to listen to stories of old women, mothers, married and nonmarried women, widows, and women without children. There is a tremendous traditional wisdom there!

Spreading Information

In order to make the struggle against sexism efficient it is a duty for any man involved in the struggle to spread information to other men and to try to explain to them the evil of sexism in our society. I suggest that centers of "women studies" be created in various African universities to foster the study of African traditions and modern cultures in matters pertaining to the welfare of women. Schools and churches should be involved in providing female role models to young people and in challenging some taboos. Without an appropriate antisexist education, it is difficult to expect significant changes in society. The study and teaching of African history should take special care to identify both seeds of sexism and antisexism.

Challenging Our Fellow Men

The struggle against sexism should not be abandoned to women's organizations alone. It is a duty for every man to challenge any man involved in sexist behavior. This is the best way to show solidarity with our mothers, sisters, and friends.

Learning to Listen Carefully

We should start everywhere we are (home, school, job, church, etc.) to listen carefully to women. Listening with a loving heart, without judging, listening with respect. One way of listening to women is also by reading works by women authors. For the sake of justice, a man committed to gender equity should strive to always quote a substantial number of female authors in his writings. This way we can stop the tradition of "silencing women." As women rightly put it, men blame women for not writing. And when women write, men do not read. When I say women authors, I mean in all the domains, not only on specifically feminist issues. Women's voices should be heard everywhere.

Redefining "African Tradition" and Inventing New Traditions

For a genuine gender justice to take place, we need to liberate African tradition itself from the bondage of patriarchy and from its narrow and selective definition of the tradition of the ancestors. History shows that African tradition has always been dynamic, polysemic, and polyphonic, open to critique and change. Contrary to widespread opinion, criticism was an important component of African tradition as summarized by this proverb from Kenya: "He who has not traveled thinks that his mother is the best cook in the world."[72] Among the Akan people, for instance, beside the sign *matemasie* (symbol of wisdom and insight) another Adinkra symbol called *ofamfa* was created to express the notion of critical examination and excellence.[73] This symbol literally means "searching rod or measuring rod." And this case is not unique in Africa. Among the Baluba, the master of critical thinking is called *Ntenda Mambo* and praised as the sage par excellence. The Baluba make a distinction between *Mukulu* (venerable and wise old person) and *Kikulu* (unwise old person). A proverb states clearly that it is not "white hair" that makes somebody a wise person, for there are the wise among young people and the unreliable among old people. This notion shows, for instance, that tradition does not mean blind obedience to old people. There are numerous cases of rupture within the tradition in African history. King Njoya of Cameroon invented a writing system and broke with oral tradition. Chaka put an end to circumcision and to several rituals of passage and imposed celibacy on soldiers while incorporating women into the army. King Agadja (1708–1732) of Abomey created an army of the famous Amazons, called the "virgins," who could not marry as long as they were soldiers.

African tradition has always changed in order to meet new challenges. This openness to change and transformation is already embedded in African cosmogonies. There is a strong traditional belief in the periodic rebirth of the universe. According to their calendar and to their *sigui* ritual the Dogon of Mali had to change everything, including the high priest and the king, during the sign of the "star of fonio" that appeared once every sixty-years. The Baluba, like the Dogon, think that creation is not finished; God continues to create whenever he wants. In Luba cosmogony, God forges a new sun each day; and is, for that reason, called *Kafula moba*.[74] This worldview is even expressed in the proverb: *Kosepa lemena Vidye muntanda ukipanga* (Do not laugh when you see a handicapped person; God continues to create). Regarding the issue of sexism, it is clear that what is needed most today is the creation of new traditions through creative interpretations of the old legacy.

Contrary to a prevailing male understanding of tradition, African tradition cannot be reduced to patriarchy and gerontocracy. It was neither monolithic nor static; it was dynamic, changing constantly in view of new challenges; indeed it was polysemic and rooted in a pluralistic worldview that transcended the limits of such false dichotomies as "asynchrony versus diachrony," "tradition versus modernity," "religion versus science," "past versus present," "determinism versus freedom," and "male versus female." Thus my first conclusion is that antisexism should start by subverting men's definition of tradition. Since tradition itself has embodied this power of self-transformation, it is neither antireligious nor antitradition to reestablish new traditions more consonant with respect for human rights, especially the rights of women to a genuine human existence. I see tradition as the dynamic interpretation of the will of the ancestors in the light of the *Bumuntu*. Contrary to a widespread belief among men, I argue that it is indeed patriarchy that is against tradition in two ways. First, it obliterates and alienates tradition by reducing the whole to particular fragments of historical social codes set up to protect male privilege. Secondly, by applying literally a "traditional worldview" in different social circumstances patriarchy betrays the *raison d'étre* of tradition by making it meaningless where new challenges require dynamic solutions instead of mute, deaf, and static customs. Tradition was about the protection and flourishing of life, and life is dynamic in Bantu philosophy. Indeed African tradition is rooted in the notion of vital force, which implies constant dynamism and metamorphosis. The best way to preserve tradition is not through mummification, but rather through dynamic interpretation, through a reinvention of new expressions. Thus by reinventing tradition, the antisexist movement is more faithful to tradition than patriarchy. After all, the will of the ancestors is about the goodness of life and not about the perpetuation of evil and antisocial behaviors. This brings us to the crucial issue of criteria in the struggle against sexism.

Bumuntu and the Golden Rule: A Fundamental Criterion

This whole debate rests upon one crucial question, Why should a man be involved in the struggle against sexism? As said earlier the key to gender justice is the notion of *Bumuntu*. This concept of personhood, harmony, and wholeness should convince men that the will of the ancestors is not about exploitation. Instead sound tradition entails respect *(Buleme)* of one's life and the life of others *(Bumi)*; it involves the praxis of enhancing the life of others in the genuinely African spirit of *Ujamaa* (oneness in family). I have insisted that critical thinking was indeed part of the tradition. All customs and practices have to undergo critical examination in the light of the *Bumuntu* (humanness), which as the embodiment of *Mucima muyampe* (good heart) condemns patriarchy as the power of domination and oppression. In this spirit my analysis of sexism in Africa was inspired and guided all along by the centrality of the African critique of personhood found all across Africa in such expressions as *Yao ke muntu* (He or she is not a human being) used in relation to a person of bad character who mistreats women. I have argued that "the art of critical examination" and "moral excellence" as criteria of humanness were central to the dynamic nature of African tradition. The core of the will of the ancestors or tradition was *buswe* (love), *Buleme* (respect for others and for oneself), and *bumi* (the protection of the dignity of human life) in all *Bantu* (human beings). The rest was pure commentary and a set of fallible interpretations never intended by any ancestor to last forever unchallenged.

The struggle against sexism is not a charity but a duty, indeed a matter of justice and common sense. As Yoruba wisdom puts it: *Iwa lesin*[75] (Good character is the essence of religion). Such is the African formulation of the "golden rule" and the main spirit of African tradition. And sexism is a good test for the humanity of any man and the credibility of his faith and obedience to the will of the ancestors.

NOTES

1. The concept of *Bumuntu* used by the Baluba people of Central Africa refers to the fundamental traditional vision of what it means to be truly human. It embodies the ideal of human dignity, autonomy, liberty, personal responsibility, and relationality. Contrary to the Western egocentric vision of the self and the Buddhist nothingness or selfless self *(Sunyata* and *anatta)*, the notion of *Bumuntu* embodies the notion of a self that finds the holistic meaning of its selfness in the interconnectedness with the community and with the whole cosmos. Indeed Bantu ontology is very different from the notion of being articulated by Plato, Aristotle, Kant, or Hegel. This concept of *Bumuntu* is found in South Africa under the terminology of *Ubuntu*. In West Africa, the Yoruba use *Iwapele* to refer both to "existence" and to the "moral character" of human beings.

2. In a conversation, Maguy Kabamba (Democratic Republic of Congo), Ruth Heckelsmuller (University of Fribourg, Switzerland), and Myriam Cartine (Montclair State University, United States), told me that the dilemma, what men owe to women, should be understood first of all as a matter of "what men owe to themselves." It is interesting to note that coming from different cultures (Congolese, German, and American) these women reached the same conclusion.

3. John Mbiti summarized this point in his famous statement,

> Africans are notoriously religious. Religion permeates into all the departments of life so fully that it is not easy or possible always to isolate it. . . A study of these religious systems is, therefore, ultimately a study of the peoples themselves in all the complexities of both traditional and modern life. . . To ignore these traditional beliefs, attitudes and practices can only lead to a lack of understanding of African behavior and problems. Religion is the strongest element in traditional background, exerts probably the greatest influence upon the thinking and living of the people concerned.

(Mbiti, *African Religions and Philosophy*; [Portsmouth, NH: Heinemann, 1990], 1).

This position is widely supported by the majority of scholars, even though few people like Kwame Gyekye reject it in order to show that African thought is as philosophical as Western philosophy. Gyekye rejects not only the notion that religion is central to the African worldview, but that it is also the religious foundation of African morality and conscience:

> It should be clear from my analysis that the Akans hold moral-
> ity, to be logically independent of nonhuman (supernatural) pow-
> ers . . . the important point to note is that in Akan thinking about
> the foundations of morality, consideration is given solely to human
> well-being . . . I maintain that tiboa (conscience) whether as moral
> sense or as moral will, is not innate to man, but something acquired
> through socialization, through habituation . . . thus I interpret tiboa
> as nothing mysterious or supernatural in its origins.

(See Gyekye, *An Essay on African Philosophical Thought: The Akan Conceptual Scheme* [Philadelphia: Temple University Press, 1995], 136, 143.) This should be perceived as the effect of Western secularism on some African thinkers.

4. African Christian theology is based upon the key assumption that African traditional religions are a sine qua non for locus theologicus. See T. Tshibangu, *La théologie Africaine: manifeste et programme pour le dévelopement des activities théologiques en Afrique* (Kinshasa, Zaire: Saint Paul-Afrique, 1987); Tissa Balasuriya, "Les luttes des femmes comme lieu théologique," in *Spiritualité et liberation en Afrique*, B. Mveng, ed. (Paris: L' Harmattan, 1987), 95–103.

5. See *Les religions africaines comme source de valeurs de civilization: collogue de Cotonou. 16–22* Août 1970 (Paris: Présence africaine, 1972).

6. Kofi Appiah-Kubi and Sergio Torres, eds., *African Theology en Route* (Maryknoll, NY: Orbis Books, 1979); specifically the "Final communiqué of the Pan-African Conference of Third World Theologians" that defined "sources for African theology."

7. See Mercy Amba Oduyoye, "Commonalities: An African perspective," *Third World Theologies: Commonalities and Divergences,* K. C. Abraham, ed. (Mary-knoll, NY: Orbis Books, 1990), 101. These statistics were given in December 1986 at the General Assembly of the Ecumenical Association of Third World Theologians. I cite them here to offer a certain idea of a very complex and dynamic situation of religious pluralism.

8. I use the term *African traditional religion* in the singular to refer to the common set of values and worldviews that characterize traditional religions in various cultures of Africa. The issue of the "cultural unity" of Africa has been the object of hot debate. Rejecting the two extremes of a uniform Africa and a completely chaotic universe of radically isolated tribes, serious scholarly works have highlighted the core values beneath the diversity of cultural modes

of expressions. Mbiti's conclusion that African religion has the notion of one supreme being, for instance, is based on a study of nearly three hundred different peoples, and about twelve thousand proverbs. (See his books: *Concepts of God in Africa*, [New York: Praeger, 1970]; and *African Religions and Philosophy*, [Portsmouth, NH: Heinemann, 1990]); also see Cheikh Anta Diop, *L'unité culturelle de l'Afrique noire* (Paris: Presence Africaine, 1960); Kwame Gyekye, *An Essay on African Philosophical Thought: The Akan Conceptual Scheme* (Philadelphia: Temple University, 1995); particularly interesting is the section on "Common Features in African Cultures" in chap. 12. E. G. Parrinder, *African Traditional Religion* (New York: Harper & Row, 1962). Our knowledge of traditional religions depends largely on data collected since the end of the nineteenth century by Western anthropologists. African scholars joined the field of study after the Second World War and increased their publications in the seventies. All of this literature is dominated by an interpretative framework inspired by Western secularism and Christian theology. However, some practitioners of traditional religions have begun to emerge with significant publications. See, for instance, Malidoma Patrice Somé's books, *Of Water and the Spirit: Ritual, Magic, and Initiation in the Life of an African Shaman* (New York: Penguin, 1994); and *Ritual, Power, Healing and Community* (New York: Penguin, 1997). While using written literature, my interpretation of traditional religions stems from my personal experience within my own family where Christians live under the same roof with relatives who pour libation for the ancestors and practice divination and other traditional rituals.

9. An excellent collection of texts of African traditional religions is found in Andrew Wilson, ed., *World Scripture: A Comparative Anthology of Sacred Texts* (A Project of the International Religious Foundation, New York: Paragon House, 1995). In this book, African texts are selected according to various themes and put side by side with the sacred texts of Abrahamic religions and other world religions.

The Yoruba religion has now a kind of "Bible," a written collection of sacred texts called *Ifa*. See Afolabi Epega and Philip John Neimark, *The Sacred Ifa Oracle* (San Francisco: HarperCollins, 1995). Mbiti in Anglophone Africa and Vincent Mulago in Francophone Africa have created important centers for the study of African traditional religions. Thanks to their effort, various texts are available today. See, for instance, Mbiti, *The Prayers of African Religion* (London: SPCK, 1975); and Mulago Gwa Cikala, *La religion traditionnelle des Bantu et leur vision du monde* (Kinshasa, Zaire: Presses Universitaires du Zaire, 1973).

See also L.V. Thomas and René Luneau, *Les religions d'Afrique noire: textes et traditions sacrées*, Fayard Denoël, ed. (Collection trésors spirituels de l'humanité, 1979).

10. For a general picture of sexism throughout the world, see the *1995 Human Development Report* of the United Nations Development Program.

11. See M. A. Oduyoye, *Daughters of Anowa: African Women and Patriarchy* (Maryknoll, NY: Orbis Books, 1995).

12. See an interesting study on this topic by Ogbu U. Kalu, "Gods as Policemen: Religion and Social Control in Igboland" in *Religious Plurality in Africa,* Jacob K. Olupona, ed., (Berlin and New York: Mouton de Gruyter, 1993), 109–130.

13. See Pierre Bourdieu, *Language and Symbolic Power* (Cambridge: Harvard University Press, 1994). His theory of "authorized language" and "effectiveness of ritual discourse" can well be applied to the African context. In societies based on oral tradition, language is particularly important and powerful.

14. Among the best studies of the issue see Engelbert Mveng, "Impoverishment and Liberation: A Theological Approach for Africa and the Third World," in *Parts of African Theology,* Rosino Gibellini, ed. (Maryknoll, NY: Orbis Books, 1994), 154–165.

Also see the excellent study edited by John W. Harbeson and Donald Rothchild, *Africa in World Politics: Post-Cold War Challenges* (Boulder, CO: Westview Press, 1995), specifically Thomas M. Callaghy, "Africa and the World Political Economy: Still Caught Between a Rock and a Hard Place." See also R. McAfee Brown, ed., *Kairos: Three Prophetic Challenges to the Church.* (Grand Rapids, MI: William B. Eerdmans, 1990); Ulrich Duchrow, *Global Economy: A Confessional Issue for the Churches?* (Geneva: World Council of Churches, 1987); Jack Nelson-Pallmeyer, *The War Against the Poor* (Maryknoll, NY: Orbis Books, 1988); and Franz J. Hinkelammert, *The Ideological Weapons of Death: A Theological Critique of Capitalism* (Maryknoll, NY: Orbis Books, 1986).

Regarding the issue of globalization as a threat, see the excellent analysis of "capitalist lies" by John Dalla Costa, *The Ethical Imperative: Why Moral Leadership is Good Business* (Reading, MA: Addison-Wesley, 1998). On the specific issue of wealth disparity and the power of corporations, see David C. Korten, *When Corporations Rule the World* (West Hartford, CT: Kumarian Press, 1995).

15. John S. Mbiti, *Concepts of God in Africa* (New York: Praeger, 1970), xlv.

16. F. Eboussi Boulaga, *Christianity Without Fetishes: An African Critique and Recapture of Christianity* (Maryknoll, NY: Orbis Books, 1984), 78.

17. Anne Nasimiyu-Wasike, "Polygamy: A Feminist Critique" in *The Will to Arise: Women, Tradition, and the Church in Africa,* M. A. Oduyoye and M. R. Kanyoro, eds. (Maryknoll, NY: Orbis Books, 1992), 112.

18. Cheikh Anta Diop brought to the attention of African historians the role of women in traditional kingdoms in *L'Afrique noire prècoloniale* (Paris: Prèsence Africaine, 1960).

19. Joseph Ki-Zerbo, *Histoire de l'Afrique noire d'hier á demain* (Paris: Hatier, 1978).

For the role played by queens and prophetesses in various struggles for African dignity and liberty see the excellent *General History of Africa. Vol. 7* (Paris: UNESCO, 1990).

20. For an African approach to feminism, see Ifi Amadiume, *Reinventing Africa: Matriarchy, Religion, and Culture* (London: Zed Books, 1977) and her other

book, *Male Daughters, Female Husbands: Gender and Sex in an African Society* (London: Zed Books, 1988).

From a theological perspective the most systematic critique of African traditions has been articulated by Mercy Amba Oduyoye. Particularly important are the following books by Oduyoye, *Daughters of Anowa: African Women and Patriarchy* (Maryknoll, NY: Orbis Books, 1995), Oduyoye and M. R. Kanyoro, eds., *The Will to Arise: Women, Tradition, and the Church in Africa* (Maryknoll, NY: Orbis Books, 1992). Oduyoye has also introduced into African feminist discourse a critique of global capitalism.

21. V. Y. Mudimbe, *The Idea of Africa* (Bloomington: Indiana University Press, 1994) 191.

22. Oduyoye offers an excellent critique of African proverbs and myths of creation in her book *Daughters of Anowa*.

23. Lloyda Fanusie, "Sexuality and Women in African Culture," in *The Will to Arise: Women, Tradition, and the Church in Africa,* 143.

24. Ibid.

25. Oduyoye, "Women and Ritual in Africa" in *The Will to Arise,* Oduyoye and M. R. Kanyoro, eds, 22.

26. Fanusie, "Sexuality and Women in African Culture," in *The Will to Arise.*" Also Mbuy Beya, "Human Sexuality, Marriage, and Prostitution" in *The Will to Arise,* 159.

27. Oduyoye, *Daughters of Anowa: African Women and Patriarchy* (Maryknoll, NY: Orbis Books, 1995), 82.

28. Kajsa Ekholm Friedman, *Catastrophe and Creation: The Transformation of an African Culture* (Philadelphia: Harwood Academic Publishers, 1991), 1–2.

29. See Bénézet Bujo, *African Theology in Its Social Context* (Maryknoll, NY: Orbis Books, 1992).

30. Takyiwaa Munah, "Law and Society in Contemporary Africa" in *Africa,* Phyllis M. Martin and Patrick O'Meara, eds., (Bloomington: Indiana University Press, 1995), 340.

31. Ibid.

32. Kwame Gyekye, *An Essay on African Philosophical Thought: The Akan Conceptual Scheme* (Philadelphia: Temple University, 1995), 19.

33. Segun Gbadegesin, *African Philosophy: Traditional Yoruba Philosophy and Contemporary African Realities* (New York: Peter Lang, 1991), 33.

34. Ibid., 82.

35. Ibid., 27.

36. Ibid., 38.

37. Wandé Abimbola, "Ifa: A West African Cosmological System" in *Religion in Africa* T. D. Blakely, ed. (Portsmouth, NH: Heinemann, 1994), 111.

38. Ibid., 114.

39. Gbadegesin, *African Philosophy*, 27.

40. G. M. Setiloane, "Civil Authority from the Perspective of African Theology" in *Religious Plurality in Africa*, J. K. Olupona and S. S. Nyang, eds. (Berlin: Mouton de Gruyter, 1993), 146.

41. Cited by George Anastaplo, "An Introduction to 'Ancient' African Thought," in *The Great Ideas Today: Britannica Great Books of the Western World* (London: Encyclopedia Britannica, 1995), 176.

42. Oduyoye, "Women and Ritual in Africa," in *The Will to Arise*, 21.

43. Geoffrey Parrinder, *A Dictionary of Non-Christian Religions* (Philadelphia: Westminster Press, 1971), 162.

44. See Modupe Owanikin, "The Priesthood of Church Women in the Nigerian Context," in *Will to Arise*, 212.

45. See Nzuzi Bibaki, *Le Dieu-Mère: l'inculturation de la foi chez les Yombe* (Kinshasa, Zaire: Editions Loyola, 1993). This book is a doctoral dissertation presented at the Gregorian University in Rome in 1992 by the Congolese Jesuit Nzuzi on the theme of God as Mother. See also Sr. Edet, "Pour une Théologie de Dieu comme Mère" in *Spiritualit et libération en Afrique, B*. Mveng, ed. (Paris: L'Harmattan, 1987), 65–69.

46. Quoted from Mbiti, *African Religions and Philosophy* (Portsmouth, NH: Heinemann, 1990), 34.

47. See Ngugi wa Thiong'o, *Decolonizing the Mind: The Politics of Language of African Literature* (London: James Currey, 1986), 5, 8–33.

48. See "Gender-Free God Language," in *Daughters of Anowa: African Women and Patriarchy*, M. A. Oduyoye, ed. (Maryknoll, NY: Orbis Books, 1995), 110–113.

49. See Thomas Pakenham, *The Scramble for Africa. White Man's Conquest of the Dark Continent from 1876 to 1912* (New York: Avon Books, 1991). Yesterday, missionaries such as Livingston and Tempels supported the colonial enterprise in the name of bringing the light of civilization to poor natives. The question today is whether theologians and other missionaries are critical enough of the growing tentacles of global capitalism. All signs show that the concentration of wealth in the hands of few leads to the end of democracy, women's rights included.

50. Edward Said, *Culture and Imperialism* (New York: Vintage Books, 1994), 23.

51. Crawford Young, "The Heritage of Colonialism" in *Africa in World Politics: Post-Cold War Challenges*, John W. Harbeson and Donald Rothchild, eds. (Boulder, CO: Westview Press, 1995), 25.

52. Naomi Chazan and Robert Mortimer, eds., *Politics and Society in Contemporary Africa* (Boulder, CO: Lynne Rienner, 1992), 315.

53. Ibid., 310.

54. Ulrich Duchrow, *Alternatives to Global Capitalism* (Utrecht, Netherlands: International Books and Kairos Europa, 1995), 12. It is not a secret anymore that some industrial countries are dumping their toxic waste in Africa.

55. See Anne McClintock, *Imperial Leather: Race, Gender, and Sexuality in the Colonial Contest* (New York: Routledge, 1995), 5.

56. *United Nations Development Report, 1993,* 35. Also see Paul F. Knitter, *One Earth, Many Religions: Multifaith Dialogue and Global Responsibility* (Maryknoll, NY: Orbis Books, 1995), 189–190.

57. Paul Kennedy, *Preparing for the Twenty-First Century* (New York: Random, 1993), 32–33.

58. *UNDP Human Development Report. 1992.* Also see David C. Korten, *When Corporations Rule the World* (West Hartford, CT: Kumarian Press, 1995), 106–107.

59. Duchrow, *Alternatives to Global Capitalism,* 14.

60. See Phyllis M. Martin and Patrick O'Meara, eds., *Africa* (Bloomington: Indiana University Press, 1995), 364. See also G. K. Helleiner, "The IMF, The World Bank and Africa's Adjustment and External Debt Problems: An Unofficial View," *World Development* 20(6): 1992.

61. For an analysis of the "patriarchal character of World Economy" and its impact on Third World countries, see Maria Mies and Vandana Shiva, *Ecofeminism* (London: Zed Books, 1993).

62. Duchrow, *Alternatives to Global Capitalism,* 14.

63. It is now widely known that some industrial countries dump their toxic waste in Africa. This situation reached such proportion that even the World Bank was alarmed. See World Bank, *Sub-Saharan Africa: From Crisis to Sustainable Growth,* 22. Also see the World Bank's *World Development Report,* 1992, which focuses on environmental issues and development; and Martin and O'Meara, eds., *Africa,* 382.

64. See the excellent study by Suzana Sawyer and Arun Agrawal, "Environmental Orientalisms," in *Sapina: A Bulletin of the Society for African Philosophy in North America* 10(1) (July–December, 1997), 59–78.

65. John Reader, *Africa: A Biography of the Continent* (New York: Knopf, 1998), 4.

66. There are people in Africa who think that the whole debate over overpopulation is a pseudo-problem. In light of what happened in the last four hundred years of contact with the West, and in the light of Western evolutionary theories on the extinction of "low races" there is fear that Africans may be wiped out one day. See, for instance, the enlightening analysis by the Swedish scholar Sven Lindqvist, *Exterminate All the Brutes* (New York: New Press, 1996).

According to the United Nations Demographic Yearbook of 1957 and Carr-Saunders's Study on World Population (Oxford: Clarendon Press, 1956), in 1650 Europe and Africa had an equal population of 100 million people or 18.3 percent of the world's population; but after the encounter between the two civilizations, in 1950 Europe had 593 million people or 24 percent, while African population declined and counted only for 7.9 percent. See L. S. Stavrianos, *Global Rift: The Third World Comes of Age* (New York: Morrow, 1981), 199. On a specific level, the Congo Scandal is well-known in the whole history of the encounter between Africa and the West. In 1900 the Congo population was estimated to be at least 20 million. An official census taken in 1911 revealed that only 8.5 million remained alive. Global capitalism at the beginning of the automobile revolution overworked local people to get rubber for tires. Edmund Morel, the leading British authority on West Africa, recorded the tragedy in a famous book titled *Red Rubber*. The situation gave way to an African proverb: "the white men's work eats people." See John Reader, *Africa: A Biography of the Continent* (New York: Knopf, 1998), 547.

67. One aspect of "colonial sexism" was the loss of economic and political power of African women. As Sheldon Gellar pointed out, the Europeans who came to live and rule in Africa invented new traditions to promote their self-esteem and respectability. Under colonial rule, white officials whose perceptions of female roles were based on their European experience worked almost exclusively through male traditional authorities and ignored female candidates for chiefships. Thus the status of women throughout much of Africa declined under colonialism, as colonial policies often reinforced patriarchal authority. See Gellar, "The Colonial Era" in *Africa*, Martin and O'Meara, eds., 139–141.

68. See *Our Creative Diversity: Report of the World Commission on Culture and Development* (Paris: UNESCO, 1996), 142.

69. Lwamba Katansi, "Women's Rights Within the Framework of Human Rights: A Socio-Judicial Essay," in *Philosophie et droits de l'homme: Actes de la 5éme semaine philosophique de Kinshasa 1981* (Kinshasa, Zaire: Faculté de Théologie Catholique, 1982), 352.

70. In their *Dictionnaire des civilisations africaines* (Paris: Fernand Hazan, 1968), Georges Balandier and Jacques Maquet have analyzed the issue of excision in various rubrics. Their conclusion, which I can confirm from my knowledge of the Baluba and from some other people, is that there are two, and even three traditions. Although circumcision is widespread, some ethnic groups practice both circumcision and excision, some practice neither of them, and in some other groups excision can exist without its counterpart circumcision, and vice versa. Among the Baluba and Hottentots of South Africa, women with a significant development of labia minora are more admired, and excision is not practiced. The case of the labia minora of Hottentot women is well known in Western literature since the publicity over the famous "Hottentot Venus" who ended up on Cuvier's dissecting table in 1815. (See Jean Comaroff and John Comaroff, *Of Revelation and Revolution: Christianity, Colonialism and Consciousness in*

South Africa, [Chicago: University of Chicago Press, 1991], 104.) Writing on the Baluba, W. F. P. Burton recalls the story of the husband of a poor woman who boasted that his wife had a bigger labia and clitoris than the wives of the local chief. This development of labia minora and clitoris is part of female initiation among the Baluba. This initiation, called *Kwikana,* is considered an important preparation to marriage. (See Burton, *Luba Religion and Magic in Custom and Belief,* [Tervuren, Belgium: MRAC, 1961], 149.)

71. Aimé Césaire, "Discourse on Colonialism" in P. Williams and L. Chrisman, eds., *Colonial Discourse and Post-Colonial Theory: A Reader* (New York: Columbia University Press, 1994), 177.

72. John S. Mbiti, *Introduction to African Religion* (Chicago: Heinemann International, 1991), 209.

73. See Kwame Gyekye, *An Essay on African Philosophical Thought: The Akan Conceptual Scheme* (Philadelphia: Temple University Press, 1995).

74. William J. Dewey and S. Terry Childs, "Forging Memory," in *Memory: Luba Art and the Making of History,* Mary Nooter Roberts and Allen F. Roberts, eds. (New York: Museum for African Art, 1996), 76.

75. Wandé Abimbola, "Ifa: A West African Cosmological System," in *Religion in Africa,* T. D. Blakely, ed. (Portsmouth, NH: Heinemann, 1994), 115.

4

Islam, Women, and Gender Justice

Asghar Ali Engineer

ISLAM MADE ITS APPEARANCE in the Arabian peninsula in the seventh century C.E. and immediately began to display its capacity for growth and change. The Islamic theologians (known as the 'Ulama) often point out that women were treated like chattel before Islam and they acquired great dignity because of the Qur'anic teachings. But what the 'Ulama do not realize is that what was done by the Qur'an to improve women's situation was, to a great extent undone, by the "patriarchization of Islamic law" in later centuries. We will discuss the process of the patriarchization of Islam not only through interpretational means but also by presenting *ahadith* (reports outside the Qur'an on what the Prophet said and did) to make our treatment more complete.

SHARI'AH LAW AND ITS EVOLUTION

First, to the meaning of what is called in Islamic law Shari'ah; this is a compilation of Islamic law codified in the second to fourth century *Hijra* (i.e., of the Islamic calendar) by the doctors of Islamic law. There are four sources of Islamic law in Sunni Islam:

1. Qur'an;
2. *Hadith;*
3. *Qiyas* (analogy);
4. *Ijma'* (i.e., consensus).

The Qur'an is a compilation of the divine revelation that occurred during the Prophet's lifetime. Hadith (plural, *ahadith*) is a report of the Prophet's sayings and doings. The *ahadith* also include reports of how the Prophet understood particular revelations and also how he acted in accordance with particular revelations. These reports were compiled more than two centuries after the death of the Prophet of Islam and are usually authenticated by referring to the chain of narrators. These narrators are judged by their reputation and character so that the possibility of forging *ahadith* by persons of loose character is eliminated. However, the *hadith* literature remained problematic despite these steps. Thousands of spurious *ahadith* were in fact forged to meet certain exigencies.

Also, the two sources, that is, the Qur'an and *hadith* were also found to be inadequate in certain situations as new problems and challenges arose. The learned doctors turned to analogy to meet such situations. For the formulations to be acceptable to the community, a consensus had to be developed among the doctors that was known as *ijma'*. Once consensus developed, it became part of the Shari'ah law.

The Shi'ah tradition differs somewhat from this mode of interpretation. The Shi'ah doctors did not accept analogy and consensus. In the Shi'ah tradition, after Qur'an and Sunnah (reports of sayings and doings of the Prophet) the people of the family of the Prophet *(Ahl al-bayt)* were the final authority. Their interpretation and *ahadith* as narrated by them were thought to be unquestionable. Thus in the Shi'ah tradition the most authentic sources of Shari'ah law were Qur'an, Sunnah (or *hadith*), and the authority of *ahl al-bayt*.

The Shari'ah law about marriage, divorce, inheritance, child custody, maintenance, equality before law, the right to work for women, and so forth, was evolved according to the methodologies just explained. Though it is maintained by many laity that the Shari'ah law in these matters is divine, most scholars would question this. Such law is human inasmuch as interpretational endeavors and concepts of analogy and consensus are involved.

As the Shari'ah law pertaining to rights of women was evolved by the 'Ulama who had deeply imbibed patriarchal values, these values were incorporated into the Shari'ah law.

THEORY OF JUSTICE IN ISLAM

Before we critique the existing gender laws it is important to say a few words about the theory of justice in Islam. There is a great deal of emphasis on justice in the Qur'anic teachings. Qur'an uses words like 'adl and qist for emphasizing the concept of justice. According to Imam Raghib Isfahani 'adl in Shari'ah means "equal retaliation" and to substantiate his point he said: "And the recompense of evil is punishment like it. . . ." (Raghib 1971, 676–677; verse 40:42). But the Qur'an also uses it in a loftier moral sense when it says further in the same verse: ". . . but whoever forgives and amends, his reward is with Allah. He loves not wrong doers." The Qur'an also uses repeatedly the words 'adl and 'ihsan, that is, "justice" and "benevolence" in a moral sense. Thus according to the Qur'an, retaliation for "justice" may be considered necessary but "forgiving" and "benevolence" are higher ideals. Allah enjoins upon all believers to be just and to do good to others (16:90). Thus, according to the Qur'an one must be quite just in trade transactions. One should weigh justly, not letting selfishness interfere (170:35, 260:182, 55:6, etc.).

In fact, economic justice in Islamic law embodies high ideals, ideals that offer moral challenges to many contemporary capitalist practices. The Qur'an strongly condemns accumulation of wealth and its unjustly uneven distribution or its limited circulation among the rich only (see 107:1-7, chap. 104, 9:34, 59:7, etc.). Also, Islamic justice insists on treating one's enemies justly. Animosity with people should not provoke one to be unjust to them. "Be just, it is closest to observance of duty" (5:8).

Similarly, gender justice is also integral to the theory of justice in Islam (2:228, 33:35). Both of these verses leave no doubt that gender justice is highly crucial to Qur'anic teachings. These verses also make it abundantly clear that gender justice cannot be realized without gender equality. "The rights of the wives (with regard to their husbands) are equal to the (husbands') rights with regard to them . . ." (2:228). According to the Qur'an, it's always necessary to favor the less powerful groups of society (and women in a patriarchal social structure also belong in this category). The Qur'an shows its preference for the poor and the disempowered (28:5).

This in short is the rich Qur'anic concept of justice. Thus all gender-based laws evolved by the Muslim jurists must be reviewed today in the light of this theory of justice. This theory is far more important than the interpretations of the Qur'anic verses under the influence of patriarchal values.

Islam and Women

It is widely thought that Islam treats women unfairly and gender justice is not possible within the Islamic law. This assertion is partly true and partly untrue. It is true as far as the existing shari'ah laws are concerned; untrue, as the existing laws were codified during the second and third centuries of Islam when the general view of women's rights was very different from today's perspective. The Qur'anic verses that are quite fundamental to the Islamic law, were interpreted so as to be in conformity with the views about gender rights prevailing at this time.

Thus it will be seen that the most fundamental values in Islam, as expounded by the Qur'an are justice, benevolence, and compassion. The Qur'anic terminology for these values is *'adl, ihsan,* and *rahmah*. The Qur'an places these values in the imperative category. Another Qur'anic verse testifies to this. "And surely Allah enjoins justice and benevolence (to others)" (16:90). Thus it will be seen that justice is very central to the Islamic value system—as central as love to the Christian ethics and Tsedaqah in the Jewish tradition. No legislation in Islam that ignores this value can be valid. The meaning of this for men's obligations to women should be clear.

It is because of this concern for justice that the Qur'an shows deep concern for the weaker sections of society. "And We desire to bestow a favour upon those who were deemed weak in the land, and to make them the leaders, and to make them the heirs" (28:5). The Qur'an desires to bestow the mantle of leadership of this earth upon the weak. Islamic jurisprudence has to imbibe this compassionate spirit toward the weaker sections of society. And, again, women certainly belong to this category as far as the patriarchal society is concerned.

SCRIPTURES AND SITUATIONAL CONSTRAINTS

It is important to note that scriptural injunctions are always mediated through the prevailing social ethos. Also, and it is fundamental in the framing of laws based on Scriptures, that Scriptures both reflect the given situation and also transcend it. There cannot be any Scripture— revealed or otherwise—which is unidimensional, that is, merely descriptive, reflecting only the given situation. Scripture is normative. Every Scripture tries to go beyond what is given, pointing to a better, more just society. Of course, it faces stiff opposition from those who lose out if these transcendental and challenging perspectives are spelled out and enforced. The Scriptures condemn prevailing social evils and provide a new vision. Those who benefit from the new vision embrace the new faith. Those who lose privileges oppose it tooth and nail. But, the vested interests and those who want to perpetuate the old order have their own strategies. Soon they find ways and means to hijack the religious tradition to their own benefit. This is done in a number of ways:

1. They capture political power, and religion becomes part of the political establishment and loses its initial revolutionary thrust as it is appropriated by the ruling classes.

2. They convert religion itself into an institutionalized establishment and a power structure develops around it; religion is then used more for the distribution of favors than for spiritual enrichment.

3. Intellectual resources are used to resist the judgments of true justice, and this is done chiefly by interpreting the Scriptures in a way that robs it of its transcendental thrust.

Thus a theology is developed that is supportive of the status quo.

One must distinguish between what the basic scriptural pronouncements are and what the theology is that is woven around it. Scriptural pronouncements are divinely inspired and hence transcendental, and theological formulations are human and hence often contradict divine intentions. Scriptural pronouncements are a source of hope for the weaker and disempowered peoples, whereas theological formulations are weapons in the hands of powerful interests. It is therefore necessary that theological formulations be continuously challenged by scriptural pronouncements. One must strive to build up creative tension between the theological and the scriptural. While Scripture remains immutable with its transcendental spirit, theology must change, facing new challenges and newly emergent situations.

THEOLOGIANS AND OPPOSITION TO CHANGE

Those who oppose any change in theological formulations and in Shari'ah laws are those who would lose their dominant position. This is also true for the priesthood who monopolize theology since religion for them is instrumental in promoting their interests rather than the spiritual source of inner enrichment. The priesthood, while monopolizing theology, projects it as divine and immutable. The run-of-the-mill faithfuls' understanding of religion is mediated through the priesthood and hence they are made to believe that theology as formulated by the priesthood or by their predecessors is divine and hence immutable. Any change will amount to changing the divine will.

IS SHARI'AH IMMUTABLE?

In Islam, it is widely believed that the Shari'ah is divine and hence immutable. Whenever any measures for gender justice are proposed one meets with this stock argument. It is important to note that Shari'ah, though undoubtedly based on the Holy Qur'an, is a human endeavor to understand the divine will. It is an approach to, rather than divine will itself. The priesthood, that is, the community of 'ulama projects it as a divine end itself and hence refuse to admit any change. "The Shari'ah is divine" has become a commonly accepted position. Thus what was thought of women's rights during the early period of Islamic history has come to be final and immutable. Even to think of changing it, much less actually changing it, is presented as interfering with the divine, and hence is an unpardonable sin.

As just pointed out, there is a big gap between the scriptural, that is, the Qur'anic pronouncements, and Shari'ah formulations. While the Qur'anic pronouncements are purely transcendental in spirit, the Shari'ah formulations have been influenced by various human situations and interests as well as by human thinking on all related issues. Women were in a subordinate position in the patriarchal societies and this relationship came to be reflected in the Shari'ah laws relating to women's rights. The transcendental divine spirit was conveniently ignored, and the prevailing situation was rationalized through contextual Qur'anic pronouncements. As was just pointed out, there is always a creative tension between what is and what ought to be in Scriptures. However, this tension is often resolved in favor of the prevalent rather than the emergent, and the prevalent is eternalized by rationalizing certain divine pronouncements.

ON THE METHODOLOGY OF CREATING ISLAMIC LEGAL STRUCTURE

If we want to effect necessary changes in the Shari'ah laws, it is important to understand the methodology of creating Islamic law. The Islamic legal corpus is known as "Shari'ah." As Shari'ah is, after all, a human approach to divine will as reflected through the Scripture, that is, the holy Qur'an, it is not uniform but has several variants. In Sunni Islam itself there are four different schools of jurisprudence, that is, *Hanafi, Shafi'i, Hanbali,* and *Maliki.* Besides these schools there is what is known as the *Zahiri* school. Also, there are several schools in the Shi'ah Islam as well, the *Ja'fari* or the *Ithna 'Ashari,* the Isma'ili, and the *Zaidi* schools.

Sunni Islam bases Shari'ah—besides the Qur'an—on *Sunna* (i.e., the sayings and doings of the Holy Prophet), *qiyas* (analogy) and finally *ijma'* (consensus). However, except for the Qur'an, the remaining three sources, that is, *Sunna, qiyas,* and *ijma'* are controversial. Some *ahadith* (sayings of the Prophet) are accepted by some while they are rejected by others. Some *ahadith* are considered weak *(da'if),* some of doubtful origin, and some appear to be outright forgeries. Also, *qiyas,* analogical reasoning, varies from jurist to jurist. There is controversy about *ijma'* as well. The crucial question is, Whose *ijma'*? Is it a consensus of the jurists and the 'Ulama, or of the entire community? Also, has the determination of *ijma'* ever been possible? Have all 'Ulama, let alone the entire community, ever developed consensus on any issue? There are hardly any instances of this nature in the history of Islamic jurisprudence. Thus it will be seen that except for the Qur'an that is divine (i.e., the belief of all Muslims), the three other fundamental sources, that is, *Sunna, qiyas,* and *ijma'* are human and hence controversial.

It is also important to point out here that there is controversy about the Prophet's pronouncements, that is, the Prophet's *ahadith,* about whether they should be considered as divine or human. The Ahl-e-Hadith (i.e., the followers of *Hadith*) consider *hadith* as divine like the Qur'an, while many others do not give it that status and consider it as human and hence not eternal.

THE SHI'AH JURISPRUDENCE

The Shi'i jurisprudence (Shari'ah) is based on the Qur'an and on the Prophet's sayings as reported by Imams, that is, the male descendants of the Prophet's daughter Hazrat Fatima and her husband 'Ali. The Qur'an as interpreted by these Imams is considered the only right interpretation, while every other interpretation is considered mere conjecture or opinion *(ra'i).* And *tafsir bi'r ra'i* (i.e., Qur'anic interpretation or exegesis through human opinion) is rejected outright in the Shi'a Islam. But there is controversy in the Shi'ah Islam as to who is rightfully appointed Imam. The Ithna 'Asharis ("twelvers"), the Isma'ilis (also referred to as "seveners"), Zaidis, the Qaramitas, and the Alavids, all differ on this issue. All of these sects have Imams of their own and consider others as not rightfully appointed and hence have no legitimacy. Also, at times, the juridical pronouncements of these Imams differ from each other even on matters of principle.

Thus the important conclusion is this: had it been immutable the Shari'ah would not have differed from one school to the other and from sect to sect. The Qur'an, being divine, does not differ and is immutable. It admits of no change. However, its interpretation differs from sect to sect and from one school to the other. Thus the Qur'an is divine and its interpretations are human, and what is human admits of change. The Shari'ah, being based on human interpretations of divine word, can and does admit change.

What was thought to be just in respect to women's rights in medieval ages is no longer so. The idea of justice also changes with changing consciousness; what is just in one age may not necessarily be just in the other. We will throw more light on this aspect a little later. This is in fact a very important aspect as far as the Qur'anic concept of law is concerned.

HADITH AND SHARI'AH

There are two types of controversies about *hadith* and Sunna:

1. Whether *hadith* is divine or human;
2. Whether it is authentic, weak, or forged.

The Qur'an is unanimously accepted as divine and there is no controversy about it. Also, its contents are accepted with unanimity and without any controversy. No one maintains that this or that verse of the Qur'an is inauthentic, or added later, or of doubtful origin. But it is not so as far as *hadith* literature is concerned. There are several *ahadith* that are controversial. Either they are considered of doubtful origin, or weak, or outright forgery. It is said that Imam Abu Hanifa, the founder of the Hanafi School of Law, accepted only seventeen *ahadith* as true and authentic and yet he used many more while giving his juridical opinions.

There are Muslims who maintain that *ahadith* (Prophet's sayings) are divine like the Qur'an. They believe that the Qur'anic verse: "Nor does he speak out of desire. It is naught but revelation that is revealed" (53:34) applies to all of the Prophet's pronouncements, including his *ahadith*. These Muslims believe that *ahadith*, too, are divine and hence above any human controversy. Thus this source of Shari'ah also becomes equally divine for them. However, there is no unanimity about it. Many Muslims do not believe that *hadith* is divine. *Hadith* is not above controversy as to its origin. Imam Bukhari, one of the greatest collectors of *ahadith*, is said to have collected more than six hundred thousand *ahadith* of which he accepted only four thousand and rejected others as of doubtful origin or outright forgeries. This clearly shows how some people with special interests were producing *hadith* literature to serve their own ends. Unfortunately, many of these *ahadith* went into juridical formulations in general, and formulations about women, in particular. These formulations reflect the prejudices and dominant thinking of the time rather than the Qur'anic principles. These formulations, therefore, cannot be treated as immutable.

Also, there is yet another problem about *hadith* literature. And this problem remains, even if *hadith* literature is treated as divine and immutable. The Qur'an, which is unanimously held to be divine by all Muslims, contains many sayings that are directly related to the then prevailing Arab social structure. These pronouncements also reflect social norms or social problems as they existed then. They cannot be of universal application in other societies and cultures; for example, there was a practice called *zihar* among Arabs that is mentioned in the Qur'an (33:4 and 58:2–3). It was a practice among Arabs to declare their wives like their mothers and to abandon them. "Allah has not made for any man two hearts within him; nor has He made your wives whom you desert by *Zihar*, your mothers. . . ." (33:4). Edward William Lane defines *Zihar* in his Arabic-English Lexicon as a husband telling his wife "thou art to me as the back of my mother." "Those of you who put away their wives by calling them their mothers—they are not their mothers. None are their mothers save those who give them birth, and they utter indeed a hateful word and a lie. . . ." (58:2). "And those who put away their wives by calling them their mothers, then go back on that which they said, must free a captive before they touch one another. To this you are exhorted. . . ." (58:3).

From these two verses we come to know that Arabs used to desert their wives, saying they were now like their mothers, and some used to go back on that vow and wanted to touch their wives again. The Qur'an prescribed that they free a captive (i.e., a slave) before breaking their vow. This practice was unique to the Arab society of that time. We do not find such practices in other societies. Also, today there is no institution of slavery. It has already been abolished. If an Arab today pronounces *Zihar* on his wife and wants to take back his vow, there are no slaves available to free. Thus such verses in the Qur'an should be treated as contextual, that is, revealed in the context of that society, and are no more valid because social practices have changed. Similarly, there are several pronouncements about slaves and slavery in the holy

Qur'an but they are no longer applicable as the institution itself does not exist anymore. But in Shari'ah, as formulated in the second and third century *Hijrah* (Islamic calendar), these practices prevailed and hence elaborate laws were made by the jurists based on Qur'an or *hadith*. But they are totally irrelevant today. Thus the proposition that Shari'ah laws are immutable is not maintainable.

CATEGORIES OF QUR'ANIC VERSES

The Qur'anic verses thus should be divided into two categories, contextual and normative. The normative pronouncements of the Qur'an are eternal and while rethinking issues in Islamic Shari'ah, particularly pertaining to women's rights, the normative pronouncements will have precedence over the contextual. But during the early centuries contextual often had precedence over normative and it was quite "normal" then. And hence these formulations became widely acceptable in that society. These laws were thought to be normative then and hence struck deep roots in society as well as in the hearts and minds of the people. They came to acquire the status of immutability with the passage of time.

Thus even if *ahadith* is accepted as divine, its contextuality will have to be kept in mind. It is also said, and rightly so, that the Prophet explained the Qur'anic verses through his words and deeds, and who knew the meaning and import of the Qur'anic verses better than the Prophet? Quite true. But the question of contextuality remains. The holy Prophet, while dealing with the given society, could not have gone beyond its context in explaining and practicing the Qur'anic pronouncements. It can best be illustrated with an example of women's status in that society. While explaining the cause of revelation of the Qur'anic verse 4:34, all classical commentators like Tabari and Fakhruddin Razi maintain that the Prophet allowed a woman (daughter of his companion) the right to retaliate against her husband who had unjustly slapped her but, because of the prevailing social ethos, it led to unrest among the men and the Qur'an reversed the Prophet's decision. This once again shows that the question of contextuality is highly relevant in all judicial pronouncements be they those of the Prophet or of other Islamic jurists. There is room for change and growth.

Another example in this respect is that of *milk-e-yamin*, that is, legitimizing sexual relations with a slave girl. There was near unanimity among the ancient Islamic jurists that it was permissible to have sexual relations with slave girls and that the Prophet himself had such relations with a Coptic Christian slave girl. The modernists and some other commentators, of course, challenge this formulation and maintain that the Prophet had married her. But Maulana Maududi, a contemporary Islamic thinker and founder of the Jam'at-e-Islami, maintains in his commentary on the Qur'an *(Tafhim al Qur'an)* that the Prophet had relations with the slave girl without marrying her. Most of the eminent medieval jurists concur with this. But this view that sexual relations with a slave girl is permissible could not be approved by contemporary society. Thus the Prophet's Sunna cannot be seen as acceptable outside of its social context.

SCHOOLS OF LAW IN ISLAM

There were four great jurists in Sunni Islam who founded four different schools of jurisprudence. All four differ from each other on many issues. The modern scholars maintain that one important reason was their differing social situations. Imam Hanbal and Imam Malik lived in Medina and thus were quite close to the social ethos of the society in which the Prophet himself lived. They were closer in their juridical formulations to what the Prophet said and did in that society. Imam Shafi'i and Imam Abu Hanifa, on the other hand, lived in Egypt and Iraq, respectively. There were confluences of many cultures in these countries and thus writers were seen as unorthodox in the method they used to arrive at juridical opinions. While Imam Malik and Hanbal mainly relied on *Hadith*, Imam Sahfi'i and Abu Hanifa used *qiyas* and *ijma'* more liberally, apart from *Hadith*. Thus while the former two Imams' formulations were closer to Arab practices in Mecca and Medina, the latter two Imams' formulations had been largely influenced by other practices. This clearly shows that Shari'ah is influenced by human situations and can incorporate situational changes. The Arab *'adat* (customary law) also became an integral part of the Shari'ah law.

Applying all this to women, it can be seen that the then prevailing opinions about women in Arab society greatly influenced the Shari'ah laws pertaining to women. The Arab *'adat* cannot certainly be considered as divine injunction and hence immutable. In fact, the Arab *'adat* had great relevance as long as Islam was confined to Arab society. But once it spread out to far off areas, the need to incorporate other practices also became equally important. And now the changed consciousness about women's rights can also not be ignored. This is an important conclusion.

Problems of Hadith Literature

There is yet another problem about the *hadith* literature that is, as just pointed out, an important ingredient of Shari'ah. The *ahadith* were generally passed on by the Prophet's companions. In this respect even the most authentically reported *ahadith* present different kinds of problems. First, most of the *ahadith* reported by the companions were not the exact words of the Prophet but the overall meaning of what he said. There are few *ahadith* that can be said to be the exact words of the Prophet. Second, the *hadith* literature also incorporates the reports about what the companions saw the Prophet doing. Thus the prophetic Sunna includes both what the Prophet said as well as reports about what he did in different situations.

Now among the Prophet's companions there were all kinds of people. There were companions who had sharp memories and good comprehension of the problems. There were companions who had very poor understanding of the complex issues, and also there were companions who had poor memories. And there were companions who spent several years with the Prophet and there were companions who spent only a few hours with him, and there were those who saw and heard him from a distance. All that these companions reported having heard from the Prophet became part of *hadith* corpus that then was used for formulating Shari'ah laws.

Not only that. There is yet another problem. The *ahadith* have been reported by people who heard it from the companions of the companions *(tab'i tabi'in)* and from the companions of the companions of the companions of the Prophet. Thus there is a whole chain of narrators known as *rijal* (narrating men or women). The collectors of *ahadith* did try to develop the science of *rijal* (i.e., *'ilm al-rijal*) criteria to judge the honesty and integrity of the narrators. But this criteria judged the honesty and integrity of the narrators rather than his or her comprehension or intelligence. Moreover, there were often missing links. Also there were cases wherein much was not known about one or more of the narrators in the chain. Many narrators were of totally different cultural backgrounds—some narrators being Arabs and others non-Arabs not properly acquainted with Arab affairs. Also, many narrators had their own biases for or against women (also about other matters), and these biases definitely affected their narratives or reports.

It was for this reason that the Prophet had strictly prohibited his followers from compiling his sayings. He knew very well that his sayings may not be reported faithfully to future generations for various reasons. Also, he was fully aware of the fact that future generations would insist on strictly following what reached them as the sayings of Allah's Messenger though they may be facing different circumstances. Even the first caliph Hazrat Abu Bakr did not permit compilation of *ahadith* for similar reasons. Still, people did compile these *ahadith*, though much later. And by the time they were compiled, spurious ones had mixed up with authentic ones.

Thus it will be seen that *hadith* literature, even if entirely authentic, presents several problems. It cannot be considered a highly reliable source of Islamic legislation. But the Islamic *juris corpus* is as much based on the problematic *hadith* literature as on the holy Qur'an. Still, the 'Ulama present it as unquestionably divine and hence immutable. They refuse to admit any change even though sweeping changes are taking place in the social, cultural, economic, and political circumstances. The doctrine of *taqlid* (mechanical imitation) is emphasized by many contemporary jurists in the world of Islam. They maintain that rethinking the formulations of the great Imams is not permissible. In fact, these formulations are treated as divine. Also, most of the 'Ulama do not even permit taking more favorable views of women drawn from other schools of law. They insist that only one school should be followed in its entirety. Some 'Ulama follow such a rigid approach but they are fewer in numbers today. Now, more and more 'Ulama are coming around to permitting this approach that has given some relief to women. The Ottoman rulers had adopted this approach in the nineteenth century, but still it is not widely accepted. The rigid *Taqlid* is the more generally established rule. This is causing a great deal of hardship to Muslim women everywhere.

CONCEPT OF *Ijtihad*

The holy Prophet had anticipated the problems that would arise in the future. He took care to leave some guidance in this respect. First, he encouraged what is known as *ijtihad* (i.e., exerting oneself to solve newly arising problems if no precise guidance was available in the Qur'an and in the Prophet's Sunnah). The *hadith* regarding Ma'adh bin Jabal is a good example of this. When the Prophet appointed Ma'adh as governor of the Yemen, he asked him how he would govern. "According to the Qur'an," Ma'adh replied. And if it is not in the Qur'an? the Prophet asked him. "According to the Prophet's Sunna," replied Ma'adh. And if he does not find anything of the sort in the Sunnah? the Prophet inquired. "Then I will exert myself to solve the problem" *(Ana ajtahedo)*. The Prophet patted his back in approval. Also, the Prophet is reported to have said that even if one makes a mistake in doing *ijtihad* he or she will earn one merit and if one does not err he or she will earn two merits. The Prophet did this to encourage Muslims to solve problems that were likely to arise in the future. This would be very helpful in treating the status of women today.

Many modern scholars argue that we should use *ijtihad* to solve new problems and issues, including women's issues. However, the orthodox 'Ulama argue that the gates of *ijtihad* were closed long ago and that now there are no qualified persons to do *ijtihad*. They feel that the great Imams and some of their followers had the requisite qualifications and none today has such impressive merits. Some 'Ulama do feel the need for *ijtihad* but they too stop short of resorting to it for fear of the consequences. Some who did faced the wrath of the fellow jurists and were even ostracized. The debate is raging in the Islamic world for and against *ijtihad*. And when it comes to women's issues and rights, the resistance to change and to rethinking is much greater in the male-dominated Islamic world.

Dr. Muhammad Iqbal, a noted Urdu poet and thinker from India (d.1938), was greatly in favor of *ijtihad*. He wrote in his *Reconstruction of Religious Thought in Islam:* "The ultimate spiritual basis of all life, as conceived by Islam, is eternal and reveals itself in variety and change. A society based on such a conception of reality must reconcile, in its life, the categories of permanence and change. But eternal principles when they are understood to exclude all possibilities of change which, according to the Qur'an, is one of the greatest 'signs' of God, tend to immobilize what is essentially mobile in its nature" (Iqbal n.d, 147–148).

Iqbal also stated very boldly: "The only alternative open to us, then, is to tear off from Islam the hard crust which has immobilized an essentially dynamic outlook on life, and to rediscover the original verities of freedom, equality, and solidarity with a view to rebuild our moral, social and political ideas out of their original simplicity and universality" (156). Iqbal thus maintains that *ijtihad* is necessary to rebuild the law of Shari'ah in the light of modern insights and experience in the realm of morality.

My own position is that *ijtihad* is even more necessary today in respect to Shari'ah laws pertaining to women. It is highly regrettable that the Shari'ah laws are neglected in many other respects (e.g., property and contract laws, criminal laws, financial transactions) but when it comes to women's issues, these laws are strictly applied. In several Muslim majority and minority countries, modern secular laws are applied in respect to all other things except laws pertaining to marriage, divorce, maintenance, and inheritance, in the sphere of what is called "personal law." The greatest resistance, in the name of Shari'ah, is manifested by men when it comes to according better status to women. In this respect the Shari'ah becomes sacred and immutable and arouses great passions. The Islamic world, if it will ever come to understand the dynamic spirit of Qur'an, and to enact it in real life, will have to enact changes in the Shari'ah laws and accord women an equal status. In fact, the time has come to put the grand Qur'anic vision of sexual equality in practice.

BASIC ISLAMIC TEACHINGS

Permit me here to set out certain values that are fundamental to the Islamic teachings. Any legislation that ignores these fundamental values would be anything but Islamic. It is necessary to understand that the classical jurists did not ignore these fundamental values, but the application of these values was constrained by the social ethos of the age.

It is important to note that values like justice and compassion cannot be applied abstractly and independently. In the medieval period the very understanding of the concept of justice was very different from what it is today. Our era is a democratic era and justice in our era is not a condition of society if equality of all humans irrespective of sex, race and creed, is not ensured. Discrimination between one and another human being on any ground, including the sexual one, will be perceived as injustice. But in medieval ages these discriminations were thought to be quite natural and nonviolative of the concept of justice. Even slavery was thought to be natural and in keeping with the principles of justice. In fact, if a slave ran away from the master it was thought to be an unjust act. Today, slavery, bonded labor, and child labor are considered as grossly violative of justice. Thus the concept of justice varies greatly in a democratic era from that of a feudal one. And yet justice as a value remains important in both ages. The expression of the concept of justice in a particular era will vary but justice as the ideal of giving to each person what is his or her due perdures. However, religious traditions, including those of Islam, may give permanent status to expressions of justice from the past, expressions that do not do justice to our understanding of what justice entails in our time. What was thought to be just during the classical period of Islam is thought to be just even today. Because of this, some of the orthodox think the contemporary expression of the notion of justice is violative of divine will. It is this attitude that impedes a change in Islamic legislation so as to accord women equality with men.

GENDER JUSTICE IN THE QUR'AN

One finds in the Qur'an full support for sexual equality in several verses. The Qur'an was certainly mindful of what was just in the era when it was revealed and what ought to be just in the transcendental sense. When the Prophet permitted a Muslim wife retaliation against her husband as a measure of justice, the Qur'an overruled him and permitted a measure of conditional male domination (see 4:34). It would have been thought to be unjust if the Qur'an had permitted the wife to retaliate against her husband; it would not have found acceptability in that society.

However, the Qur'an also did not intend to eternalize the then acceptable notion of justice. The dynamics of "is" and "ought" or interaction between history and eternity informs the whole spirit of the Qur'an. Unfortunately, the orthodox miss this very spirit while reading the Qur'an from their own perspective. The Qur'an is much more fundamental in this respect as it clearly accords women equality with men in all respects (33:35). Another verse is informed by the spirit of that era (4:34); another verse deals with the eternal dimension (33:34). The orthodox, however, do not wish to go beyond the divine injunction (4:34). They have frozen their minds in the classical age of Islam. What was temporal has become permanent for them, and what is permanent is just brushed aside as of no consequence.

The Qur'an must be reread and reinterpreted in today's context as the classical jurists read and interpreted it in their own context. Otherwise no reformation is possible. The real intention of the Qur'an—that of sexual equality—comes through several verses. Those verses need to be reemphasized. . . . The rights of the wives (with regard to their husbands) are equal to (husbands') rights with regard to them. . . (2:228) is quite definitive in this respect. It hardly needs any comment. Maulana Muhammad Ali, a noted Pakistani commentator, says of this verse that it must have caused a stir in a society that never recognized any rights for women. He notes that this was a truly revolutionary change since, to that point, Arabs had regarded women as chattel. This Qur'anic verse gave women a position equal to that of men. This change not only affected Arabia but the whole world since the equality of women with men had never been recognized by any nation or reformer. A woman could no longer be discarded by her husband, and she could now claim equality and even demand a divorce (Muhammad Ali 1973, 97).

However, much of this spirit of justice and equality was lost when the Islamic doctors legislated under the influence of their own social ethos. The Qur'anic categorical imperatives were ignored, as pointed out before, in favor of those verses that were actually concessions to the mores of that age. There are many instances of this. Polygamy is an example. First, it was seen as a protective measure in some circumstances (there were large numbers of war widows and orphans to be taken care of as many men perished fighting in the battle of Uhud) and there was great emphasis on justice to all the wives (their number not to exceed four). It was a great advance over the pre-Islamic practice of marrying an unlimited number of women without any obligation toward the wives. Second, the verse on polygamy (4:3) is preceded by a verse that emphasizes sexual equality in these words: ". . . the Lord Who created you from a single being (*min nafsin wahidatin*) and created its mate of the same (kind) and spread from these two many men and women. . . ." (4:1). There is a reference to justice for orphans and widows (4:2). Polygamy is permitted provided one marries widows and orphans (and not just any woman). And when one was permitted to marry more than one woman, there had to be true justice for all the wives. If one could not meet the demands of justice for all wives, then one must marry only one. No one before had insisted on such moral conditionalities regarding a plurality of wives. Third, and more importantly yet, another verse states that even if you desire to do justice to all your wives, you cannot do it (4:129). The verse says that you cannot do justice between or among the wives. There will be disinclination toward one and a preference for the other, leaving the first in suspense. If two of these verses (4:3 and 4:129) are read together, the implications are clear: *polygamy is as good as not permissible.* But the jurists, in order to avoid the implications of reading the two verses together invented various explanations and resorted to *hadith* to keep the possibility of polygamy open. And, much worse, in practicing it, the claims of justice toward the wives were hardly enforced. In today's conditions, polygamy should be done away with in order to implement the Qur'anic conditions required by justice. Abolition of polygamy will serve the end of justice far better than its practice today. The various arguments (men are more sexual, or there are more women than men and so we should permit polygamous marriages to avoid immoral relations, etc.) are all attempts at human rationalization rather than expressions of divine intention. These arguments do not hold much water as there may be an excess of women over men in one country and an excess of men over women in another. And prostitution and immoral sex thrived even when men could marry any number of wives and also keep slave girls without limit.

RIGHTS OF WOMEN IN ISLAM

Normatively speaking, the Qur'an concedes all rights to women that were available earlier only to men. They could exercise their rights to divorce their husbands as men could divorce them at will. The Prophet permitted a woman called Jamila to divorce her husband—against his will and without consulting him—just because she did not approve of his looks! While a woman was permitted to liberate herself from an unsatisfactory marriage by suitable compensation to her husband (i.e., returning the dower amount; 2:229), she had the right to appoint an arbiter of her own to settle the marital dispute or agree to divorce (4:35). Also, the Qur'an requires men to keep their wives in a goodly manner and to leave them, if it is necessary, in a benevolent manner. And another verse lays down the law that women could not be inherited or taken as wives against their will (4:19). Men are also exhorted in this verse not to take a portion of what they have given to their wives and to treat them kindly. It was also emphasized that believing men and women are each others' friends, they enjoin good and forbid evil (9:71). Thus both enjoy equal obligations. From this verse, jurists like Abu Hanifa have concluded that a woman can become *Qadi*, that is, a judge, as it is also her obligation to enjoin good and forbid evil.

It is argued that a daughter inherits only half that of a son and hence this shows that man is superior (4:11). Some modern commentators also argue on the basis of this verse that this shows injustice to a daughter as she has been given half that of the son and hence it is bias against the female sex. Neither interpretation is correct. What can be said is that this verse was a cautious reform in favor of daughters. In pre-Islamic society daughters did not inherit at all, and now they were given the right to inherit half that of a son. From another perspective it could be argued that it was not bias against the daughter to be given only half that of the son because daughters were duly compensated by *mehr* (dower amount at the time of marriage) whereas sons had to lose out by paying dowers to their wives. Also, they argue, wives do not have to spend anything by way of maintenance as it is enjoined upon the husbands to maintain their wives. Also, a woman inherited as both a wife and a mother. Moreover, she did not contribute to family wealth in those days by way of earning but now she does and her portion could be increased in view of the changed conditions. Thus, the Qur'an properly understood has done no injustice to her even in matters of inheritance.

Another question is of *hijab* (veil). *There is no injunction in the Qur'an that women should veil their faces.* It only lays down the law that women should not display their adornment and fineries publicly and that they should cover their breasts (tribal women in those days used to leave their breasts uncovered) and that they should not cover their ankles with ornate anklets in public so as to draw attention to their adornments. In these verses both men and women have been asked to lower their gaze (24:31 and 4:30–31) and to restrain their sexual passions. As for what constitutes adornment and what should and should not be displayed, there are sharp differences of opinion. These differences are human and every commentator has his views. But Abi Ja'far Muhammad bin Jami'-al-Bayan Tabari, the noted classical commentator, has summarized the views of many eminent jurists in his *Jami'-al-Bayan*. According to Tabari adornment means:

1. adornment of dress or the clothes that a woman wears—in other words, she is not required to cover the clothes she wears;

2. adornment which the woman is not required to cover, such as collyria, rings, bracelets, and her face.

This is more lenient than the veiling regulations in some Muslim countries.

CULTURE AND MODE OF DRESSING

What to cover and what to reveal and what to wear is highly culture-sensitive and culturally conditioned. There can be no universal norm in this respect. The mode of dressing that is quite acceptable in the West may be rejected by the people of the East. And what is considered a sexually exciting mode of dressing in one society may not be so in another society. Even in Islamic countries, mode of dressing (for women) varies greatly. What is acceptable to Indonesian or Thai Muslims by way of dressing for women may be scandalous for Arabs. Dress and sexual stimulation are certainly culturally conditioned.

The opinions of theologians have varied over the ages. Today the sensibilities in this respect are very different and the scope of the exception can be made much wider, subject to—and that is the intention behind it—restraint of sexual passion and protection of one's chastity. To prevent extramarital sex is the responsibility of both men and women and not of women alone, as per the Qur'an. Also, both should avoid wearing sexually stimulating dress. They should wear dignified dress. Covering of the face by women is not required in the Qur'an at all. It was a cultural practice of some post-Islamic societies. The Qur'an also does not require women to be confined to their homes. On the contrary, they could earn and what they earned was theirs alone (4:32); thus women can benefit from what they earn. The cultural practices like confining women to home were sought to be legitimized later by inventing suitable *ahadith* or by farfetched interpretations of the Qur'an.

CONCLUSION

In conclusion, it should be said that if one goes by those verses of the Qur'an that belong to the normative category or that are of the nature of laying down principles and basic values, *men and women should enjoy equal rights in every respect.* It would be necessary to reread and reinterpret many verses that were used for centuries to subjugate women in Muslim societies. This subjugation was more cultural and patriarchal than genuinely Islamic or Qur'anic. The whole *corpus juris* of Islam relating to women needs to be seriously rethought on the basis of the Qur'an and understood in the light of the powerful Qur'anic sense of compassionate justice. When this is done, the genuine beauty at the heart of Islam would be more visible to all.

REFERENCES

al-Tabari, Abi Ja'far Muhammad bin Jarir. 1988. *Jami'-al-Bayan 'An Ta'wil Aya al-Qur'an*, Beirut, Lebanon: Dar al-Fikr.
Holy Qur'an. 1973. Trans. by Maulana Muhammad Ali. Lahore, Pakistan.
Iqbal Muhammad. *Reconstruction of Religious Thought in Islam.* Lahore, Pakistan.
Isfahani, Imam Raghib. 1971. *Mufradat al-Qur'an* Lahore, Pakistan: Ahl-e-Hadith Academy.
The Message of the Qur'an. 1980. Trans. by Muhammad Asad. Gibraltar: Dar Al-Andalus.

5

A Jewish Perspective

ZE'EV W. FALK

WHY TORAH?

ISRAELI SOCIETY IS LARGELY SECULARIZED and lives by Western standards. Most Israelis would respond to the dilemma of "what men owe to women" according to secular concepts of human rights and equality. However, the state of Israel depends on political consensus between secular politics and religious parties that demand that the Torah be incorporated into the law. Even most secularists feel the need of the Jewish state for cultural continuity and religious identity, which, again, calls for an accommodation between the secular norms and Torah in the law of the state of Israel.

Jewish traditionalists maintain that the community of Israel was chosen and defined by divine will, as expressed in the Torah and interpreted by the rabbis. According to them, divine law cannot be changed by human beings. Hence, the claim is made that the distinctions between the sexes are eternal, including the rules keeping women from the study of great parts of Torah.[1]

Indeed, rabbinic tradition approached issues like "what men owe to women" by submitting to the will of God, as expressed in the Torah and as interpreted by custom and teaching. Both men and women were created to serve God and to put the interest of community and family above their own. Such a position is taken by many traditional women who are ready to submit to patriarchy in the interest of the community and in responsibility toward God.[2]

During the nineteenth century rabbinic law was criticized by the Reform and Conservative Judaism that emerged in Western Jewry and in the state of Israel during the last decades. Both movements aim at meeting the religious needs of women for full participation in religious life. A more extreme stand is that of twentieth-century Reconstructionism, which declares all *halakhah* (rabbinic law) to have lost the character of law, since it lacks legitimation by the people. Instead the emphasis is laid on individual autonomy, on pluralism, and on the values of democracy.

Orthodoxy and traditionalists react to these critiques by stressing the immutability of Torah, even at the expense of women's rights. The rabbinic courts in the state of Israel, composed exclusively of Orthodox rabbis, stand by when thousands of wives of recalcitrant husbands are unable to obtain a divorce, and their lives are ruined. At the same time there is an effort to maintain the Orthodox monopoly in matters of Jewish religion and to block any attempt by non-Orthodox rabbis to help these unfortunate women.

On the other side, Jewish feminists, comprised of Orthodox as well as non-Orthodox Jews, seek changes in interpretation, some of them asking only for partial reforms in woman's religious status, while others demand radical solutions in and outside of Torah to erase its patriarchal rules and attitudes.

Our question is, therefore, whether the concepts of God, Israel, and Torah, which were developed in biblical and rabbinic sources as part of a patriarchal system, can be changed or reinterpreted in a meaningful yet faithful way for postpatriarchal society. Moreover, the rights and protection of women in the present must be discussed for a society that no longer relies on the extended family and on its moral sanctions. In modern (and postmodern) society an individual woman stands vis-à-vis an individual man, while rabbinic law still takes for granted the communal presence and the moral authority of tradition.

We will address here mainly the Orthodox opinion, as represented by the official Israeli rabbinate. We will try to show that a negotiation between its assumptions and the equal status of women is necessary and possible, not because God and Torah have changed, but in order to meet the supreme demand of God and the Torah: *to do justice,* which must therefore override any other consideration.[3] This principle calls for recognition of the case presented by many feminist writers and speakers. We must show the necessary empathy and use all intellectual and spiritual resources for a possible solution.

Feminist literature has, indeed, opened our eyes to many aspects that have heretofore been overlooked and without which the study of Torah cannot be complete. No rabbi can now speak about women in Judaism without relating to their arguments, such as those in the brilliant analysis of Judith Plaskow.[4] For justice demands an open mind by Jewish judges for the views of all parties: *shamo'a ben 'achekhem ushefatetem tsedeq* (Deut. 1:16: *audiatur et altera pars*).[5]

GOD AND PATRIARCHY

Jewish feminists have shown that a great part of Torah interpretation and rabbinic theology depends on patriarchal theological concepts, which need revision before the status of women can be equalized. Their harsh critique of religious life often extends to a rejection of God's being, which therefore limits any dialogue and renders difficult the hope for compromise with the orthodox.

To speak as I do from faith in Israel's God, means that we must have the greatest respect not only toward God, but also toward Scripture and tradition that speak of God. We must really take off our shoes, for the place on which we are standing is holy ground.

Moreover, God has no meaning for us without being infinite, eternal, uncreated, creator of all, personal, and self-revealing.[6] Hence, an orthodox man, who is bound by Torah, will have difficulties accepting those particular feminist views that insist the traditional "images of God as male and as dominating Other" always mean that God must be seen as "judge and oppressive."[7] While an orthodox man will certainly feel enriched by such images of God as "lover and friend," he might fail to understand why the infinite God could be criticized by some feminists as "male and as a dominating Other." There is a rich theology of God in Israel and it must be examined in depth.

Taking for granted that the tradition of Israel was steeped in a faith in a personal God, a perception of God *imago humanis*, as an image for humans became necessary. If God was to be seen as active and close to human beings, and if language was that of ordinary people, not philosophers, he had to be described either as male or as female. The fact that goddess worship was practiced in Israel's neighborhoods must have strengthened the patriarchal and androcentric reaction and self-perception of religious thinkers. Thus the feminine aspects of Israel's God concept[8] were downplayed or ignored by law (though not by mysticism), in order to prevent any reception of the goddess theology. Israel, moreover, perceived God as being in time and history, which, again, invited into its theology the reigning concepts of its patriarchal society.

While God is obviously not male, there is no justification, in my view, for a goddess cult or "Queen of Heaven" worship (Jer. 7:18,

44:17–18). Feminist calls for a "transformation" or "reconstruction" of Judaism, of "creating a new Torah," or for "moving beyond images of God's domination"[9] sound presumptuous and seem to be counterproductive.[10] To be heard in biblical and Jewish religious discourse, the speaker must be extremely humble and present a personal model of his or her teaching. My criticism of some feminists in this regard does not close the door to dialogue. It states a problem that I with my faith in a compassionate God feel deeply. The purpose of dialogue is to deal sensitively with problems deeply felt and honestly expressed, and then to walk humbly in our conversation.

On the other hand, God was seen even by patriarchal people as bound by human ethics and expected to be a righteous judge, whose acts could be assessed by human beings. Abraham was said to have been chosen in order to impose an obligation of *imitatio dei*, that is, observing equity and justice (Gen. 18:19). This concept was derived from human reason and feeling, not only by divine will, and could, therefore, be used by human beings to question divine decrees (Gen. 18:25).[11] Even divine statutes were subject to criticism and could be questioned in the forum of reason and conscience (Exod. 32:11–14; Num. 14:13–20). Therefore, the wisdom of the divine commandments was perceived as reasonable and as being appropriate vis-à-vis humanity (Deut. 4:6–8). The characteristic of God's judgments was said to be truth and justice (Ps. 19:10), for he was a "lover of justice who established equity and executed justice and righteousness in Jacob" (Ps. 99:4).[12]

The status of women by divine order could be questioned and, as a result, be changed (Num. 27:1–11). The daughters of Zelophehad, said the rabbis, had sensed that men lacked the necessary empathy with women's feelings. Therefore they had asked for a review of the divine rule by the Creator, who certainly would show compassion for all creatures.[13] Any other law that is perceived to be unfair toward women should therefore be referred back for reconsideration, just as the law of the daughter's inheritance had been returned to God. The goal and strategy of this would be the elimination of discrimination in the light of the overriding principle of justice and equality.

TORAH AND PATRIARCHY

According to Orthodoxy, the Torah was addressed to women as well as to men, but it was given to men alone to be studied and interpreted. The Orthodox claim that Torah could be understood only by male rabbis trained in traditional academies, and they are unwilling to recognize the competence of women to participate in the interpretation of Torah.

No doubt, biblical and rabbinic traditions reflect patriarchal concepts, which are in conflict with our own contemporary feelings on justice and equal rights. Many modern women, including Conservative and Orthodox women, feel offended that Torah and tradition address men, and only exceptionally women. They complain about the study of Torah and about the transmission of tradition, which are primarily the prerogative of males and are denied to the other sex.

However, many passages of the Torah present a more balanced attitude toward women and should be remembered while women's status is under consideration. We should not look for modern statements of feminism in these ancient texts but see them as they were: ameliorations of the harsh conditions of women in those times. Right at the beginning of humanity's story, we find the principle of gender equality. "Therefore shall a man leave his father and his mother and cleave unto his wife; and they shall be one flesh" (Gen. 2:24). This probably represents an emphasis on the need for love between the sexes in order to effect procreation.

Hence, although women were not addressed, they were included by implication in the divine commandment to their husbands. Take for instance the Sabbath and the Festivals, which were days of rest for the whole family, so that there was no need to mention the wife along with the rest of the extended household (Exod. 20:8–11; Deut. 5:12–15, 16:14). Obviously, the husband was to include his wife in the celebration. The Passover sacrifice also included women and daughters (Exod. 12:3ff.). Wives sometimes participated in the annual pilgrimage to the central sanctuary (Deut. 14:26, 15:20, 16:11; 1 Sam. 1:9), though they were often exempt because of pregnancy or care of the children (Exod. 23:17).

Moreover, a wife could develop her own form of spirituality, independently from her husband. She could, for instance, take the Sabbath or New Moon meal at the table of the Prophet, while her husband stayed at home (2 Kings 4:22).

Women were mentioned among the participants celebrating the covenant between God and the people under Joshua (Josh. 8:35) and under King Assa of Judah (2 Chron. 15:13). The public reading of the Torah, at the time of Ezra included the participation of women as well as of men (Neh. 8:2). Their presence in the sanctuary and their noble donations for the building were taken for granted (Exod. 38:8; 1 Sam. 2:22). Women sang in choirs of the Temple (Ezra 2:65; Neh. 7:67; cf. Exod. 15:20).[14]

The Torah takes notice of women's experience.[15] Oddly enough, even the laws of war include an inchoate understanding of female feelings and needs. "When you go forth to war against your enemies . . . and see among the captives a beautiful woman . . . then you shall bring her home . . . and she shall . . . bewail her father and her mother a full month; after that you may go in to her, and be her husband, and she shall be your wife. Then, if you have no delight in her, you shall let her go where she will; but you shall not sell her for silver, you shall not treat her as a slave, since you have humiliated her" (Deut. 21:10–14).

Likewise, every man was expected to show respect for the feelings of his wife, even before fulfilling his civil duties. "When a man has taken a new wife, he shall not go out to war, neither shall he be charged with any business; but he shall be free at home one year, and shall bring cheer to his wife which he has taken" (Deut. 24:5). Though, originally, marriage was perceived as a unilateral act of the bridegroom, acquiring rights over the bride's sexuality from her father or from herself, it transformed into a covenant relationship, imposing duties upon the husband as well as upon the wife: ". . . because the Lord was witness to the covenant between you and the wife of your youth, to whom you have been faithless, though she is your companion and your wife by covenant" (Mal. 2:14). Although this was not necessarily an egalitarian solution, this covenant carried with it moral and religious duties in favor of the woman.

Rabbinic literature testifies that the rabbis showed respect for woman's feelings. "The wife ascends to the status of her husband, but does not descend to his status . . . R. Elazar interpreted Gen. 3:20; 'And Adam called his wife's name Eve, because she was the mother of all living'—she was given to live, not to suffer."[16]

Torah scholars realized their debt to their wives who enabled them to spend time outside the house for study. Thus, "R. Aqiba said to his disciples about his wife: All that is mine and yours is actually hers."[17] Advice was given in the academy to love and honor one's spouse. "If you love your wife as yourself and honor her more than yourself, . . . the blessing that 'you shall know that your tent is safe' (Job 5:24) will be fulfilled in you."[18] Rava taught his disciples: "If you want to become rich, honor your wives,"[19] perhaps as a result of their being induced to save. A moral lesson was drawn even from an exceptional tale about reconciliation. "And her husband arose and went after her (Jud. 19:3)—that is, he followed her words and advice" (BT Berakhot 61a). Attitudinal changes come slowly in cultures and these moves in the direction of justice.

Thus, rabbinic law was meant to serve as a means of promoting family values. It was said that the sages spread peace in the world by

innovative amendments of the Torah. An example is the rabbinic measure to prevent suffering of women, to liberate them from being
"chained" to their husbands and in need of contention. Due to these
considerations, the sages in some cases annuled the duty of a childless
widow to undergo the ceremony of "unshoeing" her brother-in-law or
the obligation to marry him under the rule of the "levirate marriage."[20]

Torah Dynamics

The Torah itself includes certain forms of dynamism, which may help
us, even today, to abolish discrimination on the basis of gender and to
promote equality. There was no hesitation among the rabbis to abrogate
some mandatory norms of the Torah, if their observance would lead to
the violation of a higher norm of the Torah. Take for instance the blowing of the horn on New Year; if falling on a Sabbath,[21] it was abolished,
lest it lead to the violation of the Sabbath. The rabbis even abrogated
certain prohibitive norms of the Torah by way of *Hora'at Sha`ah* (tempo-
rary measure), so as to prevent the violation of other norms, which they
considered to be of a higher order.[22]

The abrogation of Torah norms was justified, among other things,
by following the principles: "It is time to act for God, for your Torah has
been violated;"[23] "Better to abrogate one single norm of the Torah than
risking desecration of the Name of God;"[24] or "It is wrong to risk violation of Torah's ultimate goals."[25] The rabbis claimed to have the authority for abrogating an injunction of the Torah *lemigdar milleta* (to close the
breach in a special case).[26] Here again we see the dynamics of progress.

Finally, abrogation of Torah norms is also justified, if their observance would endanger life.[27] This reason is indeed special, authorizing
not only the rabbis, but also laypersons to disregard the law in order to
protect life. "Everything necessary to save life permits violation of the
Sabbath, the quickest is praiseworthy, and no permission from the court
is necessary."[28] In our view, this means that immediate action regarding
the position of women may be justified even against rabbinic opposition. Many of the women murdered in recent years by their husbands
would still be alive, if the rabbinic courts had been more efficient in the
dissolution of their marriages.

We may therefore say that the Torah, according to rabbinic concepts, does not claim to be perfect but aims toward perfection. Indeed
the God of Israel, unlike the God of the Philosophers, is shown in the
Torah as changing his mind according to the situation. God is seen as
changing his will according to human needs. While Bileam is said to

have claimed that "God is not human, that he should repent" (Num. 23:19), Moses said: "God shall repent for his servants" (Deut. 32:36).

Indeed, R. Joseph Albo (fifteenth century) stated clearly: "I see no evidence nor any necessity, from Maimonides' arguments, that the immutability and irrepealability of the law should be a fundamental principle of a divine law generally or of the law of Moses in particular."[29]

The rabbinic recognition of the dynamic character of Torah finds special emphasis in mystical thought. For Jewish mystics perceived Torah as an organic and developing discipline. According to the *Sefer haTemunah* (Book of the Image), written during the thirteenth century in Catalonia, both the letters of the Torah and its contents will be changing their meaning from time to time. While the current aeon of seven thousand years knew a Torah of God's stern judgment, in the next aeon it would get to know the Torah based on the divine attributes of loving kindness, which would change its meaning.[30] The author assumes that Torah had expressed loving kindness in an earlier cosmic cycle, that in the present cycle it had been transformed into an expression of justice, and that in a future cycle it was going to be based on mercy.[31]

This mystical tradition was accepted and popularized by Chassidism. R. Israel Baal-Shem-Tov (1700–1760) explained how Solomon's wives could have turned away the heart of the wise king. "Every word of the Torah permits different interpretations, so man has to decide whether to turn toward mercy or toward stern justice."[32] Torah was open-ended and could be the result of the argument of women. R. Levi Yitschaq of Berditchev (1740–1809) made use of the already mentioned idea: "We comprehend only the meaning of the black letters, but not the white gaps between the letters. There will come a time when God will reveal even the white hiddenness of the Torah."[33]

Moreover, the community of Israel is called *Malkhut Peh* (God's mouthpiece), according to their understanding and inner light.[34] It is their understanding, from time to time, which represents Torah, rather than the immutable text and tradition based on rabbinic understanding, even though derived from revelation.

An amendment of Torah doing justice to women would therefore be in line with mystical expectations that the *Sefirah* (divine manifestation) of loving kindness, will prevail over that of stern judgment. It would, likewise, represent the divine manifestation of "kingdom," which corresponds with Knesset Israel (Community of Israel) as well as with the *Shekhinah* (divine presence), both of which are perceived in the female gender.[35]

Even texts that have been interpreted against change may be reinterpreted to support a review of women's status. R. Simchah Bunem of Przyscha (1765–1827) quoted an opinion about holiness and gave it a novel and dynamic interpretation. "And you shall be to me a Kingdom of Priests and a Holy Nation. These are the words which you shall speak to the children of Israel" (Exod. 19:6), to which a rabbi of the second century had remarked: "Neither less nor more."[36] This conservative and classic statement is usually interpreted to prohibit change. R. Simchah Bunem, however, turned it into the romantic and dynamic idea of an ongoing moral process. "Moses in his benevolence had intended to reveal more than that to the people, but was not allowed to do so. God wanted the people themselves, not Moses alone, to interpret Torah beyond its revealed text, so as to find Him in the act of creative interpretation."[37] These ideas give great hermeneutical openness to those who search for justice for women in the spiritual traditions of Judaism.

Similarly, R. Mordekhai Joseph Leiner (d. 1854) of Izbica called upon the husband to follow the advice of his wife, even against the rule of the Torah, if he knew that he acted exclusively for God's sake and not for his (or hers).[38] If God enlightened man, he should act even against the rule of Torah.

Hence, the incorporation of the concepts of human rights and of women's equal rights into the law of Torah would be examples for the dynamics of Torah and be in line with traditional Jewish thought.[39]

JUSTICE

Obviously, men's relation to women should follow the rule: "Justice, justice shall you pursue" (Deut. 16:20). This means first of all to have an open mind and to listen to complaints of women that their rights are being violated. Orthodox religious authorities can no longer disregard the growing voice of Jewish feminists. This rule also means that we must examine all religious and social institutions under the criterion of justice. If a man is supposed to pray to God: "Behold, I long for Your precepts; in Your righteousness give me life" (Ps. 119:40), a woman has equally been endowed with the right of life,[40] and every man owes a woman his life and his righteousness.

Rabbinic law must not be allowed to conflict with justice, the implied rule of the second order. If a divine decision could be questioned by Abraham for violating his criteria of justice (Gen. 18:25), rabbinic law is definitely not beyond the scrutiny of human justice. Amos would have addressed the contemporary scene of the rabbinic courts: ". . . I take no delight in your solemn assemblies. . . . Take away from me the noise of your songs, to the melody of your harps I will not listen. But let justice roll down like water, and righteousness like an everlasting stream" (Am. 5:21–24). Likewise, Jeremiah could have spoken to the present establishment. "The priests did not say, 'Where is God?', and those who handle the law did not know me. . . ." (Jer. 2:8).

Justice as well as utilitarian considerations now call for a change of patriarchal attitudes. If the rabbis throughout two millennia have disregarded the intellectual potential of Jewish women, and, as a result, reached many unjustified conclusions in the interpretation of Torah, it is now our duty to step in and correct this injustice.[41]

Take, for instance, the exemption of women from time-bound commandments[42] that explain why men have priority over women in various matters (Mishnah Horayot 3:7). Hence, an argument could be made on behalf of women that they did not want to enjoy the protection of this rabbinic ruling: *'ee 'efshi betaqanat chakhamim kegon zu.*[43] Most people would, probably, opt out of such an exemption, if it was the cause of discrimination. Perhaps, this was the reason Maimonides omitted the rule of men's precedence.[44]

Our sense of justice has difficulty with the father's control of his daughter's marriage, nor do we feel justification for the husband's control of his wife during the marriage ceremony, in married life, and even after the termination of marriage (e.g., by long absence or by the rule of levirate marriage). Our sense of justice is violated by the rabbinic double standard demanding the consent of the bride for marriage (BT Qiddushin 2a), but disregarding the wife's will in divorce proceedings (BT Gittin 77a). Likewise, the double standard of permitting polygyny, while prohibiting polyandry cannot easily be justified.

There is no justification for Orthodox rabbis' refusal to listen to non-Orthodox arguments in favor of equal rights for women. If rabbinic law and practice deny equality of women, they thereby violate the principles of human rights,[45] which are both part of municipal and international law. It represents a failure in the search for justice.

HISTORY

It was probably in 64 C.E. that elementary schools were created in Judea and Galilee by the high priest, Joshua ben Gamla, which gave access to boys only. The program led the students up to a number of Talmud academies for gifted graduates, which again gave access to male students only.[46] Girls, though often taught Scripture and prayers,[47] were not eligible for regular education and were to find their satisfaction in the preparation toward the role of homemaker and mother.

The irony is, however, that on strict legal grounds, there was no justification for this discrimination. The question of women's Torah study had arisen within the context of the ordeal of jealousy (Num. 5:11–31). The discussion was whether women should be informed about the teaching that the ordeal would sometimes be ineffective. For the teaching was that, though she had been unfaithful, a woman could be saved from the effects of the ordeal if she had otherwise acquired some merit. Ben Azzai (second C.E.) thought general knowledge of this teaching was obligatory, while R. Eliezer thought it would undermine the discipline of women.[48] Though Eliezer's views are never followed in other areas of Torah interpretation, this particular one was accepted and even extended to prevent all study of Torah by women.

Hence women were discouraged from study, lest it lead them to immorality, misuse of their knowledge, and to a critique of the established views. As a result, women were also exempt and excluded from donning phylacteries, from observing time-bound commandments,[49] from the quorum needed for public prayer,[50] and from playing a role in public religion[51] or in public administration. Probably, for the same reason they were disqualified as witnesses,[52] judges,[53] and leaders.[54]

In practice, however, Jewish women enjoyed a much better status.[55] Already in the early Middle Ages women joined men in the observance of time-bound commandments such as drinking wine on Passover night, lighting Hanukkah candles, reading the Megillah, and reciting the blessing that women were obliged by divine commandment to do so.[56] According to some authorities, women could even lead the service and read the megillah to the congregation.[57] In the thirteenth century, R. Simchah of Speyer allowed women to be counted among the minyan (quorum) of ten to recite the Name before the grace after the meal.[58] The traditions were not all negative and should not be presented as such.

While Halakhah exempted women from Torah study and from observance of time-bound commandments and thereby diminished their status, women, over the course of time, practically emancipated themselves. They invaded the areas reserved by Halakhah for men, such as the reading of "Shema," the prayers, participation in the seder,[59] counting the "Omer," hearing the blowing of shofar, sitting in the sukkah, and taking the Lulav.[60]

This process of "autoemancipation" has accelerated in recent years. The Orthodox feminist Blu Greenberg noted that the confluence of women's learning in Orthodoxy with the model of female rabbis in the other movements will lead to women becoming Orthodox rabbis, although probably not pulpit rabbis. In her view, the impact of feminism on Orthodoxy is a revolution of small signs. These include individual women chanting the blessing over wine and the Havdalah at home and reciting some "words of love," usually from the Song of Songs, at their weddings; and saying the mourner's prayer during the year-long mourning period. In Greenberg's hopeful view, a female presence in sacred settings is becoming normal, natural, familiar, everyday and the taboos against seeing and hearing women perform communal acts of holiness are steadily being lifted.

Among many Orthodox Jews, women are engaged in the study of Torah and Halakhah.[61] Lately, women have been taught, examined, and certified by the Chief Rabbinate of Israel as "Rabbinic Pleaders" to argue before, and therefore participate in, rabbinic courts and in the decision-making process. Likewise, the "Derishah Institute" for women's Torah study organizes tuition, examination, and certification about the study of rabbinic law.

Although Orthodox women's prayer groups were supported around 1980 by two Orthodox rabbis Avi Weiss and Saul Berman of New York, their prayer groups were attacked in 1984 by five Orthodox rabbis of Yeshiva University, who rejected even this form of women's activity in public liturgy. Women's groups worshiping at the Western Wall in Jerusalem were likewise censured and attacked by the Orthodox rabbinate.[62]

Instead of a reform of Jewish divorce law, a number of palliatives have been administered. Rabbinic courts in Israel may now impose certain sanctions against a recalcitrant husband to get his consent to the divorce. He may forfeit his right to hold an Israeli passport or driver's license; he may lose his right to run for public office or engage in various professions; he may be prevented from having a bank account and, if he is in prison, he loses the right of leave.[63] The Modern-Orthodox Rabbinical Council of America in 1993 introduced a prenuptial agreement imposing financial and liturgical sanctions against the recalcitrant husband.[64]

Jewish mysticism long ago had the insight that a purely male concept of God was unbalanced, and therefore had introduced the feminine element into its theology. This was actually an important precedent for the feminist critique of sexist language. The status of ordinary women cannot have remained unaffected by mystical speculations about the "unification of the Holy One and his Presence," a kind of *hieros gamos*, giving direction to the observance of rites as well as to prayer.[65]

Meanwhile, non-Orthodox synagogues have set many precedents for more or less equal access for women, even to leadership positions. New liturgies for the birth of a daughter and for other life events are gradually becoming part of the non-Orthodox Jewish lifecycle. Discussions about sexist language in prayer, Scripture, and tradition are quite common and have led to various liturgical reforms.[66]

Pluralism

To do justice to women does not mean emancipation by force, that is, that every woman be forced into an egalitarian lifestyle. Judaism allows the traditional model of the homemaker as an option open for those who freely choose it. At the same time, other options must be open to women who are willing and able to play a more active role in religious life and in the public and social aspects of religious life.

Pluralism in women's religion was recognized long ago and met with rabbinic approval. There was a tradition mentioned during the second century C.E. that Mikhal, King Saul's daughter and wife of King David, used to don phylacteries without encountering any rabbinic protest. Likewise, the wife of the prophet Jonah was reported to have participated in the pilgrimage to Jerusalem, without encountering rabbinic opposition.[67]

The model for pluralism of behavior is indeed the very God. The one and only God of Israel and of the universe is also unique in uniting other attributes and phenomena. He is seen as a king but also as a father, as a judge but also as a friend; he is the creator of light and darkness as well as of good and evil. Sometimes God's acts are seen as punishments of the wicked, while at other times he appears as a compassionate and loving being. We should trust him and his word, which expresses both power and loving kindness (Ps. 62:12). The psalmist thereby makes reference to the hermeneutical freedom and pluralism in the study of the divine word.

But pluralism is also cherished among human beings when Torah is studied in public. Hence God is to be lauded as the fountain of wisdom, whenever one sees a great number of Israelites together. For "just as their faces differ from one another, their opinions differ," and a multiplicity of interpretations is essential for the discovery of the riches of Torah.[68]

Pluralism is, actually, a *conditio* sine qua non of unity and monotheism. The dichotomy of patriarchal and feminist thoughts resolves itself in God, so that only a pluralist and inclusive understanding of the issues is adequate to his infinity. Feminist dialogue in Judaism should be full of hope. The principles for progress are solidly grounded in the tradition.

THE FUTURE

In any case, morals and justice as well as utilitarian considerations now call for a change of patriarchal attitudes. If the rabbis throughout two millennia have disregarded the intellectual potential of Jewish women and, as a result, reached some unjustified conclusions in the interpretation of Torah, it is now our duty to step in and correct this injustice.[69]

This historical task is, indeed, beyond the power of men alone and needs the full participation of women scholars and women leaders. A systematic reexamination of all sources should be carried out by men together with women (as well as with secularists and non-Jews). Such a discourse will probably lead to a reinterpretation or overruling of those texts, tradition, and rituals violating women's feelings, and the same applies to the feelings of non-Jews and non-observant Jews.

Since women so far have not had a chance to participate in the development of Jewish law and tradition, they need affirmative action to promote their rabbinic education. Scholarships should be provided for women's study of Torah, and homemakers and mothers should be given the opportunity for the regular study of all sources. Beside the creation of special Torah programs for women, both full- and part-time, the existing Torah academies should admit women and thereby expose male Torah scholars to the wisdom of their women colleagues. Every encouragement must be given to promote women's creativity,[70] experimentation, and complementarity of Torah and tradition. Their work should be included in the prayer books and public liturgy.[71]

Indeed, examples of both types of Torah study already exist. Even Jewish Orthodoxy now encourages women to study Torah, though often with a limited syllabus, with a stress on studying secondary sources. Other institutions of Higher Torah studies include all aspects and sources and are open to Orthodox and non-Orthodox women alike. Coed study of Torah exists both in a number of special institutes (e.g., the Conservative Yeshivah and Pardess, both in Jerusalem), at the various universities, at programs of adult education, and in non-Orthodox programs of rabbinic education.

Justice demands recognition of the fact that women were denied access to priestly and public office and that their voices and experience may not have been recorded in Scripture or incorporated into the oral tradition.[72] Surely they contributed, but their contribution is not acknowledged. The rabbis counted forty-eight prophets and seven prophetesses who were mentioned in the Bible, but they assumed that there were actually many more ("double the number of those leaving Egypt"). They assumed that "only prophecies needed in future had been recorded in Scripture," and that the other prophecies were therefore unknown.[73] In other words, the redactor of the Bible had been selective in the preservation of his texts, and had not included any prophecy of a woman (e.g., of Miriam or Hulda) in his canon.

A belated effort should therefore be made, at public expense, to give women access to public texts, teaching, liturgy, print, and the media. Women's biographies, writings, and experiences must be preserved and studied by men as well as by women, to restore a sense of balance and to do justice to our mothers, sisters, and daughters.

Even outside the realm of religious law proper, a common effort is needed for the promotion of gender equality in all administrative and social structures of Judaism. The opposition of the religious parties to women's representation in the religious councils has no justification, and is rightfully overruled by the Supreme Court of Israel. Women should be welcomed into all frameworks to make use of their contribution toward the religious, spiritual, and administrative development of Judaism.

In general, rabbinic law must incorporate by an express *taqqanah* (rabbinic statute) the concepts of human rights and dignity according to the basic law: human dignity and freedom.[74] Until such a *taqqanah* be made by the Chief Rabbinate of Israel, there should be the possibility of petitioning the Supreme Court of the state of Israel for the protection of human rights in a rabbinic court.

This would not be totally new, for Moses had been ready to listen to women's complaint against discrimination by the divine law (Num. 27:1–11) and Amos had already criticized those "who cast down righteousness to the earth . . . who hate him who reproves in the gate and abhor him who speaks the truth (Am. 5:7, 10). The rabbinic courts in the state of Israel need to listen to the divine accusation that "the priests do not say 'where is God', those who handle Torah do not know Me and the pastors transgress against Me" (Jer. 2:8).

The most urgent part of human rights, personal freedom, should be expressed in a special *taqqanah* in favor of the wife of a recalcitrant husband. The court needs to have the jurisdiction to annul a marriage, if the husband refuses to authorize the delivery of a traditional letter of divorce.[75] Until such a *taqqanah* be made by the Chief Rabbinate of Israel, jurisdiction should be vested in the Supreme Court of the state of Israel to issue an order of dissolution of marriage.

Obviously, responding to the feminist challenge should lead also to a reconsideration of "the Other" in general, of "chosenness" and of the non-Jew in particular.[76] A basic solidarity should be felt not only with the other gender, but with those differing from us in any respect. Every being is an *imago dei*.[77]

Openness on the part of the rabbinic establishment is also needed for an understanding of sexuality in authoritative writings and in tradition.[78] There has been a considerable output of literature on these topics, which needs discussion and resolution by Jewish thinkers, institutions, and organizations. While many assumptions and rules must be understood within their patriarchal and androcentric context, there may also be a need for limits of sexual autonomy in the interest of other ends.[79]

The demographic interest of the Jewish people, for instance, cannot be overlooked, when decisions are made regarding the toleration or morality of homosexuality. The future of the Jewish people depends on the prevalence of heterosexual families and procreation, and nothing should be done that would endanger this future. But subject to this overriding interest of national existence, homosexuals as individuals are welcome members of the Jewish community and their human rights must, obviously, be respected in the synagogue.

In any case, those rules and disqualifications of women based on their reputed eroticism cannot be justified.[80] Rules of modesty should not violate the rights of women. This means lifting any control of women's sexual attraction and appearance in public beyond that which applies to men.

Nobody should be forced to compromise his or her conscience or sensitivity. If, therefore, women feel offended in a synagogue following the traditional separation of gender, a separate but equal service must be introduced for women simultaneously with the male-centered service. The same should apply to the form of marriage and divorce, the rules of levirate marriage, and other rituals. Reforms are obviously possible from all that has just been said.

Furthermore, a combined effort must be made by both sexes to grant women equal access to public office, to share political power, to make women members of the rabbinate and of rabbinic courts, to let them share in public worship, and to be involved in religious administration.

In general, everything must be done to recognize the female gender as an equal and integral part of the covenant with God and of the people of Israel. Men must be conscious of their responsibility toward the soul as well as toward the body of women and to take care of their daughters' and wives' feelings.

The most striking discrepancy between the male- and family-oriented attitude of Judaism and the changed self-perception of modern woman is felt by single women.[81] Matching problems, later marriages, a rising divorce rate, longevity, birth control, and the industrial revolution have opened new opportunities of self-realization in social, economic, academic, and professional careers that certainly should not be denied to single women. Halakhah (rabbinic law), so far, has not created any goal for woman beyond that of wife- and motherhood, while, oddly enough, it exempts woman from the duty of procreation.[82]

Only a serious study of this problem as well as of Jewish law and tradition in general, carried out by men and women together, may help us to achieve justice.

Notes

1. In this framework, we can only deal with the rights and protection of Jewish women and will have to leave the duties of Jewish men to non-Jewish women for another occasion.

2. Cf. Tamar Frankiel, *The Voice of Sarah: Feminine Spirituality and Traditional Judaism* (San Francisco: Harper, 1990).

3. Cf. My `erkhey mishpat weyahadut (Legal values and Judaism: towards a philosophy of Halakhah) (Jerusalem: Mesharim, 1980), 91–115.

4. Judith Plaskow, *Standing Again at Sinai: Judaism from a Feminist Perspective* (San Francisco Harper, 1990), 2ff.

5. BT Sanhedrin 7b.

6. John H. Hick, *Philosophy of Religion, 4th ed.* (Englewood Cliffs, NJ: Prentice Hall, 1990), 14.

7. Plaskow, *Standing Again at Sinai,* 121ff.

8. Cf. Is. 42:14, 66:13; Plaskow, *Standing Again at Sinai,* 124; Tikva Frymer-Kensky, *In the Wake of the Goddess; Women, Culture and the Biblical Transformation of Pagan Myth* (New York, Macmillan, 1992).

9. Plaskow, *Standing Again at Sinai,* 9f.

10. Cf. my article "Gender Differentiation and Spirituality," *Journal of Law and Religion* 12 (1995–1996): 85ff.

11. See my book, *Religious Law and Ethics; Studies in Biblical and Rabbinical Theonomy* (Jerusalem: Mesharim, 1991).

12. This point was a central idea of R. Menachem Mendel Morgenstern of Kotzk (1787–1859): cf. Abraham Joshua Heschel, *A Passion for Truth* (New York: Farrar, Straus & Giroux, 1973).

13. Sifrey Num. 133 (Horowitz, 176).

14. This is quoted by Walther Eichrodt, *Theology of the Old Testament,* J. A. Baker, trans. (Philadelphia: Westminster, 1961), 1:131.

15. Contra Plaskow; *Standing Again at Sinai,* 174.

16. BT Ketubbot 61a.

17. BT Nedarim 50a.

18. BT Yevamot 62b.

19. BT Baba Metsia 59a.

20. R. Samuel Eliezer Halevi Edels (1555–1631): Chiddushey 'Aggadot, Yevamot, end.

21. BT Rosh Hashanah 16a; cf. R. Solomon ben Aderet ad loc.

22. Maimonides: MT Mamrim 2:4.

23. BT Berakhot 63a; cf. Joel Roth, *The Halakhic Process; A Systemic Analysis* (New York: Jewish Theological Seminary, 1986), 169ff.

24. BT Yevamot 79a; cf. Roth, 176.

25. T Menachot 99a; cf. Roth, 178ff.

26. BT Yevamot 90b; Maimonides: MT Mamrim 2:4; cf. Roth, 194.

27. BT Yoma 84b; Sanhedrin 74a; cf. Roth, 181ff.

28. BT Yoma 84b; Maimonides: MT Sabbath 2:16; Shulchan Arukh, Orach Chaim, 328:13.

29. R. Joseph Albo, *Sefer Ha-Iqqarim (Book of principles)*, Isaac Husik, trans. (Philadelphia: JPS, 1946), 148.

30. Gershom Scholem, *Major Trends in Jewish Mysticism* (New York: Schocken, 1961), 178ff.

31. Scholem, *Pirqey Yesod beHavanat haQabbalah uSemaleha.* (Jerusalem: Bialik, 1976), 77ff.

32. Quoted in R. Jacob Joseph of Polnoy (d. 1782): Ben Porat Joseph, 14c; 23d.

33. Samuel Dresner, *Levi Yitzhak of Berdichev: Portrait of a Hasidic Master* (New York: Hartmore House, 1974), 168f.

34. R. Tsadoq Hakohen of Lublin: Liqqutey Ma'amarim, 114b.

35. Scholem, *Major Trends in Jewish Mysticism,* 213.

36. Mekhilta deR. Ishmael, Bachodesh, 2.

37. Mordekhai Martin Buber, *Or Hag; Sippurey Chassidim* (Jerusalem: Schocken, 1957), 420.

38. Mey Hashiloach, Bney Braq, 1995, 1:25.

39. See also my book, *Dat Hanetsach weTsorkhey Sha`ah (Religious law between eternity and change)* (Jerusalem: Mesharim, 1986), passim.

40. BT Ketubbot 61a.

41. Cf. BT Chullin 7a.

42. Mishnah Qiddushin 1:7; BT Qiddushin 33b; cf. Biale: Women, 10–43.

43. BT Ketubbot 83a.

44. Mishneh Torah, Mattnot 'Aniyim 8:15; Gezelah 12:2; cf. Albeck: Hashlamot Horayot 3:7.

45. But see the thesis of Simon Ben Azzai that Gen. 5:1, namely, *imago dei* was the supreme principle of the Torah (Sifra Lev. 19:18 [89b]).

46. BT Bava Batra 21a.

47. Mishnah Nedarim 4:3.

48. The view of R. Eliezer ben Hyrcanos prevailed, while his colleague Ben Azzai had made Torah study of women obligatory: M Sotah 3:4; BT Sotah 21b; Maimonides: MT, Talmud Torah 1:13; R. Josef Qaro: Shulchan Arukh, Yoreh De`ah 246:6. Cf., Saul Berman, "The Status of Women in Halakhic Judaism," *Tradition* 14, 2 (1973), reprinted in E. Koltun, ed., *Jewish Woman*, 114–128.

49. M Qiddushin 1:7; R. Joseph Qaro: Shulchan `Arukh, 'Orach Chaim 17:2; Menachem M. Brayer, "The Jewish Woman in Rabbinic Literature" (1986), 2:149.

50. Shulchan `Arukh, 'Orach Chaim 55:1.

51. Although from the point of view of Halakhah, women may act as readers of Torah: R. Moses Isserlis: Shulchan `Arukh, 'Orach Chaim 282:3.

52. M Bava Qama 1;3; cf. my introduction to *Jewish Law of the 2nd Commonwealth* (Leiden, Netherlands: Brill, 1972–1978), 261; Sifre Deut. 19:17 (190); Brayer, vol. 2. 151.

53. R. Joseph Qaro; Shulchan `Arukh, Choshen Mishpat 7:1; but see Tosafot Niddah 50a, s.v. kol; Encyclopedia Talmudit, 2:253.

54. Sifre Deut. 17:15 (157); this claim was probably raised by the Pharisees when Salome Alexandra became queen, though she became, then, supportive of the Pharisees. But see Maimonides: MT, Melakhim 1:5; Brayer, 2:152.

55. See on the status of Jewish women my book, *Jewish Matrimonial Law in the Middle Ages* (New York: Oxford University Press, 1966); Tevi`at Gerushin mitsad ha'Ishah beDiney Israel. Jerusalem, Hebrew University, Faculty of Law, Institute of Comparative Law, 1973; Die Stellung der Frau in der Halakhah. Freiburger Rundbrief 25 (1973) 206–211; *The Jewish Family and Jewish Family Law. Dictionary of the Middle Ages* (New York: Scribner, 1983); Jewish Family Law. International Encyclopedia of Comparative Law, vol. 4, chap. 11, 28–53; "Gender Differentiation and Spirituality," *Journal of Law and Religion* 12 (1995–1996): 85–103.

See also inter alia, Louis Jacobs, *The Jewish Religion; A Companion* (New York: Oxford University Press, 1995), 592f; id.; *A Tree of Life; Diversity, Flexibility, and Creativity in Jewish Law* (New York: Oxford University Press, 1984), 128ff., 147f.; Robert Gordis, *The Dynamics of Judaism; A Study in Jewish Law* (Bloomington: Indiana University Press 1990), 145–200; Berman, "The Status of Women in Halakhic Judaism."

56. Tosafot `Eruvin 96 s.v. dilma.

57. R. Nissim: Megillah 2a.

58. Mordekhai Berakhot 3:158; likewise decided R. Judah Hakohen, quoted in R. Judah ben Asher: Tur Orach Chaim 199; Brayer, 248 n. 20.

59. Mordekhai, Pesachim 10; R. Moses Isserles: Orach Chaim 472:4.

60. M. M. Brayer, *The Jewish Woman in Rabbinic Literature* (Hoboken, Belgium: Ktav, 1986), 2:197ff., 247 ns. 10–11.

61. Cf. Vanessa L. Ochs, *Words on Fire: One Woman's Journey into the Sacred* (San Diego: Harcourt, 1990).

62. Cantor, *Jewish Women, Jewish Men,* 431.

63. Rabbinical Courts (Execution of Divorce Judgments) Temporary Provision Law, 5755-1995.

64. Cantor, *Jewish Women, Jewish Men,* 432.

65. Gershom Sholem, *Major Trends in Jewish Mysticism* (New York: Schocken, 1961), 229ff.

66. Cantor, *Jewish Women, Jewish Men,* 433ff.

67. BT `Eruvin 96a.

68. BT Berakhot 58a; R. Samuel Edels: Novella ad loc.; Gershom Scholem, *Pirqey Yesod Behavanat HaQabbalah uSemaleha* (Jerusalem: Bialik,1976), 16ff.

69. Cf. BT Chullin 7a.

70. Cf. Cantor, *Jewish Women, Jewish Men,* 433–437.

71. On sexist language in prayer cf. Cantor, *Jewish Women, Jewish Men,* 437–438.

72. Plaskow, *Standing Again at Sinai,* 1ff.

73. BT Megillah 14a.

74. Laws of the State of Israel, 1994.

75. See my chapter, "The Jewish Family and Jewish Family Law," in *Dictionary of the Middle Ages* (New York: Scribners, 1983); "Jewish Family Law," in *International Encyclopedia of Comparative Law,* vol. 4; Teviat Gerushin mitsad haIshah bediney Israel. Jerusalem, Hebrew University, Faculty of Law, 1973; and see Rachel Biale, *Women and Jewish Law.* 1984; Cantor, *Jewish Women, Jewish Men,* 123–147.

76. Cf. my book, *Law and Religion: The Jewish Experience* (Jerusalem, 1981), 97ff.; Plaskow, *Standing Again at Sinai,* 96–107.

77. BT Sanhedrin 27b; Shavu`ot 39a. R. Moses Cordovero, *Tomer Devorah* (Palmtree of Deborah), Louis Jacobs, trans., (London, 1960), c. 1.

78. Cf. Plaskow, *Standing Again at Sinai,* 170ff.

79. Cf. ibid., 205ff.

80. A prayer of a woman was overheard by R. Yochanan in the third century as follows: "Lord of the Universe, you created Paradise and Hell, righteous

people and evildoers, may it be your will that no men go astray because of me" (BT Sotah 22a).

81. Cf. Laura Geller and Elizabeth Koltun, "Single and Jewish: Towards a New Definition of Completeness," in *The Jewish Woman: New Perspectives*, E. Koltun, ed. (New York: Schocken, 1976), 43–49.

82. Brayer, *Jewish Woman in Rabbinic Literature*, 1:179f., 293 n. 216f.; 2:205.

6

A Roman Catholic Perspective

GERARD S. SLOYAN

What men owe to women is a dilemma that can easily be resolved: their existence, their very life. But in this they do not differ from women themselves, for all come from a woman's womb. All women are suited to exercise a mother's role, whether they marry or not. They are also capable of everything men are, short of, in some cases, muscular capacity. What must be borne in mind is all that they have been kept from doing by what is termed their *biologic destiny*. Consciously or not, men have been responsible for this repression from the dawn of humanity.

Some in our day tend to be impatient of history, knowing it to be their captor and nothing but. Understandably angry about what went on over the centuries, they desire immediate redress. They maintain that a century that has witnessed the demise of slavery and the rise of much civil and political freedom is capable of such redress through gender equality. If women have achieved a voice and a vote in many areas of the world under Caesar, why not under God? Spelling out anything the church has done to achieve gender equality will seem to some a fruitless exercise because of the legitimate concern for what the church has not done. The writer can only ask that neither the first century of the common era nor any subsequent century be judged by a late-twentieth-century standard. Some persons of vision in every age break out of the mold into which they were born. Speaking or writing against this mold has invariably resulted in their being pilloried for views which, often enough, become common teaching after fifty or a hundred years, and common practice two or three centuries later. It has happened and will continue to happen; this is the subject of this chapter. The church in this discussion does not mean ordained persons or theological writers, influential as they are. It describes all the baptized, notably the nobility or political leader class along with the clergy, but also the laity who by the force of their numbers and action or inaction achieve more change—or lack of it—than princes or the clergy can ever do.

Christianity came to birth as a reading of the religion of Israel in Roman Palestine. It shortly made its way to Greek-speaking Jewish communities of the Diaspora, to Syria, Egypt, Greece, and Rome—wherever Jews lived—and almost immediately to Gentiles. There it encountered Greco-Roman social mores, a certain modified Jewish conduct, and interpretations of the Jewish Bible not found in the heartland. If Jesus and Paul showed themselves more open to relationships with women in public than the few rabbinic teachers reported on, the fact should be noted. The observation should immediately follow that such conduct was an easier matter in the Jewish Diaspora than in the heartland. The silences of the Mishnah and Talmud a few centuries later prove little. While these writings by Jewish teachers took positions on all sorts of domestic problems and disputes, they did not propose any major changes in family organization, public conduct, or sexual life. The Pauline correspondence and the gospels that followed (plus Luke's vol. 2, the Acts of the Apostles), establish that the leading figures of the Jesus movement thought like men of their time with a few important departures. How the leading women figures in Jesus' itinerant band (see Luke 8:2–3) or in the early churches described in the Acts and in Paul's letters thought of their roles, or were thought of in them, is not recorded. The important fact is that there were such women remembered in a role other than that of spouse. Given the fact that women were considered subordinate to men in the two cultures in which Christianity came to birth, and among all the peoples to whom the gospel was preached in the next millennium, the only question worth exploring is whether woman's role was improved, worsened, or left unchanged by Christianity's advent. A second question is what Christianity should have done to achieve gender equality.

It is not easy to document male treatment of females or female self-assertion in the era of Christianity's beginnings for two reasons: the paucity of sources and the near-identity of the situation among Hellenized Jews (which at the time meant all Jews, even of Palestine). The only extant Jewish record of that period in Greek are Philo's religious tractates written in Alexandria, Josephus' chronicle of the War of 67–70 produced in the imperial court at Rome and his much later history of his people, *The Antiquities of the Jews*, and a variety of apocalyptic treatises that elaborated imaginatively on biblical texts. None deal with our question. The domestic situation in Jewish households was as it had been for centuries, the man theoretically the dominant partner although often it was the woman in virtue of her intelligence and forceful personality. The twenty-seven books of Christian commentary on the forty-five sacred books of the Jews in Greek translation came to be known as the "New Testament." They were probably composed between the years 50 and 135 and by 200 or so were accepted as authentic records of the apostolic teaching that had been delivered orally from 30 onward. These contain numerous references to the relations between men and women.

WHAT JESUS THOUGHT "MEN OWED TO WOMEN"

The first four writings in the Christian collection were later termed *gospels,* after the word in the earlier correspondence of Paul/Saul of Tarsus to describe the good tidings (Gk. *euaggelion* = Heb. *besorah*) that he and heralds like him proclaimed. They were based on reminiscences of Jesus' brief public career. They existed in the form of collections of his sayings, miracles, and exorcisms assembled for teaching purposes that the gospel writers had for sources. The men known to history as "Matthew," "Mark," "Luke," and "John"—all presumably Hellenized Jews or Jewish proselytes — wove their narratives with theological concerns uppermost in their minds. Nonetheless, a consistent picture of Jesus of Nazareth and his teaching emerges. He is portrayed as fully at ease in the company of women, although as a man of Semitic culture he would have spent much more time in the company of men. A few examples from the gospels should suffice.

Jesus is presented as a man who never married. This fact would have been unusual enough for his milieu. But the same appears true of John, son of Zechariah, known as the "Baptist" (baptizer), who preceded Jesus as an immensely popular preacher of repentance.[1] Jeremiah the Prophet is alone among the figures of the Jewish Scriptures in not having taken a wife.[2] The totality of talmudic literature reports only one scholar, Simeon ben Azzai, who did not marry so as to devote himself completely to the study of Torah.[3] John's apparently celibate life was probably the result of his single-minded attention to his mission. With Jesus that may also have been the case. He was utterly devoted to proclaiming the rule or reign of God that would overtake Israel in God's mysterious future. But this absorption with a prophetic calling did not make him flee the company of women. Rather the opposite.

The gospel writer Luke reports that women—he names three "and many others"—accompanied the band that Jesus led, supporting it out of their means.[4] Jesus is remembered as the houseguest for an occasional meal with two adult sisters.[5] He was also the guest of a Pharisee where a woman who was "a sinner" (in Pharisee vocabulary perhaps a thoroughgoing nonobservant of oral Torah) gave emotional expression of her feelings for him.[6] She brought an alabaster jar of ointment and mixed it with her tears as she applied it to his feet, then dried them with her hair. This display was well remembered. The various gospels report it with no mention of Jesus' embarrassment.[7]

Jesus' *miraculées* were women in several cases and once a little girl.[8] He could speak brusquely to a woman who was of pagan stock.[9] Another, a Samaritan, he engaged in conversation at length in a public place, contrary to Jewish convention. In the latter two instances the gospel writers use historical reminiscences for their teaching purposes, the first to show that non-Jews were as much the subjects of God's concern as Jews,[10] in the story of the woman at Jacob's well to make a point of the fittingness of Samaritans having been accepted into the company of Jesus as fellow Jews, a revolutionary move at the time.[11] A widow's dead son is restored to life like the twelve-year-old child above, in a replication of the miracles we read of in the lives of the "holy men of deeds," Elijah and Elisha.[12] Similarly, a response to his mother's request to relieve the embarrassment of the host families at a wedding party is what any obedient son would do at his mother's behest. A difference was that here the change of water into wine is described as the beginning of his miraculous "signs."[13]

It is recorded that his mother and two other women stood by him in the crowd at his execution while all his men friends but one had fled.[14] And one of the women "out of whom he had cast seven devils"[15] (extreme psychosis? diabolic possession?) lunged at him in an embrace of joy when she encountered him risen from the dead.[16]

More important was Jesus' hard line against male divorce as permitted according to Deuteronomy.[17] He normally supported biblical teaching at every turn but here he taught that a text in Genesis prevailed over a concession that "Moses" (the presumed author of this book, composed ca. 600) had made to the male ego. Jesus evidently was not alone among his contemporaries in insisting on lifetime fidelity in a monogamous union. A scroll from the Dead Sea sectarians records the same position.[18] In the case of Jesus' refusal to sanction the dismissal of a marriage partner, the tradition that came of his teaching would prohibit this kind of unilateral divorce for any reason. Matthew and Luke follow Mark in disallowing it, Moses' concession notwithstanding, as St. Paul had done before them.[19] Matthew in two places writes an exception to the blanket prohibition.[20] What his use of *porneia* meant in this context, which not only would have permitted divorce but perhaps required it, is uncertain. This umbrella term for various shameful behaviors is not unlike Deuteronomy's *ervath*, something *indecent*. An offense against some Mosaic precept concerning marriage in Matthew's milieu is certainly intended. It is probably not the woman's adultery or else the evangelist would have used the word for it. A Jewish or a pagan couple whose close blood relationship would have been a barrier to their marriage, which they either disregarded or knew nothing of, is a likely explanation (see Lev. 18:6–18 on the prohibition of the marriage of the closely related). Not only could such a couple divorce, they would be expected to do so. Another less likely explanation is that Matthew in his Mosaic-observant milieu is letting the woman's adultery stand as the sole cause justifying divorce but no other. In any case, while Christianity has had many practices and laws about a second marriage while the first spouse lives, it has never sanctioned the dismissal of a partner to marry another. Such is the essence of Jewish divorce by a husband. Christianity looks to Jesus' teaching as its warrant for this and sees in his condemnation of male callousness a protection of women. Their lot in that culture was perilous once they were repudiated.

Whether Jesus' teaching or that of Deuteronomy, which goes on to describe the remarriage of the divorced as "abhorrent to the Lord? (Lev. 4), hence a deterrent to repudiating one's wife, is the better protection for women, the good effect of Jesus' stance regarding them cannot be denied. The downside of the various Christian legislations on divorce over the centuries—and they have varied widely—is that there is no relief offered in the Catholic West except to separate when life with either partner becomes intolerable and when continued life together is destructive of the children.

It would be a mistake to attribute to Jesus' stance a conviction of full social equality. Other teachers of Torah may have adopted a similar position to his on the obligations of men to women but we do not have a record of it. He, at least, is remembered as taking a stand favorable to women.

Paul of Tarsus in Relation to Women

We have one such record, however, in the letters of a disciple of Jesus who called himself "an apostle," that is, one "sent" by him, even though he experienced the risen Christ only in a visionary appearance. Paul or Saul (he would have had both names from birth in that time, as often today) seems to have been a widower or else living apart from his wife.

The youthful Pharisee he confesses himself to be is unlikely never to have married.[21] He is in any case at perfect ease in his current celibate state and would wish certain of the anxious Corinthians to be the same, namely sexually at ease whether they be unmarried, widowed, or married.[22] Paul writes of many friendships with women, occasionally with mention of their husbands. The couples are generally devoted to the same evangelizing mission as he. The names that survive from his correspondence are the Jews Priscilla or Prisca and her husband Aquila (Akyla), Chloe, Syntyche and Euodia, Nympha, Phoebe, and those other women at Rome whom he knows: Mary; Junia; Tryphaena and Tryphosa; Persis, the mother of Rufus; Julia, the sister of Nereus; and Olympas.[23] Luke's second book tells at length of Paul's friendship with a certain Lydia at Philippi. The modern village adjacent to that city's ruins is named for her. He and others stayed at her home.[24] She does not occur in the letters that we have.

Despite these comfortable relationships with the opposite sex, Paul is modernly dismissed as a misogynist because of several passages in his correspondence. Like anyone of his time, Jew or Gentile, he took the pattern of family organization he was familiar with to be ordained by God or in the Gentile case to be sanctioned by Greek custom and Roman state religion. Headship was the prerogative of the husband and father; a subordinate position was awarded the wife and mother.[25] Women of the present age derive little comfort from the all but unanimous conclusion of critical scholarship that the author of the Epistle to the Ephesians was a later disciple, not Paul. They know that in another place Paul is the author of a passage that puts the husband symbolically in the place of Christ and the wife subordinated to her spouse as the church is to him.[26] This is not the introduction of a new teaching about the relation of spouses but the placing of an old one taken for granted in both cultures on a new basis by way of new imagery. This helps little in view of what Paul does say on the subject. For in his first letter to Corinth he writes as if it were axiomatic that "Christ is the head of every man, and a husband the head of his wife, and God the head of Christ."[27] He would have thought in such a hierarchical pattern even if there were no Jesus Christ. Not long after, Paul says in the same letter to illustrate the mutual dependence of the two sexes: "Woman is not independent of man or man of woman in the Lord [meaning Christ]. For just as woman came from man, so man is born of woman; but all things are from God."[28] This reference to the story in Genesis of how Eve came to be is part of the ancient conviction of the firstness of the man in the family by God's design. Having said roughly the same a bit earlier, Paul loses all credit with many Christians by naming its corollary: "nor was man created for woman, but woman for man."[29]

The author of a first letter addressed to Timothy is an earnest second- or third-generation teacher who writes pseudonymously as Paul. He understands the thought of his master less well than the author of Ephesians but knowing some of the Pauline correspondence he feels quite confident in giving instruction as if he were the apostle. He assigns to men the office of lifting up their hands in public prayer but to women the obligation of adorning themselves with proper conduct, not jewelry or expensive clothes. The epistle goes on:

> A woman must receive instruction silently and under complete control. I do not permit a woman to teach or to have authority over a man. She must be quiet. For Adam was formed first, then Eve. Further, Adam was not deceived but the woman was deceived and transgressed.[30]

The writer knows that Paul was concerned with women going veiled in the assembly, that he tried to impose a Jewish pattern of headdress on the females and uncovered heads for males in the congregation in Gentile Corinth.[31] He also knows that the apostle used the Genesis account of Adam's chronological priority to Eve as illustrative, even probative of man's priority in a different sense. His reading of the Eden story, however, finds in it more than is there to be found. The snake did, indeed, convince the woman that eating the fruit of the tree would bring on not death but new, God-like knowledge. The first was a lie since the tale is proposing the reason for human mortality but the second was a bitter truth. Her passing the fruit to her husband without his word of demurrer, however, says nothing about his not having been deceived. The writer reads into it his prejudice that sees woman as temptress and man as resistant to the snake's cunning. The inclusion of this pseudonymous writing under Paul's name in the canon of Christian Scriptures has fed the male prejudice against women, to the shame of the tradition ever since.

The same author is responsible for a second letter to Timothy and one to Titus. His prohibition of the woman as teacher that was just quoted has been immensely influential over the years. It may even account for what seems to be an interpolation into an authentic letter of Paul that much resembles the stricture in Timothy. It reads:

> As in all the churches of the holy ones, women should keep silent in the churches [namely, assemblies], for they are not allowed to

speak, as even the Law says. But if they want to learn anything they
should ask their husbands at home. For it is improper for a woman
to speak in the assembly. (1 Tim.)[32]

The context in this epistle to Corinth is order in the assembly. It has
been reported to Paul that noisy interruptions have been made that the
prophets (i.e., teachers, especially for their comprehensibility as contrasted with speakers "in a tongue") cannot control. The text as it stands
is in flat contradiction to the letter's earlier assumption without comment that women are praying aloud and prophesying—teaching—
through an impulse of the Spirit (11:5). Such is the reason for thinking
that an early editor of Paul's correspondence inserted the stricture
about a woman having nothing to say in public, which must have been
the discipline of that writer's late-first-century church (1 Tim.). Paul in
his young manhood in Tarsus would have been quite familiar with universal female silence in the synagogue but his Diaspora experience
among Gentile populations, newly Christian, would have been quite
different.

It is not easy to assess the impact of the Pauline teaching over the
centuries, understood broadly as including the epistles to Ephesus,
Timothy, and Titus. Since it was essentially the rabbinic view of
woman's place in the household and in the congregation, there would
have been no noticeable impact for the two centuries in places where
there were Christian Jews in numbers. The understandings in Greco-
Roman and in other cultures would have been largely identical among
the peasantry. Not so the highborn, beginning with the women who
hosted house churches or those given special responsibilities by Paul,
like the assistant *(diakonos)*, Phoebe of Cenchrea.[33] It is impossible to
know what her designated duties were in the house church of her city
but from her title it is clear that she had a position of authority in her religious community.

It is even harder to track the effect of this collection on second-
through seventh-century Christian thought for which we have any extensive documentation. This would be the homilies of the Church "Fathers" of the East and West. Most had the office of bishop but some
were learned laypeople or monastics. So far as we know, males were the
writers of all of the surviving Christian treatises and documents. Some
contemporaries, however, see feminine authorship of the romances
known as the acts of various apostles, notably the most widely circu-
lated of them, *The Acts of Paul and Thecla*, because this literature hints at
freedom from male control. When writers of the patristic age commented on passages from the Pauline corpus they assumed its inspired
character and took it for granted that households and churches should

be organized this way. That was because they already possessed the social understandings they shared with their contemporaries, for which they now had biblical warrant.

Male leadership of the earliest Christian communities (churches) would have been taken for granted, given the spirit of the times. Women would have been the backbone of the communities, as in the reports contained in acts and in the Pauline epistolary corpus. The few instances that tell of women as charismatic prophets on a par with men, or having hands placed on them in ordination, are at the same time, accounts of heretical groups. The heresy in each case was not a matter of such activity only. We have scanty records of groups whose theology was that of the Catholic or Great Church proposing women for ordained office, after which they were soon censured. The early order of widow and later in the West of deaconess did not include ordination but rather designation. One certifiable effect of the New Testament teaching that was just spelled out was the assumption that Eve had disobeyed first and then had led Adam astray. This substantiated the already held male conviction that women were unstable and, worse, would lead men astray if they could. The interpretation put upon the Genesis story is found in all of the patristic writings and was probably more influential on the subordination of women by men than anything Paul wrote on his own.

The lack of documentation for the early centuries precisely on the man-woman relation as lived out in local churches makes generalizations on what Christian men thought of women a chancy affair. St. Paul responds to some questions put him by the community at Corinth about courtship and marriage. He takes a strong stand against the false asceticism reported to him in the euphemistically quoted phrase that "It is a good thing for a man not to touch a woman."[34] Paul counters this with the eminent good sense that marriage is the normative choice for the unmarried. Within marriage, he says, each partner has the duty of fulfilling the other's sexual needs. Authority over the body belongs not to oneself but to the other. If either spouse should deprive the other, injustice is done. If a couple thinks they can do without sex, he writes, they deceive themselves. Abstention must be mutual and then only "for a time." The unmarried and the widowed should marry if the opportunity presents itself and if they find they cannot live a celibate life. Paul is convinced that he is able to do so but this is not for all. A believer in Jesus Christ and an unbeliever, he instructs, should live in conjugal harmony. Their marriage is holy because their offspring are holy. But if the unbeliever will not live at peace with the believer, separation (probably meaning divorce with the right to remarry) is an acceptable resort. But this is the only justifying cause he cites.

Paul is convinced that remaining in one's present condition, married or single, is best. "For the world in its present form is passing away."[35] This expresses his expectation of the final age experienced from early youth as somehow imminent. Such was the spirit of Jewish apocalyptic. It was fortified for Paul by his conviction that with it Christ would come in glory. But he is immediately practical in proposing that, despite this expectation, men do justice to women by marrying them rather than risk sin by an unfulfilled promise or the couple's misplaced confidence in their ability to remain continent. The net effect of his counsel is an exhortation to men to live justly in relation to women, whether married to them or not. Over the ages this counsel has not been followed by men who sin against their wives through infidelity or through unjust sexual demands. It has been strangely overshadowed by Paul's clear favoring of his own celibate situation that he made clear was not for many.[36] He naively assumed that the married live a "divided life," that is, one inferior to that of the unmarried because the latter have more time for prayer. This led to the later Catholic position that the virginal or celibate life is superior to the conjugal but it had no such effect in earliest Christianity. The ascetic ideal of the pagan philosophers who taught complete control of the passions, and the desert solitaries of both sexes who lived it out, were the major influences in that tradition. The sixteenth-century reformers denied the worth of the unmarried state vigorously, declaring the vowed life useless. Only as recently as the Second Vatican Council (1962–1965) did the Catholic West put the two states along with that of the unmarried on a par by speaking of all three as a return to the sources of Christian life.[37]

The apostle Paul did something basic in his letter to the churches of the cities of Galatia by declaring that among the baptized there is no longer "Jew or Greek, there is no longer slave or free, there is no longer male and female; for all of you are one in Christ Jesus."[38] The Colossian letter makes the same point regarding ethnicity and slavery but omits the phrase about the sexes.[39] It is argued to this day in the Catholic Church what consequences the full equality of baptized men and women have for positions of ordained and jurisdictional (i.e., deliberative rather than consultative) authority. Was male dominance meant to be brought to an end by this passage of Scripture, and did men immediately disregard its intent? Clearly all such offices and functions have always been in male hands, as in Christianity's parent first-century Judaism. The question continues to be argued by men and women theologians even though the current Patriarch of the West and the Ecumenical Patriarch of the East by implication say it is beyond argument: in virtue of Jesus' will in the matter (thus Pope John Paul II) and unbroken tradition (orthodox practice). Interestingly, the equality of lay-men with laywomen in spiritual powerlessness in both communions—a much more important matter for the churches—is not made part of the debate. The rights of Catholic women in Church life have surfaced only lately and have focused in the West on their access to priestly ordination.

St. Paul concludes his brief response to the quandaries put to him by the Corinthians by saying that, while widows are free to remarry, he thinks they are more blessed to remain as they are.[40] This preference was complemented by specific instructions from a later pen on how widows should conduct themselves and how the local church should view them.[41] Luke's second volume had already recorded a certain dis-cord in the Jerusalem church over the favoritism shown to Hebrew (Aramaic) speaking widows over the widows of Hellenist Jews.[42] The author of Timothy makes such a sharp distinction between "real" wid-ows who are presumably without resources and hope of remarriage and younger, self-indulgent ones that we see here the roots of a special class that the church must protect (1 Tim.). There are also in the passage grounds for disfavoring a second marriage by the widowed, a position without biblical basis but one that became an important ascetic trend by the third century and subsequently faded from view.

Two further second-century fragments tell us something about the protection afforded to women or at least open to them from church teaching. The first is the reiterated prohibition from the Jewish tradition that is nowhere biblically reported of "murdering a child by abortion or killing a newborn infant."[43] This stricture in a brief handbook of moral and liturgical practice, with its requirement that fetuses come to term and that the swift dispatch of newborns (infanticide) be forbidden, may be presumed to have been the more usual desire of women than men. For reasons of economic hardship or out of simple anger, especially at the birth of an unwanted female, men may well have favored the de-structive practices over women who normally wish to keep their babies.

THE GNOSTIC THREAT TO CHRISTIAN FAITH

An important threat to early Christianity was imposed by Gnosticism, a religion that long preceded it and that made its way among Jews first, then among Christians. In the late second century it surfaced at Rome as the reading of the apostolic tradition favored by an intellec-tual elite, who found the Scriptures of both Testaments too crass for their taste. The content of the gospels was given a symbolic reading in the realm of spirit with a total contempt for matter. This thoroughgoing dualism looked down on sex and childbearing, although some of the canonical gospel characters and narratives were retained in the extant Gnostic treatises, some of which take the form of gospels, and are given an allegorical meaning. An important theme of Christian Gnosticism was the existence of a *pleroma* or "fullness" made up of thirty-two aeons—spirit creatures that sprang from the One (or All). They existed in pairs denominated by two Greek nouns, one masculine, the other feminine. Although some female characters like Mary Magdalene appear in the Gnostic gospels, they have no reality as women of flesh and blood. The content of Gnostic thought had until recently been known only in the writings of Christian apologists like Irenaeus of Lyons (d. ca. 200) in his *Exposition and Refutation of Knowledge Falsely So-Called*. Their account was understandably suspect. But in 1945 an entire library of Coptic writings, some four dozen treaties, were discovered at Nag Hammadi in Upper Egypt. They vindicated the Church Fathers as to the fidelity of their reports on Christian Gnosticism. None of the four canonical gospels was found in the collection. Those that were betray, in most cases, a Gnostic tinge. Important in them in the context of this chapter is the view that the perfection of humanity is maleness. This came as part of the conviction that in the final days all opposites would be reconciled. Thus, the last saying in a collection attributed to Jesus, *The Gospel of (Didymos Judas) Thomas*, reads: "Simon Peter said to them, 'Let Mary leave us, for women are not worthy of life.' Jesus said, 'I myself shall lead her in order to make her male, so that she too may become a living spirit resembling you males. For every woman who will make herself male will enter the kingdom of heaven.'"

The opinion that women would have to be made men in the resurrection of the dead is found only rarely in the Church Fathers. How widespread the influence of this view held by Coptic solitaries is hard to know, beyond the fact that Gnostic Christianity in Greek—the original language of the Nag Hammadi writings—was deemed a sufficient threat to warrant refutation by Irenaeus, Epiphanius, and others. This body of writings puts numerous speeches on the lips of Mary Magdalene, a fact that gives rise to the claim that women were honored as teachers in the early church before men stilled their voices.[44] To conclude: the New Testament cited so far led to the early conviction that since these writings were the word of God, they were authoritative. Examining them critically was not in those times an option. They served to confirm with divine authority what was already taken to be women's subordination to men in society. Women's positions were improved in certain respects by Christianity but there was nothing like gender equality, least of all in roles of leadership in the Church.

MARY IN EARLY CHRISTIAN WRITING

Something of men's view of women that can be documented early in the tradition is the elevation of Mary, the mother of Jesus, to a position of importance in the scheme of salvation. She is mentioned infrequently in the New Testament but in situations touching on the infancy, youth (one incident), then public life of her Son (see Matt. 1:18–25, 2:13, 21; Mark 3:31–35; Luke 1:26–56, 2:5–19, 27, 34–35; John 2:1–12, 19:25–27; Acts 1:14; Gal. 4:4.) The first postbiblical reference to Mary we have is that of Justin in his exposition of Christian faith written some time after 155 that took the form of a dialogue with a fictional Jew, Trypho. There he contrasts Mary favorably with Eve as the obedient mother of life, not as the disobedient mother of death.[45] The *So-Called Epistle to Diognetus* of uncertain date, perhaps by Quadratus of Asia Minor, takes up the theme as he counsels adherence to the teachings contained in his letter. These are described as a fruit that "the serpent cannot touch nor deceit defile. Then Eve is not seduced, but a Virgin *[parthenos]* is found trust-worthy."[46] Tertullian writing in Latin will stress the same contrast be-tween Eve and Mary.[47] Nothing is done by this literary conceit to provide an accurate reading of Eve's role in the garden story but it is the root of all later devotion to the mother of Jesus. She was obviously seen as the "new Eve" by way of expansion of Paul's typology of Christ as "the last Adam" to fulfill the failed promise of "the first man, Adam."[48] It seems safe to say that men were softened in their harsh treatment of women by the picture that was held out to them in homilies and in artistic representations.

We know from patristic and medieval sermons what a favorite topic Eve as temptress was. It is impossible to conclude whether this made the deeper impression on the male psyche—men being the preachers and writers—than the pulpit idealization of the "God-bearer," as the Council of Ephesus (431) called Mary. The title was a christological rather than a Mariological statement but "Mother of God" made its way into Western Christian vocabulary as its translation. Among other results of this devotion were the mosaics, the icons, and depictions of the Mother in every medium, most often carrying her in-fant Son. Roughly one hundred cathedral churches were dedicated to Mary in France over the century that spanned the thirteenth and four-teenth. Men were their architects and builders. Knighthood among the upper classes was often conceived as a consecration to Mary. The wider effect of this piety on the male peasantry is hard to document, beyond observing that men and women came to places of Marian pilgrimage in great and equal numbers.

Some contemporary Catholic women have said that the devotion to Mary of both East and West depressed the condition of women more than it elevated it. Mary has consistently been proposed as something exclusively of her Son and always in a posture of lowliness or subjection. That the term *lowliness* stems from the canticle of praise attributed to her following the angel's message, the Magnificat, does not impress them.[49] Some say that men of the church have promoted the cult of Mary precisely as a means to remind women of their lowly status,[50] that her self-description is the male ideal for the place of the female in the family and society. Such a calculated strategy on the part of the men who wrote the liturgies, preached the panegyrics, built the cathedrals, and led the pilgrimages to Marian shrines is doubtful. Their veneration of the Virgin called "blessed among women" by her kinswoman Elizabeth probably stemmed more from the desire to have her as an advocate with her Son "now, and at the hour of our death," as the medieval Western prayer, *Ave, Maria* (Luke 1:28) has it. The medieval period was an age extremely conscious of sin, death, and judgment. The biblical typology that sees in Christ the male spouse of the church—an extension of YHWH as the strong husband of virgin Israel—receives the same interpretation at the hands of some contemporaries.[51]

SOME FORWARD AND BACKWARD STEPS FOR WOMEN

In the second half of the second century a certain Montanus of Pepuza in Phrygia, modern Turkey, claimed that the Holy Spirit or Paraclete would shortly descend upon the church in his area.[52] He predicted this in the company of two female prophets, Prisca and Maximilla. Montanus' prophecy of the imminent descent of the heavenly Jerusalem included the claim, as reported by the later opponent of the movement, Tertullian, that he himself was the Holy Spirit. This was enough to have him declared heretical. Some have thought that women's place in local communities was set back by these events. This is part of the reconstruction of an early Christianity in which women at first enjoyed full equality with men as a result of their baptism and roles of service but were very shortly repressed by a male hegemony. The evidence for such a historical sequence is meager. It includes the designation by Paul of Phoebe of Cenchrea as *diákonos*, Junia as "of note among the apostles," and Lydia of Philippi as one who offered her house to Paul as a meeting place after her baptism, and progresses to the much later claim that a fresco of a woman in a loose garment is that of a presider at the Eucharist.[53] The apostle had many female coworkers, starting with the Jewish woman Prisca expelled from Rome by the emperor, who came to Corinth. She had a leadership role in the community such as some Christian women have had in their congregations ever since. Only in breakaway groups like the Montanists do we read of their doing the work of presbyters such as baptizing. Montanism clearly set back claims to unauthenticated prophecy and in its train may have done the same to feminine leadership. The male refusal to admit women to the order of presbyter in local congregations probably had a simpler history than one of total equality in leadership before the threefold order of bishop, priest, and deacon developed, followed by a repressive reversal. It is much more likely that those roles emerged on a Jewish pattern and that they were always accompanied by the service of strong women in the conduct of local church life, much as we find it testified to in Paul's authentic epistles.

A splinter of the Montanist movement reached Latin-speaking North Africa where it was adopted by the previously orthodox Tertullian (d. ca. 225). He was perhaps attracted by its rigorism that forbade marriage after the death of a spouse, laxity in fasting, and in other disciplinary practices. In light of his writings it is hard to imagine him as an enthusiast engaging in ecstatic prophecy. While he might have espoused such behavior it is doubtful that he engaged in it. What he did was describe the Catholics as "psychics," meaning living at a merely sentient level. They were not "pneumatics" or the Spirit-filled people of his new allegiance. Tertullian composed a beautiful tribute to his wife but in it he asked her to remain a widow after his death; if not that, then to marry a Christian.[54] This was in his Catholic period; as a Montanist he exhorted a friend not to remarry, calling such a union of the widowed "a kind of fornication.[55] One treatise attacked second marriage violently, while another written a decade before expected all virginal women to go veiled in public.[56] Tertullian was extremely influential in the Latin West both because of his defense of the faith and because of his distinguished written rhetoric. Despite his lapse into heresy he continued to be read and cited widely. His views on the modesty of women almost certainly contributed to their subjugation. The male ego that is always fragile at best took comfort in the notion that the female sex, whether wives, mothers, or virgins, should be seen and not heard.

Tertullian's Montanist commitment did enable him to make room, following Paul, for women who prophesied (see 1 Cor. 11:5) and in one treatise he reported at some length on the visions experienced by a woman of his worshiping company.[57] In his Catholic period he had fulminated against a woman "who would claim for herself any function proper to a man, least of all the sacerdotal office" (his term was *offering*).[58] An office he sanctioned because it was traditional was that of widows, whom he included in an ecclesiastical order along with virgins as members of the clergy. It was the sexual continence of widows that qualified them for this office. He listed their order after men in the order of bishop, presbyter, and deacon to whom a second marriage should not be allowed[59] and mentions seats reserved for them in the assembly that virgins should not occupy.[60] The special care for widows as a class is testified to in Hippolytus and Hermas, both writing in Greek from Rome in Tertullian's period.[61] Nowhere, however, is this order of widows assumed to be an active liturgical office except in heretical conventicles. They were to fast often and pray on behalf of the church.[62]

Writers of the East like Origen and Clement of Alexandria wrote of widows as if they were familiar with the same customs concerning them as in North Africa and Italy. Even though "washing the feet of the saints" (believers) (1 Tim. 5:10) were among the good works that were appropriate for widows and even older women were "to teach what is good," (Titus 2:3), Origen could not see in either a liturgical office or in the prophetic gift of the daughters of Philip (Acts 21:8–9) a legitimation of female prophesying in a mixed assembly.[63] In general Alexandria was completely ill at ease with permitting any public role in worship to women. A Syrian document in Greek of the first half of the third century, the *Didaskalia*, speaks of some women who were "appointed" to "the order of widows" and who sat with the older women in the assemblies.[64] Appointed widows in this document had the obligations of nuns in later centuries: a continent life and prayer for the rest of the community. Another class is mentioned here, women deacons who were appointed to assist their colleagues as male deacons did for men.[65] A liturgical function was specified in detail, namely their responsibility to anoint women candidates for baptism before they went down into the pool, normally in brief nakedness with a white baptismal robe slipped off and immediately on. If no woman deacon was available for this function a man in that order could exercise it but, for reasons of modesty, pouring the water of baptism on the head only.

SOME FEMALE DECLARATIONS OF INDEPENDENCE

A late-second-century development moving into the third saw women in the Greek-speaking culture strike back, by their claiming the right to remain virginal for the sake of the gospel. Many Christian men fell short of the Christian ideal that held that they owed women justice and the fullest measure of equality the culture allowed. Some violated it seriously by cruelty and repression. The commonest form that male dominance took was in the context of the arranged marriage in which fathers and guardians or older brothers chose "suitable" partners for young women of the family. The suitability was often totally questionable, being based on property, place in society, and the forming of new family ties. Since the women of marriageable age were treated as if they had no will of their own their husbands took their cue from this and dealt with them in the same way. The result was domestic cruelty, physical and mental, in many cases. The women revolted, claiming as Christians that they preferred being espoused to Christ over a union with a man not of their choice. They did not "hie themselves to nunneries," there being none at the time, but they claimed the privileges of widowhood, a class acknowledged and respected by local church communities.

What we know of this movement comes from a succession of popular writings that bordered on romances purporting to originate in the circle of the apostle Paul. The earliest of these, surviving in fragments, has been reconstructed as *The Acts of Paul*. Its components are an apocryphal reply of the Christian community of Corinth to his second epistle and an equally spurious third epistle; a *Martyrdom or Passion of St. Paul* filled with fictitious miraculous details; and the most popular of all, *The Acts of Paul and Thecla*.[66] Many of the details of the story are fantastic including one that she baptized herself. They include numerous attempts to kill Thecla by fire and wild beasts until, aged ninety, she retired to a cave at Seleucia. Her cult at that sanctuary as a result of the legend was by no means fictitious. It went on for several centuries. An outcome of equal importance was a spate of similar acts of holy women for whom a virginal consecration to Christ was claimed. Some of these narratives may have been based on fact. There were women as well as men who sought an eremitic life of prayer, many out of unmixed motives. The apocryphal accounts of "flight from the world," however, are of a literary genre that testifies more to flight from unattractive arranged marriages.[67] It has been speculated that upper-class women were the authors of some of this literature of social protest. If so, it need not have been the prospect of domestic cruelty—although such may have been present—but of an unappetizing union with a man scarcely known or whose character was all too well-known.

A cognate development stemmed from the life of female solitaries that was to reverberate down to our day. The third-century Egyptian desert and sixth-century Ireland witnessed the widespread phenomenon of Christian men and women living solitary lives of prayer and contemplation, coming together on Sunday for the eucharistic meal. Out of this life there developed the cenobitic or common life in which the two sexes lived apart from but were located close to each other. On the female side a woman of means named Macrina, the sister of Basil of Caesarea and Gregory of Nyssa, was the founder in the fourth century of nuns in community. A similar role was played in the West by Scholastica, sister of Benedict, a century and a half later. Much later, when convents of nuns became a fixture in society, they came to be populated by the highborn at first and peasantry later if a dowry could be found for them. Often the candidates came with uncomplicated motives but at times daughters were offered by well-off families as hostages to fortune. Medieval literature testifies to some of these women unhappy in their claustration. The important matter is that as a class they were treated respectfully by male monastics and by the culture generally. Bishops and abbots were their protectors against the depredations that might have threatened a house full of women. They were self-governed under an abbess of their choosing just as with the men. A few of the latter monastics were in priest's orders and served as chaplains to the female monasteries but the women maintained a fierce independence of any ecclesiastical authority or male domination. They tended to become literate and a few deeply learned in cultures where only laywomen of noble birth had such opportunities. As with Buddhist nuns today (see Puntarigvivat's chap. in this vol.), becoming a nun was the gateway to education and empowerment.

An occasional man of property would school his daughter in learning at home. The spouses and female children of the powerful often succeeded to a measure of power in virtue of their education, normally a male preserve. The learned nun of free spirit, contrariwise, was usually the product of feminine independence and initiative, if at times under the guidance of abbots and spiritual directors. The writings of some of the most gifted women in the high Middle Ages show them to be perceptive of the mood of the times. They acknowledge the men as their superiors in learning and stress the modesty of their own contributions so as to be taken seriously. It is a pose that women have had to adopt from time immemorial unless they are born to wealth and power. This discussion may strike some as of little importance since literate, sometimes highly educated Christian women were so few relative to the wives and mothers trapped on the domestic front. The phenomenon is important because the nuns in Carolingian and in later medieval monasteries, contrary to the anticonventual stereotype of women locked away and deprived of normal liberties, were often freer in mind and spirit because of their literacy than their lay counterparts.

Even into the twentieth century the educated religious Sister in the various professions was a pioneer and role model of the mentally liberated women of the West. English- and German-language writing of the Enlightenment, being Protestant, was in no condition to acknowledge the development.

How did it go in families in the centuries up to the year 700 and in the next two centuries in the West? The latter—800–1,000—have been labeled the "Dark Ages" only because we know relatively little about them. That much is true even of female monasticism, let alone of domestic relationships. Unquestionably Christian life exercised some softening influence on the tribes that came down from the north: Teutons like the Goths and Franks and Huns, later the Slavs, Magyars, and others. In the process of Christianizing them, even the semiliterate among the preachers would have proposed the women of the Bible and early saints of the church for emulation. Joseph as Mary's husband even if not the father of her child would have figured as a model for men and even more, Jesus himself. But the times were rough and the manners coarse. All men including Christian men, had been raised on a diet of male dominance. They knew something of their debt to women but on the meager evidence, not much. If their conduct was widely countercultural in a good sense we should have heard of it. No such record exists.

THE TREATMENT OF WOMEN IN PATRISTIC WRITINGS

If Christian women of the East and West have a complaint about their being kept subordinate to men on the basis of the New Testament Scriptures—admission to ordination apart—it should be lodged against the Church Fathers whose writings proved immensely influential through the prism of subsequent popular preaching. This was based on passages in the epistles of St. Paul and in the author of the first and second Timothy and Titus to which congregations, being largely nonliterate, would not have had direct access.

St. John Chrysostom was bishop and by that fact patriarch of Constantinople from 398 to 404. He wrote much, some in the form of theological treatises but most as homilies on books of the Bible or sermons. Some in the latter two genres are remembered for their harsh theological anti-Judaism but these, despite their poisonous influence, were a small portion of his total output. He left in place the social structures of the classical authors for the good ordering of the family, not letting himself be disturbed regarding women by Paul's "for freedom Christ has set us free" (Gal. 5:1). As to the effect of this text on the social relations between the sexes, he would have thought: "Does not apply."[68] He pressed the dominion of Adam over Eve to the utmost but with the interesting observation that God had created her without any authority above her. It was her sin of disobedience, freely chosen, which reduced her to slavery and thus, presumably, reduced all womanhood to subjection. There must be a ruler and the ruled in society, he wrote, lest anarchy prevail.[69] Similarly, the father must rule benevolently as king in the household. There is no room for democracy in the society of the family.[70]

Chrysostom allowed women to teach men in the privacy of the home, especially if the man was a pagan or a quite ignorant Christian, but never in public. Women must retire in face of the magnitude of the task. This seems cruelly repressive but it was of a piece with the fact that educational opportunities for women were severely curtailed. As early as Chrysostom's century, Catholic women (as contrasted with members of Christian sects) were expressing unhappiness at their exclusion from priestly functions. Some wealthy women, he reported, attempted to make and unmake priests at will.[71] Elizabeth Clark brings much of this to light, pointing out that Plato was Chrysostom's chief target. He thought that some of the suggestions in book 5 of *The Republic* were "ridiculous" and the philosopher "a foe to modesty." Having argued that a woman's subordinate position is decreed by nature and confirmed by the stories of Eve's creation and her tempting Adam to sin, Chrysostom declared that the woes of marriage only added to the miseries of a woman's servitude. There was a way out, the celibate life, which he praised without reservation. Paradoxically, he thought that the situation of women in the church had not always been such. He looked back to the freedom they had in traveling with the apostles, marveled that some were even called "apostles," and that they prophesied in the assembly. But all these privileges had been lost. The Church Fathers did not see them as retrievable, or that the domination of men was the cause of women's plight.

The Latin-speaking Jerome was even fiercer than Chrysostom, holding the bizarre position that the primary purpose of marriage was to beget virgins. Neither man was a misogynist in the sense of holding the whole female sex in contempt. Far from it. A Roman aristocrat named Paula, widowed at thirty-three and the mother of five, moved from Rome to Bethlehem with her daughter Eustochium to found a convent of nuns to be spiritually guided by the choleric hermit. Before he left Rome his most scholarly female friend was a young highborn widow named Marcella. This was a time when many men and women of social status were abjuring their wealth and becoming Christians, some few to embark on monastic or lives of solitude. Jerome departed the capital in a hail of criticism for his too close association with women, a large number of whom he corresponded with for the rest of his life. This did not keep him from writing sarcastic invectives against women, a situation with which—as with Chrysostom—modern pop psychologists have had a field day. Attributing the outlook of either to his repressed celibate status, however, does not quite do it. Many of the most antifemale writers of history have been married men. Chrysostom's chief source of consolation was a certain widowed aristocrat named Olympias who, like him, was learned and pious, and also extremely supportive of the clergy out of her means.[72] If challenged, both he and Jerome might have said in praise of any woman friend: "She thinks just like a man."

A clear indication of where women stood in fifth-century Latin culture can be found in the view of the learned rhetorician Augustine, bishop of Hippo Regius (Annaba in modern Algeria). He kept a mistress for sixteen years, who bore him a son. We know the boy's name, Adeodatus (Gift of God) from Augustine's adult memoir, but tellingly not the mother's.[73] In reporting the union he is at pains to deplore the long-standing grip that sexual desire had on him, without expressing any compunction for the injustice done to the woman. When his mother counseled him to send her away in the interests of making a suitable marriage he dutifully complied, reporting the woman's tearful vow that she would never know another man. About his feelings for her he reports that his heart "still clings to her" and was "pierced and wounded" within him, drawing blood. In the event, he took another woman but never married, saying that marriage and a family had no attraction for him.

Augustine was a devotee of the syncretistic Persian teacher Mani at the time, whose dualist doctrine held that spirit was of value and matter was not. When as an adult he adopted the Catholic faith of his mother he did not manage to shake off completely his Manichean abhorrence of sex. It took the form of a theoretical, scarcely Catholic position that the will was never quite successful in governing the passions in the marriage act. A later Catholic morality would call this healthy urge "concupiscence" but not sin. Augustine defined the uncontrolled element as sin. This conviction was at the heart of his theory of how the sin of the primordial pair was transmitted. He called the guilt *peccatum originale*. This became *original sin* in Western theology. The term has never been used in theology to describe the disobedience of Adam and Eve as "*the* original sin," a popular misconception. Happily, the church did not accept Augustine's bizarre theory of race guilt via the sex act when at the Council of Arausicanum II (Orange in southern France) in

529 it defined the humanity-wide tendency to sin and the power of grace to overcome it.[74] But so great was the man's influence in the Western church that a theory that never attained the status of dogma became a widespread assumption. If any Christians, Protestant or Catholic, have erroneously supposed sex in marriage to have something of the character of sin, Augustine is the one responsible. He is to be repudiated thoroughly in this matter.

This is not to say that the dogma of our age has merit that holds that no exercise of the sex act in marriage can be morally wrong. Adultery is still thought to be such an offense but in some Christian traditions it is not alone. According to Catholic morality, what is, in effect, rape in marriage, premarital sex including the "protected," and sex completely divorced from childbearing can be grave injustices to both parties. Modernity accepts the validity of the first of these as wrongdoing but is in no mood to acknowledge the other two. Augustine's part in all this is not that he set an example of callousness to women by his longtime liaison that he allowed to be abruptly terminated for selfish reasons. It was that his later, lifelong categorization of sex as unwittingly having the character of sin contributed to the view that a woman cannot but be a temptress to hapless males and that her role as a mother is necessarily tinged with evil. The never fully recovered Manichee Augustine bears this burden.

Women's voices were heard in the early centuries in a different and more powerful way by their heroic behavior in martyrdom. Among those who gave witness to Christ by their lives in persecution under Marcus Aurelius in 177 or 178 was a certain Blandina. When her body was mangled almost beyond recognition by her torturers who were exhausted from the effort, she could still say: "I am a Christian. We do nothing to be ashamed of."[75] Better known is the account of a well-born woman aged twenty-two, Perpetua, the mother of an infant son, and her slave Felicitas, who gave birth to a girl shortly before her death in the arena. The year was 202, the place Latin-speaking Carthage, and the emperor Septimius Severus. This account is so movingly told that Tertullian is thought to be its author or editor, while St. Augustine two centuries later warned its readers not to put the *Acta* (account) on a level with the canonical Scriptures. The largest part of the narrative (chaps. 3–10) is Perpetua's own diary and tells of her visions in prison.[76] The Roman martyrs whose names appear in the Roman canon of the Mass include Agnes, Cecilia, and Felicitas, the latter who had seven sons.[77]

Aside from that incorporated fragment of prison literature, there are no extant writings of the women who must have been Mothers of the church. If we possessed them they would have been produced anonymously to gain acceptance. Female authorship was uncommon in the period, not only Christian but pagan and Jewish as well. St. Macrina the Younger (327–380) may have written a rule for her nuns on the family estate but we do not have it. What we do have is testimony to her skill as a theologian by Gregory in his treatise *On the Soul and Resurrection*.

Much later, St. Hilda of Whitby in Northumberland (d. 680) was the abbess of a double monastery, having jurisdiction over monks and nuns. A woman named Dhuoda or Dodena wrote in the years 841–843. We have her thoughts and word pictures on loving God but not her chapters "On the Holy Trinity" or "Faith, Hope, and Charity." Although of Frankish, that is, Germanic stock, she wrote in Latin like any person of letters in her day.[78]

Medieval and Renaissance Women of the Christian West

The writings of the women mystics St. Gertrude of Helfta (d. ca. 1302) and Mechtild of Magdeburg (d. ca. 1282) are becoming increasingly well-known in our time. They were preceded by St. Hildegard, abbess of Rupertsberg near Bingen (d. 1179), a polymath as well as a visionary.

The spiritual outreach of Hildegard was replicated two centuries later in the person of St. Catherine (Benincasa) of Siena (d. 1380), the twenty-third of twenty-five children born to the wife of a prosperous dyer. She made the vows of a member of the Dominican third order, first living at home but then moving about with a retinue that included clerics, in various peacemaking ventures. Her one political success was to have convinced Gregory XI in 1377 that he should return from Avignon, where the popes had resided since 1309. She remained committed to his successor, Urban VI who, with the popes who came after him, was challenged by a series of antipopes until 1417. Catherine, worn out by her activities and her ascetic way of life, died at thirty-three.

England's champion was an anonymous anchoress (d. after 1416) who, with a servant, lived in a cell attached to the church of St. Julian in Norwich. Her visions that she called *Showings*, as later written up, were extremely influential. The same influence is true of St. Bridget or Brigitta of Sweden (d. 1373), foundress of a double monastery at Vadstena where her daughter St. Catherine (d. 1381) succeeded her as first abbess.[79]

It needs to be asked, How did the lives of women like these affect women generally? Many more were managing households, bearing children, and going largely unlettered. The answer seems to be that they were giving a sense of what Christian womanhood could be by serving other women. The many nuns of East and West were not "walled up" in monasteries as the popular image created by post-Reformation writers would have it. Chanting the divine office in choir—the church's public prayer, composed chiefly of the book of Psalms—was these women's chief engagement. But their monasteries, single or double, were centers of service of every kind: of health care, education in the practical arts and, for gifted daughters of the area in letters. They also schooled women in how to cope with domestic cruelty and neglect. The women who lived by rule and vow were role models of the most effective kind. Having got rid of the male dominance that marked the entire culture, they showed other women how it could be done within the limits of their circumstances.

The monasteries of the feudal age were succeeded by convents of the medieval and modern eras in which "Sisters" replaced "nuns." The difference lay not in a common life of prayer and service, which continued, but in mobility. Just as the friars took to the streets and the roads, not remaining on a large monastic property, so their female counterparts would have willingly gone out among the people were not their movements limited by legitimate fears for their safety and a centuries-old tradition of their *enclosure* (a term of church law). The Renaissance saw an increased participation in the lives of the people by groups like the Ursulines, founded at Brescia by St. Angela Merici (d. 1540) for catechizing and later for schools-instruction and by the widowed. St. Louise de Marillac's (d. 1660) Parisian Daughters of Charity were founded for the relief of the sick and the poor. Two other ventures at female self-determination were less successful. These two religious congregations achieved their freedom from clerical domination with the aid and encouragement of clerics. Another widow, this time of the Burgundian minor nobility, named Jane Frances Frémyot de Chantal (d. 1641) attempted liberation from the monastic tradition by naming her group the Order of the Visitation, with home visits as their elected role of service. The departure from tradition was too much for the archbishop of Lyons who blocked the plan and forced their retreat to the contemplative life.

These four courageous females were the forerunners of the myriad societies of "women religious," as they are popularly known, in the West. Their influence since the Reformation has been incalculable. The reformers to a man had a poor view of common life for both men and women, maintaining that a healthy spiritual life in families could better achieve the same ends, but the Reformation churches were demonstrably impoverished by the disappearance from their ranks of educated, unmarried women devoted to prayer, the spiritual and corporal works of mercy, and the life of learning.

Contemporary feminism has noted the acceptance by a Dominican friar St. Thomas Aquinas (d. 1274) of the erroneous supposition of Aristotle that, in the earliest cell development in the womb, a female was an imperfectly developed male *(mas occasionatus)*.[80] Israelite anthropology, as reflected in the Bible, thought that the female womb was simply the receptacle of the male seed that slowly developed into fetal life and birth. Even with the discovery in the not so distant past that the role of sperm in the process was simply to trigger fertilization by irritating the ovum, not much was changed in the popular mind. More recently still, there's the discovery that all humans would be female were it not for early gene activity; those who now know what Aquinas and Aristotle did not know are no more able to alter the cultural perception.

The world's economies have long managed to survive in virtue of women's economic servitude. Whether they can survive on another principle remains to be seen. Catholic teaching as enunciated by its bishops and by its chief bishop has not spelled out clearly the double freedom women require if they are to be treated justly by society. This must become the subject of Catholic teaching or else nothing will change.

Women's Roles in Catholic Worship

The Catholic situation as contrasted with the Orthodox and the Protestant is marked by special difficulties. It has long been known that women are the backbone of all religious devotion and service while men have claimed for themselves most positions of ritual and administrative leadership. Many late-twentieth-century Catholics think of it as a God-ordained tradition that must be honored, but, increasingly, people of both sexes indicate their conviction that the tradition can be departed from. All Christianity defines such roles ideally as service. Some women, however, see in them the exercise of power. An initial observation about the effect of ordination in the Catholic and Orthodox churches is that a voluntary servant class is created and, at the same time, both sexes are rendered voiceless in church affairs. How things go in the Orthodox East a Western Christian can only suspect from a distance but the Catholic Code of Canon Law (1917; rev. 1983) formalizes what has long been the case.[81] Only bishops and pastors have what is called "jurisdiction" at law, meaning deliberative power in a diocese and parish respectively. That means decision making in all matters, including spending the people's money.

Some things can be changed without any disturbance of the spiritual authority that is exercised in the sacraments but other changes will mean the male clergy's yielding up a measure of power for the greater good and the Roman bishop's relaxing a centralizing power in the church that he has exercised only for the last century and a half. The immediate result would be church politics of a kind the Roman Communion has not known since an early age, replacing the politics among the higher clergy it has long been familiar with. What has evolved can devolve.

The question of ordaining women to the diaconal, presbyterial, and episcopal orders is another case altogether. Many Catholic women—not only on the North American continent and in Western Europe—ask, Why not? They are impatient with the fact of historical tradition and say, simply, that women could exercise the sacerdotal office as well as men if not better. The current bishop of Rome is on record as maintaining that women cannot be ordained to the presbyterial order because Jesus toward the close of his lifetime decided otherwise. Theologians generally think that the case for Jesus having made any such deliberation is weak or nonexistent. Bishops, out of respect for the office of the papacy or their own conviction, are silent on the matter. Pope John Paul II in his various utterances has found in Jesus' words to his disciples at the Last Supper, which authorized a ritual meal in bread and wine "in memory of me," an ordination to the priesthood that only men can pass along. He has also supported the positions that acting "in the person of Christ" in presiding at the Eucharist mean that only men can represent the man Jesus Christ, as if maleness were part of the intended qualification. The Council Fathers of Vatican II probably gave the matter no thought. They no doubt went on the supposition that two millennia of tradition provided reason enough to suppose that the sacrament of ordo, popularly "holy orders," could be conferred on men only.[82]

This unbroken tradition is the chief reason why what is in place can be presumed to stay in place for some time. There must be much cultural change in the roles of the two sexes worldwide before it can be maintained successfully that the first-century situation was a function of Jewish and Greco-Roman life at the time without a provable divine intent. Earliest Christianity could not have gained acceptance within the Judaism that was its matrix or the Greco-Roman culture where it expanded rapidly if women had presided at its mysteries. The latter term was used in Greek for the rites that a Latin-speaking church would "call sacraments." Vocabulary apart, men were dominant in the cultures where Christianity not only took its rise but where it flourished for the sixteen centuries after the emperor Theodosius I declared it the state religion (380). They consistently asserted their authority over women in all matters touching church affairs, even over nuns and other vowed women in community.

The Christian faith may be in its infancy if the world goes on for aeons. The slow approach to the equality of the sexes is a global phenomenon, not one confined by any means to the West. Bishops aided by theologians are coming to see that there is no barrier except tradition, formidable though it is, to hinder women from receiving the sacrament of orders. That barrier exists primarily in common with Eastern orthodoxy. If breached, it would make reunion with those churches an even more distant prospect even though it would remove a barrier with Protestant communions. Already, the ordination of women by many churches of the Anglican Communion has caused ecumenical strain between Rome and the churches that have their origins in Canterbury.

Catholic women frequently cite the ordination of women to ministry in most of the Protestant churches as a model for the practice of their church. The comparative recency of the practice—a bit more than a century—and the indignities that ordained women have endured at the hands of their male colleagues are no arguments against it. If designating learned women to preach publicly, to preside at nonsacramental liturgies, and to give spiritual counsel were the meaning of ordination in the Catholic Church there would be no barrier. Bishops are already free to do that and are doing it. Catholic women are presiding at funerals and at communion services (reading from the Bible, commenting on it, and distributing the eucharistic Christ from previous celebrations of the Eucharist). The question is whether there is such a worldwide emergency in the nonavailability of the eucharistic Christ to some millions in newly Christian and in longtime Christian places. Some say that for the reason of the shortage of priests if no other, the barrier of an unmarried Western clergy and of the continued nonadmission of women to orders indicates the necessity of change. This may be so but equally assured is the likelihood that popes and bishops in the immediate future will be guardians of a two-millennia-old tradition. Change will come from below, as has always been the case in a church that has been worldwide in conception from the beginning but such, in fact, with any strength only in this century. At the present writing its largest rite by far (the Roman; there are twenty-one others) is governed administratively from Italy. A parallel would be that the mode of operation of all governments in the member states of the United Nations be specified by the functionaries in its New York headquarters, all of them men and none joining their wives and children after a workday.

"What men owe to women" in this large religious society parallels "what men owe to women" in human society: a voice in its conduct and specifically their place in it. How will it come about? Through the bishops of sub-Saharan Africa, Asia, the Pacific archipelagoes, and Latin America heeding the cry of the women who are more than half of their faithful. This cry will not be primarily for representation in church councils to discuss administrative policy, but for their role precisely as women believers.

What is Catholic morality and immorality in these matters? Until now, men have decided these questions on the basis of theological principles thought basic and irrefutable. Women have long had certain other convictions but they have not been asked. It will shortly come to light that it will not be good enough for regional bodies of bishops to give women a consultative role. Women will demand and of necessity be given a deliberative role in how to live a woman's life in the church to the fullest. Needless to say, unmarried women will stand shoulder to shoulder with the married, and clergy including bishops unconcerned about their future will assist them. There will be men sufficiently prescient to know that the future of this huge, largely lay Communion is in the balance.

The steady progress of feminism is by no means the issue here. It is the progress of both sexes and many races and peoples in living humanly. St. Paul's plea to his churches was that they come to maturity in Christ. "Grow up!" in other words. Until now the men of the church have had certain limited opportunities to do so, although many have not risen to the challenge. Maturity in Christ will be a possibility for both men and women in the next century by God's doing, a God who will continue the work of justice for them that has been begun worldwide. But, for believers, God does nothing on behalf of the human family apart from humanity's free action. In Christian history—to confine ourselves for the moment to those millions—there seems to have been more rejection than acceptance of the gift held out. We speak here of social or societal sin that is much more damaging in its effects than personal sin. In the scenario just envisioned, Christian women will act corporately, impelled by grace, in concert with men. African women, so long submissive by cultural necessity? Oriental women, equally conditioned by generations of imposed respectful response? The gentle women of the Pacific Isles? Yes, in every case. All will be emboldened by God's grace to speak for justice at men's hands. The spectrum will be broad, in Latin America especially: from the indigenous women of the

Andes and its altiplano to the women of Spanish, Portuguese, and Italian immigrant stock who have no difficulty expressing themselves.

And their clergy, in particular their bishops? The courteous men of the Asian continent and its island republics like the Philippines and Indonesia, the far more numerous and vocal officeholders of Brazil, Argentina, and the Philippines? All will experience a grace to act more powerful than their mistrust of "women power" or reprisal by the Roman See. These and other Catholic bishops who are the church's teachers, aided by theologians as they have always been, will respond to the plea of their women communicants and begin to write pastoral letters that demand gender justice. The bishop of Rome, whose voice carries more weight than any individual bishop, will be among them.

Catholic writers on "what men owe to women" have up to now largely left to others the questions of domestic oppression and violence, economic injustice, and the effects on women of war and abandonment. Their concern has been with male vocabulary for God in the Bible and with all subsequent religious discourse, the subjugation of woman in church life by omission or silence and women's lack of a voice in the ranks of the ordained. But the 1995 meeting on economics and development in Beijing sponsored by the United Nations drew attention to the plight of women brought on by factors with which Christianity had something to do. A literature on these weighty problems from the standpoint of Catholic faith may be expected in the upcoming decades.

A demand of women for a rightful place in the church is needed and appropriate. But even more pressing is the demand of this church, over a billion strong, for the rightful place of women in the *world*.

NOTES

1. Mark 1:2–11, 6:14–29. This is very probably the first gospel to have been written.

2. Jer. 16:2. The Prophet lived until some time after 600 B.C.E.

3. b. Yebamoth (Sisters-in-law), a tractate of the Babylonian (thus b.) Talmud, 63b. He recommended marriage and procreation. When challenged for inconsistency he said: "My soul loves Torah. The world can be carried on by others."

4. Luke 8:2–3.

5. Luke 10:38–42.

6. Mark 14:3–9.

7. John 12:1–8.

8. Mark 5:22–43.

9. Mark 7:27.

10. Mark 7:28–30; cf. Luke 4:25–26.

11. John 4:4–30.

12. Luke 7:11–17; cf. 1 Kings 17:17–24; 2 Kings 4:18–37, writings of an anonymous chronicler in the mold of the author of Deuteronomy of the four hundred years of reigns between that of Solomon (d. ca. 922 B.C.E.) and Zedekiah of Judah, carried off into captivity in Babylon (587).

13. John 2:11.

14. John 19:25–27.

15. Luke 8:2.

16. John 12:17.

17. Deut. 24:1–4.

18. Zadokite Document (Damascus Rule) CD 4:20–5:1.

19. Mark 10:11–12; Lk 16:18; 1 Cor 7:10–11.

20. Matthew 5:32; 19:9.

21. Philippians 3:5; cf. 1 Corinthians 9:5.

22. 1 Corinthians 7:7–16.

23. See Romans 16:3–16.

24. Acts of the Apostles 16:14–15.

25. Ephesians 5:22.

26. Vv. 24–33.

27. 1 Corinthians 11:3.

28. 1 Corinthians 11:11–12.

29. V. 9.

30. 1 Timothy 2:8–14.

31. 1 Corinthians 11:5–6.

32. 1 Corinthians 14:33b–35

33. Romans 16:1.

34. 1 Corinthians 7:1; vv. 2–16 summarized above.

35. 1 Corinthians 7:31.

36. 1 Corinthians 7:7.

37. In separate documents the world's Catholic bishops at that meeting spoke at length of the holiness to which all Christians are called in virtue of their baptism, without making any comparison among the states of married life, single life, the vowed life, and priestly life. They are: Gaudium et Spes, "The Church in the Modern World," with its Sections 47–52 on married love that calls for the total mutuality of the partners; a decree on the up-to-date renewal of the vowed life, *Perfectae Caritatis*; another on the vocation of laypeople, *Apostolicam Actuositatem* and still another, *Presbyterorum Ordinis* on the ministry and life of priests. All four were promulgated in the last months of the Council, October to December 1965. The various "states of life" are each commended separately but nowhere subjected to comparison or contrast. See *The Documents of Vatican II*, Walter M. Abbott, S. J. General Editor, Herder and Herder, New York, 1966.

38. Gal. 3:28.

39. Col. 3:11.

40. 1 Cor. 7:40.

41. 1 Tim. 5:3–16. This author is concerned that women dress modestly, not braid their hair, and go without adornment (2:9–10). Cf. Peter that uses almost identical wording (1 Pet. 3:3–5).

42. Acts 6:1.

43. Didache ("Teaching" of the Twelve Apostles) 2.2 in *Early Christian Fathers*, Cyril C. Richardson, trans. and ed. (New York: Macmillan,1970), 172. Since having enough live births both to continue an ethnic tradition and ensure economic survival was the problem for most of humanity in its long existence on the planet, curbing births was always a relatively lesser problem. Hence there is no detailed exposition of Christianity's opposition to contraception, abortion, or infanticide except in a more general way: it opposed all three. Historical research is made difficult by the paucity of documentation but this very paucity seems to indicate the lack of serious censure of contraception by withdrawal or folk-medical spermicides. The small size of the families into which numerous distinguished Christians of an earlier age were born helps to raise the question. Infanticide, whether by exposure or by any other means, is a clearer matter. It is consistently repudiated. In the high-profile modern case of abortion, a careful study of various landmark writings in the history of theology is significant. A team of experts in Colombia funded by the Ford Foundation produced a thirty-seven page chapter of its overall investigation into abortion in Latin America and the Caribbean, "Problematica Religiosa de la Mujer que Aborta." It could not find a clear distinction made between intra- and extrauterine killing for sixteen centuries (although its translations from Greek and Latin are arguable). When that distinction began to be made, the chapter found saving the mother's life to be the excusing cause, long an axiom in the church's moral theology. Some Catholic theologians allow abortions in other circumstances, on the basis of the history of the practice in the church.

44. See Elaine Pagels, who hints at the probability when she writes that Christian Gnosticism emerged "as the very time when earlier, diversified forms of church leadership were giving way to a unified hierarchy of church office. For the first time, certain Christian communities were organizing into a strict order of subordinate "ranks" of bishops, priests, deacons, and laity." It is hard to date that "first time: and impossible to be sure of the exact modes of leadership in church communities that preceded it. Professor Pagels documents the Catholic resistance to Gnostic patterns of charismatic leadership and specifically women as leaders (with no mention of their ordination). See Pagels, *The Gnostic Gospels* (New York: Vintage Books of Random, 1981), 47ff. For the complete corpus of extant writings from Upper Egypt see James M. Robinson, gen. ed., *The Nag Hammadi Library in English*, (3rd rev. ed.) (San Francisco: Harper & Row, 1988), 549.

45. Justin, "Dialogue with Trypho," chap. 100. Tran. by Thomas B. Falls in *Saint Justin Martyr* (New York: Christian Heritage, 1948), 304–305.

46. *The So-Called Letter to Diognetus*, 12.8. Tran. Eugene R. Fairweather in *Early Christian Fathers*, Richardson, trans. and ed., 224.

47. Tertullian, De carne Christi, 17. See 1 Cor 15:45. A. Roberts and J. Donaldson, eds., *The Ante-Nicene Fathers*, (Edinburgh, Scotland: T. and T. Clark, 1885), 3:536.

48. See Luke 1:48.

49. Luke 1:42.

50. See Elizabeth C. Johnson, C.S.J., "The Marian Tradition and the Reality of Women," Horizons 92(1) (Spring 1985): 116–135 where she reports on six such judgments by women. Note esp. 120.

51. See Eph. 5:21–30; for Israel as a virgin ideally committed in fidelity to YHWH, see Isa. 4:4-8; Jer. 2:2, 32; Ezek. 16:8–14; and Hos. 2:9b–17, 21–22.

52. For the term *Parákletos*, "Advocate," or "Counselor," see John 14:26.

53. See Karen Jo Torjesen, *When Women Were Priests* (San Francisco: HarperCollins, 1993). The research does not support the book's title. For a developed hypothesis on how the threefold ordained office emerged in the church see James Burtchaell, *From Synagogue to Church, Public Services and Offices in the Earliest Christian Communities* (Cambridge: Cambridge University Press, 1992), esp. 272–338. Monique Alexandre assumes the character of the earliest urban communities to have been "charismatic" in their governance and in the next century "hierarchical." That requires a swift move from the many voices, some "in a tongue" of 1 Cor. to Justin's 1 Apology on the leadership of the *episkopos* while disregarding "those set over you" of 1 Thess. 5:12 and the offices of *episkopoi* and *diakonoi* of Phili. 1:1. See her "Early Christian Women" in *A History of Women in the West*, Pauline S. Pantel, ed. (Cambridge: Belknap/Harvard University Press, 1992), 1:409–444, remarkable for its scope and wealth of citations.

54. To His Wife, 1.4, written about 203. Tran. Charles Munier, *Sources Chétiennes*, no. 273 (Paris: Les éditions du cerf, 1980), 94–95 (with Latin text).

55. *An Exhortation to Chastity*, written before 207.

56. *On Monogamy*, about 217; *On the Necessity of Veiling Virgins*, probably written close to the plea for chastity.

57. *On the Soul*, ANF, 3, 188.

58. *On the Veiling of Virgins*, 9; ibid. 4, 33.

59. *On an Exhortation to Chastity*, 13.7.

60. *On Monogamy*, 11, 1; ibid., 67.

61. Hippolytus, *The Apostolic Tradition*, 23; Hermas, The Shepherd.

62. *On the Veiling of Virgins*, 9.2–3.

63. Fragments on 1 Cor., 74.

64. 3.1, 1-2. Gryson examines this text and similar "Church orders," that is, manuals of discipline, in detail. See n. 67. The late-fourth-century apostolic constitutions from Syria or Constantinople circumscribed widows' activities severely, ordering them not to perform baptisms (3, 9, 1–4) or to teach except in an elementary catechetical fashion (3, 6, 1–2).

65. 3.12, 1–3.

66. Edgar Hennecke, ed. by Wilhelm Schneemelcher, *New Testament Apocrypha*, (Louisville: Westminster/John Knox, 1992), 2:239–246. Full text in R. A. Lipsius, *Die apokryphen Apostelgeschichten und Apostellegenden, Volume 1* (Brunswick, 1883). Schneemelcher remarks somewhat harshly on "a liberated women's movement in the Church of the 2nd century": "On a sober treatment of the evidence, hypotheses of such a kind appear to be no more than the products of modern fancy, without any basis in the sources" (222).

67. See on this subject Steven L. Davies, *The Revolt of the Widows. The Social World of the Apocryphal Acts* (Carbondale: University of Southern Illinois Press, 1980). D. R. MacDonald, *The Legend and the Apostle. The Battle for Paul in Story and Canon* (Louisville: John Knox/Westminster, 1983). For a fairly exhaustive listing of the women whose names are recorded in documents of the early centuries, including those who prophesied in the various sects, see Roger Gryson, *The Ministry of Women in the Early Church* (Collegeville, MN: Liturgical Press, 1976). He provides ample quotations from Tertullian and from others.

68. Sermon 4 on Gen., 1. J. P. Migne, ed., Patrum Graecorum 54, 594.

69. Homily 23 on Romans (PG 60, 615).

70. Homily 4 on 1 Cor. (PG 61, 289–290). I am indebted for this and for the two citations to Elizabeth Clark, *Jerome, Chrysostom and Friends. Essays and Translations* (New York and Toronto: Edwin Mellen, 1979), 1, 2. Her first chapter on Chrysostom, women, and sexual relations is entitled, "The Virginal Politeia and Plato's Republic," 1–34. His horror at some of Plato's proposals for women are also spelled out (11–14). George H. Tavard cites numerous places in Chrysostom's writings in which he praises virginity but sees it as something other, and

more, than a matter of bodily abstention from sex. Tavard summarizes the teaching of Jerome, Augustine, and the more balanced Ambrose in *Women in Christian Tradition* (Notre Dame, IN: University of Notre Dame Press, 1973), esp. 72–121.

71. *On the Priesthood*, 3.9 (PG 48, 646).

72. See Palladius Dialogue 17 (PG 47, 69); on her open-handed generosity, see Sozomen, Church History 8, 9 (PG 67, 1540). I am indebted to Clark, 101, for both references. She also provides the life of Olympias in translation, op. cit., 127–44, indicating that an edition of the Latin translation is by Hippolyte Delehaye in Analecta Bollandia 15 (Brussels: Société des Bollandistes, 1896), 400–423.

73. Confessions, 4.2. 2; 6,13; 15.

74. H. Denzinger, rev. A. Schönmetzer, S. J., eds. *Enchiridion Symbolorum* (Freiburg, Germany: Herder, 1963), 132, 371–372, (canons 1 and 2 "De peccato originale").

75. The Letter of the Churches of Vienne and Lyons to the Churches of Asia and Phrygia quoted in Eusebius, *History of the Church*, 5, 1.1–2.8. See 4, 15.48 for the death of Agathonik at Pergamum in the province of Asia.

76. Herbert Musurillo, S. J., *The Acts of the Christian Martyrs* (Oxford: Clarendon Press, 1972), Latin with English translation.

77. Eusebius (d. ca. 340) produced a text that is lost, *On the Ancient Martyrs*. Also see Johannes Quasten, *Patrology*, (Utrecht, Netherlands: Spectrum, 1962), 1:176–185.

78. Dhuoda, *Liber Manualis*, Latin and French, tran., Edouard Bondurand (Paris: A. Picard, 1887). See Marie Anne Mayeski, *Dhuoda: Ninth Century Mother and Theologian* (Scranton, PA: University of Scranton Press, 1995). Suzanne Fonay Wemple in *Woman in Frankish Society, Marriage and the Cloister, 500 to 900* (Philadelphia: University of Pennsylvania Press, 1981) distinguishes between the Merovingian and the Carolingian periods, roughly beginning with Clovis (481) then with Pepin (751). In the first of these, marriages were largely not under church control but in the second their indissolubility began to be enforced, with St. Boniface as not at Pepin's ally. There was loss and gain for women in each period.

79. For a dependable, brief account of the careers of these women and those that immediately follow, see F. L. Cross and Elizabeth A. Livingstone, eds., *The Oxford Dictionary of the Christian Church*, 3rd ed. (Oxford: Oxford University Press, 1997). See, also, on the Gertrudes and the Mechtilds, Carolyn Walker Bynum, "Women Mystics in the Thirteenth Century: The Case of the Nuns of Helfta," in *Christ as Mother: Studies of the Spirituality of the High Middle Ages* (Berkeley: University of California Press, 1982), 170–262.

80. *Summa Theologiae*, 1. Question 92, art. 1, response to objection 1, citing Aristotle, De generatione animalium, 2, 3.

81. The scope of jurisdiction of the bishop of a diocese is found in canons 381–402. As to the administration of the people's money, bishops are guided by canons 1273–1278 and, in matters of passing judgment, canons 1419–1421; the rights of pastors and administrators of parishes are spelled out in canons 515–540; parochial vicars, namely, parish assistant priests, have no jurisdiction at law; the same for permanent deacons. The Code of Canon Law: Latin-English Edition, Washington, DC, Canon Law Society of America, 1983.

82. See Lumen Gentium, "A Dogmatic Constitution on the Church" (21 November 1964), section 10; cf. the "Decree on the Ministry and Life of Priests" (7 December 1965), section 2 where the phrase in persona Christi is repeated.

References

Borreson, Kari Elisabeth. 1981. *Subordination and Equivalence: The Nature and Role of Women in Augustine and Thomas Aquinas*. Lanham, MD: University Press of America.

Bynum, Caroline Walker. 1982. *Jesus as Mother: Studies in the Spirituality of the High Middle Ages*. Berkeley: University of California Press.

Carr, Anne. 1988. *Transforming Grace: Women's Experience and Christian Tradition*. San Francisco: Harper & Row.

Collins, Mary. 1987. "The Refusal of Women in Clerical Circles," in *Women in the Church*, Madonna Kolbenschlag, ed. Washington: Pastoral Press.

Fabella, Virginia and Mercy Amba Oduyoye, eds. 1988. *With Passion and Compassion: Third World Women Doing Theology*. Maryknoll, NY: Orbis.

Fabella, Virginia and Sun Ai Lee Park, eds. 1990. *We Dare to Dream: Doing Theology as Asian Women*. Maryknoll, NY: Orbis.

Graef, Hilda C. 1963. *A History of Doctrine and Devotion: From the Beginning to the Eve of the Reformation*. New York: Herder and Herder.

Isasi-Diaz, Ada Maria and Yolanda Tarango. 1988. *Hispanic Women, Prophetic Voice in the Church*. San Francisco: Harper & Row.

Johnson, Elizabeth A. 1993. *She Who Is: The Mystery of God in Feminist Theological Discourse*. New York: Crossroad.

Ruether, Rosemary Radford, ed. 1974. *Religion and Sexism: Images of Women in the Jewish and Christian Traditions*. New York: Simon and Schuster.

———. 1983. *Sexism and God-Talk: Toward a Feminist Theology*. Boston: Beacon.

Schneiders, Sandra. 1986. *Women and the Word: The Gender of God in the New Testament and the Spirituality of Women*. New York: Paulist.

Schussler Fiorenza, Elisabeth. 1983. *In Memory of Her: A Feminist Theological Reconstruction of Christian Origins*. New York: Crossroad.

Schussler Fiorenza, Elisabeth, and Mary Collins, eds. 1985. *Women, Invisible in the Church and in Theology*. (Concilium 182) Edinburgh, Scotland: T. & T. Clark.

Schussler Fiorenza, Elisabeth, and Anne Carr, eds. 1987. *Women, Work, and Poverty*. (Concilium, 194) Edinburgh, Scotland: T. & T. Clark.

Sobrino, Jon. 1984. "The Experience of God in the Church of the Poor," in *The True Church and the Poor*. Maryknoll, NY: Orbis.

Swidler, Leonard. 1988. *Biblical Affirmations of Women*. Philadelphia: Westminster.

Swidler, Leonard and Arlene Swidler, eds. 1977. *Women Priests in the Catholic Church: Commentary on the Vatican Declaration*. New York: Paulist.

Tamez, Elsa, ed. 1989. *Through Her Eyes: Women's Theology from Latin America*. Maryknoll, NY: Orbis.

Tavard, George H. 1973. *Women in Christian Tradition*. Notre Dame, IN: University of Notre Dame Press.

Trible, Phyllis. 1984. *Texts of Terror: Literary-Feminist Readings of Biblical Narratives*. Philadelphia: Fortress.

Vincie, Catherine. 1991. "Reconciliation for the Victim," Liturgy: Ritual and Reconciliation, 9(4):35–41, *Journal of the Liturgical Conference*, Silver Spring, MD.

Vincie, Catherine, Sue Mielke, and Celeste de Schryver Mueller. 1997. "Birthing Lament," Liturgy: There Is a Balm, 14(1) 1997:1–11.

7

Islam and Gender Justice

Beyond Simplistic Apologia

Farid Esack

Reflecting on the Topic

WE HAVE BEEN ASKED TO ponder the dilemma: "what men owe to women." That raises for me a set of more preliminary questions that need to be addressed before returning to the original. They are questions that may not be of interest to academic, postmodernist scholars, but they are crucial for a scholar who locates herself within a discourse of liberation theology, as the present writer does. It is often not our theological positions on the mainstream other—gendered, racial, or religious—but toward "the least" (as in "what you do to the least of my brothers . . .") which reflects the integrity of our theology, depth of commitment to justice, and breadth of our vision. Any form of theology that seeks to place justice and compassion at its core would ultimately have to respond to all manifestations of injustice—be this toward the transgendered other or to the exploited nonhuman other, the earth, and our planetary coinhabitants.

Which Men and Which Women Are We Referring To?

Is there an "essential man" who owes something to an "essential woman"? Woman as partner, comrade, lover, wife, mother, sister, and/or colleague? In confining the question to an essential man or woman (or confining the question to mothers and daughters, as some of my partners in this project seem to do), is there not a possibility of perpetuating that very stereotyping at the heart of gender injustice? One of the implications of this is that our responses to the dilemma: "What men owe to women," while recognizing the universality of gender justice, must also be culturally specific and avoid a supposed universal feminist discourse.

Who Asks the Question and Who Will Be Present When I Venture a Response?

Although I may want to offer an honest answer to my gendered other, I do not live in a sociopolitical vacuum and I may be afraid of having my honesty exploited by some religious or political other. I may also be afraid of having my faith called into question, as was done by Riffat Hassan, the Muslim respondent to a draft of this chapter. In matters that evoke such deep emotions, matters such as race, religion, sexuality, and gender, the truth is either the option of those unfettered by any sense of community, the reckless, or of those who are truly at one with themselves and with the transcendent. Alas, I am neither one of these. So, whom am I writing for? I write for myself. I want greater clarity about how and why it is possible for me to be a Muslim with a passionate commitment to both the Qur'an and to gender justice. I am aware that as I write, others will read. I hope that through my conversation with myself they will get some insight into the struggles of a Muslim male trying to be faithful to different, often seemingly conflictual voices within his spiritual/theological self. I also hope to encourage my brothers and sisters to be a bit more daring in their pursuit of truth, and to indicate that interrogating one's faith is, in fact, a condition of a living faith.

I am aware of the tensions between the political or the strategic. "How do we present our message to our people in ways that are least distasteful?" Although I value the work of my Muslim colleague on this project, Ali Asghar Engineer (chap. 4 in this vol.), I fear that this question is often presented in order to prevent the questioner herself from pushing limits and crossing boundaries, a cushion from the blows of relentless critical scrutiny.

To Whom Is the Debt Owed?

The question supposes that the debt is owed by men and to women, and that the world is neatly divided up into men and women. While the struggle for gender equality is about justice and human rights for women, it cannot be regarded as a women's struggle anymore than the battle against anti-Semitism is a Jewish struggle, or that of nonracialism is a struggle belonging only to Blacks. While violence against women may physically and legally be a woman's problem, morally and religiously it is very much that of men. In the words of Maryam Rajavi: "In a society where women are second-class citizens, deprived of their genuine rights, how can any man claim to be free and not suspect his own humanity? . . . Are men not in bondage too?" (Rajavi 1995, 31). Although I, as a male, may therefore owe women many debts, the debt is essentially to myself. I owe it to my own humanity to be free, and for this reason work for gender justice.

Difficult as it is to come to terms with, the Muslim theologian has to recognize—without necessarily affirming—the complexity of gendered and sexual otherness, and the notion that the only certainty about these is uncertainty. The fact that this otherness is based not on choice but on each person's unique nature raises profound questions about:

   a. the depth of our commitment to "the least," that is, the utterly marginalized;

   b. the nature of the God in which we profess faith;

   c. the nature of nature and its implications for the well-established Islamic theological notion that Islam is *din al-fitrah,* the "religion of nature or of humanity's natural state."

Who Is the Respondent to the Question?

First, where do I not come from? Although I have a sense of and value the immense contribution that feminism has made to gender justice, I am not familiar with feminism nor have I read literature on feminist theory of any sort. I do not feel any obligation to play to a Western or to any other gallery. Whatever convergence there is between my own ideas and fellow activists or scholars in "the West"—or anywhere else—who are committed to gender justice is a celebrated coincidence.

I am a Muslim male, the youngest of six sons and one daughter—the latter's "illegitimate" existence discovered more than ten years after the death of my mother. I am the son of a mother who died in her early fifties as, quite literally, a victim of apartheid and patriarchy and capitalism and of a father who abandoned his family when I was three weeks old. As a young South African student of Islamic theology in Pakistan with bitter memories as a victim of apartheid, I saw the remarkable similarities between the oppression of Blacks in South Africa and of women in Muslim society. Later, in my years as a Muslim liberation theologian cum activist in the struggle against apartheid, I deepened my awareness of the relationship between the struggle of women for gender justice and that of all oppressed South Africans for national liberation.

In sum, I shall not attempt to deal with the question before us in all its complexities. To begin with, I do not have the courage to do so. Furthermore, as a socially engaged theologian I accept the maxim attributed to Ali ibn Abi Talib, a cousin of the prophet Muhammad, to "address people at the level of their comprehension." I thus focus on the possible while never losing sight of the necessarily unthinkable—the equality of all people and the freedom of all people to respond to the voices of their own consciences, what the Quakers call "that of God in everyone." In the discussions leading to this publication and in the responses to it by my fellow Muslim participants and respondents, Engineer and Hassan, respectively, I understand and acknowledge that I am challenging the basis of much Muslim reformist thinking on gender justice. I do so with some trepidation and with respect for those who have charted the way for even more critical thinking.

GENDER EQUALITY BETWEEN TEXT AND CONTEXT

In the context of seventh-century Arabia, the personal example of Muhammad, also regarded as a source of law in Islam, was exemplary in encouraging a sense of gender justice and compassion toward all victims of oppression, including women. He advised that "the best of you is he who behaves best with his wives," "Listen, treat women well!" "I hold the rights of two weak types of persons sacred; the right of an orphan and that of a wife." Similarly, the Qur'an contains a number of similar exhortations. "And women shall have rights similar to the rights against them, according to what is equitable" (Q. 2:118). "Believers, men and women, are protectors, one of another: they enjoin what is just and forbid what is evil" (Q. 9:71).

Despite these, both the Islamic theological cum legal tradition as well as Muslim cultural life are deeply rooted in various forms of gender injustice ranging from explicit misogyny to paternalism under the guise of kindness. In part, this reflects the ambiguity of, and limitations to, the text itself—both that of the Qur'an and Sunnah—the pliability of all texts as contested terrain and of the resilient nature of patriarchy among the audience of these texts—the Muslims. Many Muslims acknowledge the reality of gender oppression in Muslim society but hasten to attribute this to the inadequacies of that society or to the inability/refusal of Muslims to actualize the dictates of Islam.[1] While common, the notion that Islam and gender can be distinguished from Muslims and gender is questionable. There are also limits to which one can pursue the distinction between the text and its interpretation. Whatever else Islam may be, it is also that which is interpreted, lived out, aspired toward, ignored, and debated among Muslims.

THE DEBT TO WOMEN

Finally, what, in addition to my ontological debt, is it then that I owe to women? In brief, two responsibilities: First, to call for forgiveness and, second, to center liberation, justice, and compassion in my theology and in my pastoral praxis.

The Call for Forgiveness

Each adherent of a religious tradition is simultaneously a shaper of that tradition and while one cannot assume personal responsibility for all the crimes or achievements of that tradition, there is nevertheless a sense in which we share in its inherited shame or glory. In Islam, as in most all other world religions, males are the key managers and interpreters of the sacred. As a male Muslim theologian committed to gender justice I thus have two reasons to ask for forgiveness. First as part of a privileged gender that has consistently denied the full humanity of the gendered other even as I was being nurtured and sustained by her. Secondly, for my own role—even if only by identification—in a theological tradition that fosters and sustains images of women and practices by men that deny women their full worth as human beings created by God and as carriers of the spirit of God.

The Centering of Liberation, Justice, and Compassion

I find a deep resonance with Marvin M. Ellison's belief (chap. 2 in this vol.), that "the call to justice and compassion is the animating heart of Christian piety" and see my own faith through similar lenses. Dogma needs to be interrogated by the standards of gender justice and compassion, and by every text read through these lenses. I believe that it is justified to utilize a host of hermeneutical devices ranging from contextualization and reinterpretation to abrogation in order to arrive at an interpretation that serves the ends of justice. One may well ask if this does not constitute violence toward the text. First, these devices are not unknown to the world of traditional Islam; the only difference is the starkness with which they are spelled out and the definitiveness of the criteria employed. Second, if a choice has to be made between violence toward the text and textual legitimization of violence against real people, then I would be comfortable to plead guilty to the former.

THE QUR'AN AS LEGITIMATION FOR GENDER INJUSTICE

In general, one discerns a strong egalitarian trend when the Qur'an deals with the ethico-religious responsibilities and recompense of the believers, but at the same moment a discriminatory trend when it deals with the social and legal obligations of women. With regard to both of these aspects there are two further trends:

  a. General statements are made that both affirm and deny gender equality.
  b. When specific injunctions are made, they are generally discriminatory toward women.

The following texts affirm the notion of equality in ethico-religious responsibilities and recompense:

> Muslim men and women, believing men and women, obedient men and obedient women [...] for them God had prepared forgiveness and a handsome reward." (Q. 23:35)

> And whosoever does good deeds, whether male or female and he [or she] they shall enter the garden and shall not be dealt with unjustly. (Q 219)

In the following verses, the first two frequently invoked by Muslims committed to some form of gender equality, we see how equality in a generalized manner is only seemingly affirmed. My own brief comment on the limited usefulness of invoking them for gender equality follows each verse.

  1. "They (women) have rights similar to those against them." (Q. 2:228)

Here we note that "similar" is left undefined and, as conservatives correctly argue, is not synonymous with "equal."'

2. "To men a share of what their parents and kinsmen leave and
to women a share of what parents and relatives leave" (Q. 4.7)

"A share" is left undefined and, when another verse elsewhere does define it, it becomes clear that it is an unclear share.

3. "To the adulteress and the adulterer, whip each one of them a
hundred lashes . . ." (Q. 24.2)

The fact of the inequality in the burden of proof in adultery is ignored.
Pregnancy in the case of an unmarried woman is automatic proof of
extramarital relations, while naming the male partner in the absence of
witnesses to the act is tantamount to slander. In social and legal matters, it is very difficult to avoid the impression that the Qur'an provides a set of injunctions and exhortations where women, in general,
are simultaneously infantalized and "pedastalized" to be protected,
and economically cared for by men, but also admonished and punished if they are disobedient. The following are a few examples of this:

a. Men marry their spouses while women are "given in marriage"
by their fathers or eldest brother, though they may have a say
in the choice of a partner.

b. The groom purchases her sexual favors though she may have a
choice in the amount; here we also observe the implicit notion
of a one-sided duty to fulfill the sexual needs of her husband.

c. In the matter of divorce, the right of males is automatic while
that of females is to be negotiated, contracted, and decided
upon by male judges.

d. Males may take up to four spouses though they may be compelled to treat their wives with equity, and the first wife may
leave if the marriage contract proscribes the husband from taking additional wives.

e. Muslim men may marry women from among Jews or Christians but Muslim women may not. (Q. 2:220)

The following is a text that most starkly represents the strand in
Qur'anic morality that seemingly sanctions discrimination, and according to most interpretations, also violence against women and marital
rape. Reflections on this text, I believe, will bring to the fore the tensions
between text and context, and the difficulties presented to the progressive theologian who seeks to center justice for the marginalized in his or
her hermeneutic.

> Men are qawwamun (the Protectors and maintainers) of/over ('ala) women,
> Because God has faddala (preferred) some of them over others,
> and because they support them from their means.
> Therefore the salihat (righteous) women are qanitat (devoutly obedient),
> and guard in their husbands' absence what God would have them guard.
> As to those women on whose part you fear nushuz (ill-conduct\
>   disobedience)
> Admonish them, refuse to share their beds and beat them
> But if they return again to obedience seek not means against them
> for God is the most high, Great above you. (Q. 4:34)

Fazlur Rahman (d. 1988), one of the great modernist Muslim thinkers, reflects a typical modernist apologia in reflections of the first part of this text and acknowledges that the Qur'an does allow for a division of labor and for a difference in functions. Men have to earn money and are charged with caring for women. This looks like a kind of superiority but in fact it is only functional and it would be eased if the woman suddenly acquired wealth on her own. The key point, as Rahman says, is that in the Qur'anic view, men and women as humans are equal and from a religious perspective, they are definitely equal (Rahman 1989, 49).

Looking at his reflections a number of questions remain. If the "excellence" flows from God's grace rather than from economic activity, then how does a shift in income patterns alter that excellence? Is spending a criterion of excellence? If so, then what about the economic value of a woman's labor where the husband is the key breadwinner? Is male expenditure over women purely a question of financial liability and/or social responsibility or more one of power? Why should financial expenditure by any two partners in a relationship necessarily impact on the question of equality as Rahman seems to imply? What does it mean for women who are marginalized and oppressed in all spheres of daily existence to have "absolute parity," "religiously speaking"?

In trying to understand any text one has to address a number of key issues: Who is the author? What is the nature of the text? What was the particular personal and general social context that first witnessed or gave birth to the text and its reception? Who subsequently interpreted it and thus contributed to the text by their mediation? What and how effective were the tools used in unlocking its meaning?

Who Is the Author?

Muslims believe that the author of the Qur'an is God who is Eternal, the utterly beyond, one who exists outside history. This transcendent is neither male nor female, although the Qur'an employs the masculine form of the personal pronoun *(huwa)* when referring to God and the analogy of God as a patriarchal ruler is regularly invoked in *hadith* literature. The limits that this Qur'anically rooted patriarchal portrayal of the transcendent places on the development of a truly feminist theology becomes obvious in our consideration of the following question.

What Is the Nature of the Text?

For Muslims the "eternal and uncreated Qur'an" is the *ipsissima verba* (words themselves) of God. It is God speaking, not merely to Muhammad in seventh-century Arabia, but for all eternity and to all humanity. Muhammad ibn Mukarram Ibn Manzur (d. 1312), the author of *Lisan al-'Arab*, reflects the view of the overwhelming majority of Muslim scholars when he defines the Qur'an as "the inimitable revelation, the Speech of God revealed to the Prophet Muhammad through the Angel Gabriel (existing today) literally and orally in the exact wording of the purest Arabic" (Ibn Manzu n.d. 3:42).

When the question of a text's genesis is regarded as equally unthinkable as that of God, then the problem that such gender unjust messages as those seemingly contained in the verses under discussion is obvious. First, there is no possibility of developing any notion of God as "she" and all its implications for a feminist theology, for this would be tantamount to spurning the qur'anic "he." Second, there is no way that one can ascribe "discriminatory" texts to a misogynist Paul, or to a well-meaning but time-bound David. Third, if this All Powerful Creator explicitly states that men are *qawwamun* over women because of what he had bestowed upon them, then what right does the created being have to demand equality as inherent and inalienable?

Who Is the Essential Audience of the Text?

The Qur'an's essential audience is males. While there are numerous exhortations to kindness and justice addressed toward men, and texts explicitly affirming the complementarity of women, the latter are essentially subjects being dealt with—however kindly—rather than being directly addressed. Thus, in this text, while the first verse may give the impression of the addressees being both male and female, the second verse makes it clear that this is not the case. While the text is about women, it is often addressed to men. (Cf. Q. 4:25, 4:128, 33:49, and 5:95.)

The problem of the essential audience of the Qur'an ought to present a significant problem for scholars committed to gender justice despite the scant attention, or even absence of any attention that it receives in such writings.[2] How can one be content with a transcendent who speaks about you and rarely to you? In some ways this issue is partially addressed by the following question.

What Is the Context of the Text?

In reflecting on the usefulness and/or limitations of the text in sustaining or defending a gender justice position, one has to consider a number of interrelated issues. These include the impulse of Scripture as a whole, the broader historical context wherein that Scripture was first revealed, heard, and interpreted, the place of that text within the rest of the Scripture as well as the immediate event, which occasioned its revelation. The Qur'an, wherever else it may have emerged from, as a whole has a context wherein it was revealed and so does each specific verse or set of verses.

The Historical Context of the Qur'an

The Qur'an was revealed in sixth-century Arabia at a time of enormous socioanthropological flux in the region in general, and more specifically *Hijaz*. While Arabian society had a number of distinct matriarchal features, these were now being replaced by a patriarchal system. Muslims generally hold that this was a period when women were regarded as not only socially inferior but as "slaves and cattle" (Siddiqi 1972, 16). It was a time when women "basically inherited nothing, but instead were themselves inherited. They were a part of their husband's property, to be owned by his heirs or by other men of his tribe" (Rajavi 1996, 25). It was a mark of dishonor for any man to have a daughter and many preferred to bury their female children alive rather than face social opprobrium. In the words of the Qur'an:

> When news is brought to one of them of a female child, his face darkens and he is filled with inward grief. With shame does he hide himself from his people because of the bad news he received. Shall he retain her in contempt or bury her in the dust? Ah what evil choice they decide on! (Q. 16:58–59)

The Place of this Text within the Larger Text

This text (Q. 4.34) is not regarded as having any legal significance and must be viewed within a broader scriptural context that facilitates a gentler attitude toward women, and the promise of greater legal standing than was hitherto enjoyed in Arabian society. In pre-Islamic society payments were made to the father or nearest male relative for a wife to be wedded in a direct "sale." The Qur'an altered this. Now the woman, instead of being the object of a contract, became a legal contracting party with the sole entitlement to the dowry in lieu of the right of sexual union. In the practice of divorce the Qur'an abolished the practice whereby a husband could summarily discard his wife and introduced a waiting period to work through possible ways of reconciliation before divorce and separation were effected. During this period the wife was entitled to financial support from her husband. In the question of inheritance, the Qur'an modified pre-Islamic rules that in general excluded females and minor children. "The [modified qur'anic] provision . . . qualifies the system of exclusive inheritance by male agnate relatives and in particular recognizes the capacity of women relatives to succeed" (Coulsen 1974, 16).

The Immediate Occasion of Revelation

Most of the classical exegetes believe that this text was occasioned by the Prophet's response to an incident of marital violence. Fakhr al-Din al-Razi (d. 1209) believes that it relates to Sa'd ibn Rabi, a prominent Ansari who slapped his wife, Bint Muhammad ibn Salma (1990, Vol. 10:90). She left her husband and went to the Prophet, showing him the visible marks of the physical abuse on her face. The Prophet, al-Razi says, condoned her departure from her husband and advised her against returning, and to be patient. The Prophet is also reported to have said "he would see," suggesting that he anticipated revelation for further guidance. This text was seemingly revealed in response to this anticipation. The Prophet is then reported to have said: "We [i.e., himself] wanted something and God wanted something else and what God wants is best" (ibid).

Both Abu Ja'far Muhammad Ibn Jarir al-Tabari (d. 923) (1992: Vol. 4:59) and Abu al-Qayyim Mahmud Ibn Umar al-Zamakhshari (d. 1144) (n.d.: Vol. 1:506) believe that verse was revealed about someone called Habibah bint Zayd who allegedly disclosed some confidential matters about her husband to others for which she was slapped. The Prophet, according to Zamakhshari, permitted the woman and her father to demand compensation from her husband (ibid.). Tabari adds that an additional verse was occasioned by the Prophet's advice: "Do not hurry with the Qur'an before revelation has come to you." In other words, the Prophet should not presuppose God's will (Tabari 1992: Vol. 4:60).

It is evident from this that, whatever else the qur'anic text may be or wherever else it may have originated from, it is essentially an historical document revealed in a particular time and place and often dealing with particular events in the lives of individuals. It is only when one embraces this as a given that it becomes possible to make sense of the seemingly contradictory qur'anic texts dealing with a host of different issues, including gender justice.

WHO ARE THE INTERPRETERS OF THE TEXT?

Most contemporary gender sensitive Muslim scholars rarely fail to point out that the domain of exegesis, as with virtually all of Islamic religious scholarship, is an entirely male affair. With the exception of Zainab bint Shat, few women have made a mark in exegesis, and the only relatively progressive and comprehensive exegetical work is that of Muhammad Asad. His *Message of the Qur'an* though, despite its extensive footnotes, is not nearly as elaborate as those of the standard works of *tafsir*. Exegesis is, of course, not confined to works exclusively devoted to theology, and several liberal scholars such as Nasr Hamid Abu Zayd, Wadud-Muhsin, Engineer, and Hassan have dealt with the qur'anic texts dealing with women.

These scholars have also consistently called for greater female participation in exegetical activity in order that women may reread the text through the eyes of the female experience of marginalization. This will undoubtedly be a significant contribution to the overall process of women's empowerment. Its value, however, will be limited if it does not embrace the fundamental question of the historicity of the text and the concomitant implications for the marginalization of women in the intended audience of the text.

READING AND MEANING: FOR WHOM AND WHAT?

There are considerable differences among exegetes regarding the interpretation of this text and the views of several of these have been dealt with extensively by Sa'diyya Shaikh (1997). The text deals with three interrelated notions: The *qiwamah* (superiority), of men over women, the righteous women (by implication, subservient), and the disobedient (by implication, unrighteous) women.

Qiwamah

There are slight nuances in the positions of classical exegetes. For Tabari, the *qiwamah* of men is based on the preference that God has given to men in relation to women and on specific material circumstances such as men providing the dowries *(mahr)*, financially supporting and maintaining their wives out of the wealth they earn (Tabari 1992: Vol. 4:60). Zamakhshari presents the *qiwamah* of men as a distinct duty of men as rulers over women, corresponding to the relationship between a monarch and a subject. He cites putatively essential differences in the natures of men and women and does not distinguish between biologic differences and socially constructed ones (n.d. Vol. 1:506). "The multi-dimensional and multi-causal, perceived and effective differences between men and women are indiscriminately clustered together as a natural given. What are in fact skills or culturally determined roles are constructed as "facts," "truth" and "inherent male intellectual and spiritual superiority" (Shaikh 1997, 59) Fakhr al-Din al-Razi argues that *qiwamah* is related to God-given preferences. It is fundamentally concerned with economics, and "it is as though there is no intrinsic preference given to men" (Razi 1990, Vol. 10:91). But he then proceeds to list a number of areas where men enjoy superiority over women, including "larger brains" and "greater physical prowess" (ibid.).

The text specifically states that this preference, however it is premised—economical, social, biologic, or ontological—is based on *bima faddalallah* (what Allah had bestowed). In different ways, almost all the classical exegetes have argued:

a. that men are superior;

b. that this superiority is both functional and essential to their maleness;

c. that while it is not intrinsic to their beings, it is nonetheless a gift from God.

Liberal Muslim scholars such as Abu'l-Kalam Azad, Muhammad Asad, (1980), Amina Wadud-Muhsin, and Riffat Hassan have emphasized the caring and social responsibility dimensions to *qiwamah*, and suggest that this verse is, in the first instance, a statement of the social facts as they existed in sixth-century Arabia.

In the context of this text, there is no real difference in social terms between gender relationships, whether this putative superiority is intrinsic to their biologic beings, "gifts" of physical prowess, or financial resources. God had seemingly decided to bestow it on men in a seemingly generalized manner ("Men are *qawwamun* over women") despite the fact that only some men have been given grace above some other *(ba'duhum 'ala ba'd)*—the second "other" is unspecified and gender neutral.[3]

Rather than suggesting that the text is liberating because it implies that the *qiwamah* is tied to an economic relationship that may change with time, the text in fact presents two additional problems. The first is the idea that a specific gender can acquire advantage as a group over another by virtue of some of its members enjoying some special grace or virtue (even if only economical). The second is the notion that wealth, and therefore also poverty, comes from God and that changes in the economic relationships between men and women may, in fact, be in violation of God's will for humanity.

As-Salihat wa-'l-Qanitat: The Righteous and Obedient Woman

There is agreement that the general meaning of the term *salihat* (righteous) as the upholders of the precepts of religion in a general sense is also applicable to this verse. While liberal readers insist that the second characteristic, *qanitat* (the obedient) refers to obedience to God, most of the traditional interpreters have viewed this as obedience to the wishes of the husband and suggest that this, in fact, is an extension—even a condition, of righteousness. In the words of Shaikh: "It is a relationship of obedience of female to male and thus condones marital hierarchy at a religious level. The idea of sacralized male authority and marital hierarchy becomes foregrounded in the relationship between female-believer and God. . . ."

The general tone of the verse though, as well as the following more specific requirement of the righteous/obedient/subservient wife makes it reasonable to assume that the traditional exegetes are nearer to the truth in their fusion of duty to God and to husband. The righteous wives are those who "guard in their husbands' absence what God would have them guard."

Descriptions of "what God would have them guard" include one or more of the following:

    a. the wife's sexuality;

    b. her husband's wealth;

    c. her husband's house from impropriety;

    d. her husband's secrets.

Sexual fidelity is thus portrayed as a combined duty to husband and to God and, while fidelity may also be a duty of the husband, the wife is singled out, while her sexuality is joined together with her husband's property. In the process she and her sexuality are further objectified, and notions of women as owned commodities are underlined.

Al-Nashizat: The Disobedient Woman

Having elaborated on the righteous and obedient wife, the text deals with the way in which the disobedient wife has to be dealt with.

> As to those women on whose part you fear *nushuz* (disloyalty\ill-conduct\rebellion\disobedience), admonish them, refuse to share their beds, and beat them. But if they return again to obedience seek not means against them for God is the Most High, Great above you.[4]

The Qur'an actually has a word for female disobedience, *nushuz*. Abu Hamid Al-Ghazali (d. 1111) explains that the word *nushuz* means "that which tries to elevate itself above the ground" and defines *nushuz* as "confronting the husband in act or word." Ibn Manzur defines *nushuz* in the following manner: "To protrude, to project, a hillock . . . to lift up." He describes *nushuz* in the marital relationship as "one detests and dislikes the other" and says that, in the case of the woman this occurs when she elevates herself above her husband, that she disobeys him, angers him, and withdraws from him. Classical exegetes have confined their interpretation of *nushuz* to women. Tabari, for example, defines it as "when the woman rises above her husband or removes herself out of his bed, disagrees with him regarding her obedience and is confrontational to her husband" (Tabari 1992: Vol. 4:64). Fakhr al-Din al-Razi cites Idris al-Shafi' (d. 796) as defining *nushuz* as "that which is disruptive in the wife's verbal or actual behavior" (Razi 1990: Vol. 10:92).

Several liberal scholars such as Asad have argued against the mono-gendered nature of *nushuz* and have suggested that the remedial and/or punitive measure to be taken is equally applicable to the man and that, in both cases, the implementing agent is the state. While Asad says that *nushuz* includes "mental cruelty" of the husband as well as ill-treatment in the physical sense toward his wife he, nevertheless, acknowledges that this verse refers to "a wife's 'ill-will' [which] implies a deliberate, persistent breach of her marital obligations" (Asad 1980, 109).

Three steps are suggested/prescribed for dealing with the *nashizah*:

    a. admonish them;

    b. refuse to share their beds;

    c. beat them.[5]

Although there has been much discussion on the first two sugges-
tions/prescriptions, I wish to focus on the last one.

The overwhelming majority of exegetes—liberal and traditional—
accept the translation of d-r-b as physical chastisement and restrict the
debate to advisability or otherwise, intensity, form, and implementing
agency without questioning the legitimacy of physical chastisement itself. The way in which these issues are addressed seems to suggest that,
despite the inevitable rendition of d-r-b as "beating," scholars of all per-
suasions were cognizant of its inherently detestable nature as a means
of resolving marital conflict, and were desperate to find ways of limit-
ing its negativity. One can, in fact, argue that given the many limitations
that these scholars placed on the enactment of this bit of advice that,
had they had recourse to any linguistic device to render d-r-b as anything but "beating," they would have found a way to do so.[6]

Before dealing with the resource for a gender-just approach to the
Qur'an that goes beyond liberal apologetics, a few comments about this
text and its interpretation are needed.

    a. The Qur'an does sanction violence against women. However it
       does so as a last resort to subjugate the wife within a culture of
       violence against women where this was often the first resort.[7]

    b. The immediate context for the occasioning of this verse is still a
       problematic one. The Prophet had seemingly defended the
       right of women to be free from physical abuse but God had
       seemingly condoned it.

    c. In the text we find a reflection of what Shaikh describes as "a
       three-tiered spiritual hierarchy . . . in interpretations [of this
       text]." But the truth is that this hierarchy is evident *in the text it-
       self.* Allah occupies the pinnacle of this hierarchy. Men come
       next as primary believers addressed in the *tafsir* (who in terms
       of the language, addresses men directly as "you"). Then the
       bottom echelon is occupied by women, who are seen in rela-
       tionship to men and only after that in relationship to God. In
       terms of the language of the *tafsir* women are referred to as
       "they," "the third party," and "the other."

    d. While this verse legitimizes violence against women, in classical
       and contemporary societies where violence against women is

the norm it does appear to be placing limitations on the abuser. Here Shaik draws attention to the reminder at the end of the text that "God is above you" and argues that this was really an attempt to instill accountability, to reduce the sense of power that men enjoyed "both psychologically and practically," and, in effect, to deflate their god-complexes in relation to women.

RESOURCES FOR GENDER JUSTICE

Despite my own critique of the apologetic approaches to the Qur'an in general and, more specifically, to those texts affirming gender inequality as interpreted by many liberal and modernist gender sensitive scholars, I identify with, and invoke many of the resources for gender justice that they have articulated for so long. I believe that while the Qur'an is not the human rights or gender equality document that Muslim apologists make it out to be, it, nevertheless, contains sufficient seeds for those committed to human rights and gender justice to live in fidelity to its underlying ethos. The following four approaches need to be cultivated by gender activists for both our intellectual and theological integrity, as well as for advancing the cause of gender equality. These four approaches are:

a. to God;

b. to humanity;

c. to the text and revelation;

d. to interpretation.

Approaches to God

The Qur'an affirms the centrality of God in a believer's life and not the law that is the contextual means of achieving the pleasure of God. This affirmation is both explicit in the text, in the meaning of the word *shari'ah*, and implicit in the attention being given to God in the Qur'an rather than to the law. Here I want to address three aspects to the nature of God and relate them to the quest for gender justice: *Tawhid* (divine unity), *Rubu-biyyat* (lordship), and *subhaniyyat* (transcendence).

Tawhid (Divine Unity)

Tawhid is usually understood to refer to God's absolute unicity. For those committed to progressive values it has also come to mean a principle of holism that permeates all of creation and a struggle to repair the

wholeness of creation destroyed by racism, environmental mismanage-
ment, economic exploitation, and sexism. Belief in the unity of God can
only become meaningful if we display a concern for the way in which
its manifestations are being damaged. Sexism and the discrimination
against women fly in the face of the holism of *tawhid*, which is in direct
contrast to the misogynistic worldview where man replaces God for a
woman, and where a male-female relationship is expected to mirror
that between males and God.

Subhaniyyat (Transcendence)

Although we acknowledge that the entire creation is a reflection of
God's presence and nature, as Muslims, we also believe that God is beyond whatever is ascribed to him. God is above that community which,
perhaps invariably, limits him by their preconceptions and socioreligio-
political horizons. Ultimately, God is even above Islam. This God is *Ak-
bar*—the eternally greater than, the eternally transcendent. In the words
of the Qur'an: "God is free from what they ascribe unto him." For our
present purposes this has two implications: First, God is greater than
the law. Thus to elevate the law to the level of the divine and the immutable is in fact to associate others with God, the antithesis of *tawhid*.
Second, God is greater than any gender construction or the inescapably
human device of language. Patriarchal portrayals of God are thus also a
negation of God's *subhaniyyat*. This means that every expression of the
law—including Muslim personal law—must be subject to the requirements of justice and compassion. Because the law, wherever it may
originate from, is always approached and interpreted by historical human beings, it must be interpreted in terms of the ever-approximating
and developing notions of justice and compassion.

Rububiyyat

This God is *rabb al-nas*, the *rabb* of humanity. *Rabb* is "that being who
brings into life and nurtures until perfection." This *rabb* is just, compassionate, and gracious and prescribed mercy upon Himself (Q. 2:243,
10:60, 12:38, 13:6). While this *rabb* does prescribe some laws, which are
very few in relation to the contents of the Qur'an, he is not a lawyer. On
the contrary, we get the impression of a Being who is essentially concerned with taking society from a given point and moving it further
along the path of self-actualization and recognition of his all-pervading
presence. The law, dynamic even in the limited period of revelation,
serves as a means (*shar'ah*) to reach him in their lifetimes.

Approaches to Humanity

The Qur'an places humanity in a "world of *tawhid* where God, people, and nature display meaningful and purposeful harmony" (Shari'ati 1980, 86). According to the Qur'an, the spirit of God covers all of humanity and gives them a permanent sanctity (e.g., Q. 15:29, 17:22, 70, 21:91). The human body, being a carrier of a person's inner core and of the spirit of God, is viewed as sacred. Physical concerns are, therefore, not viewed as incidental to the Qur'an.

In the context of gender relations two inviolable elements are of specific concern: the intrinsic dignity *(karamah)* of all people—including women and that of justice *(`adalah)*. Both concepts are firmly rooted in the Qur'an, while the law is a means to facilitate their actualization. When the law fails to do this then it must be reinterpreted, amended, or abandoned in order to fulfill this objective. People, as the repositories of God's spirit, precede the law.

I acknowledge that both of these concepts are not uncontested. Indeed, many Muslim misogynists seek refuge in the concept of the dignity for women as a means to support an ideology that regards women as minors who have to be eternally protected from themselves, and from the "naturally predatory" behavior of males. I, however, use these terms within a broader context of progressive values where people make—and have the freedom to do so—informed decisions about their lives and bodies based on the availability of knowledge and options. In some ways, this severely limits much of what has just been written, for the vast majority of women in Third World countries live in conditions of abject poverty, ill health, illiteracy, and political repression. In these conditions a benign male guardianship behind *chador aur char diwari* (the cloak and four walls) may even be the preferred option of many women rather than the gender equality amid starvation. This only serves to underline the interconnectedness of the quest for dignity and justice. There is no gender justice without access to the economic resources, and the political freedom that enables it. The point that I seek to make here is that humanity, rather than a canon or a set of laws, are the repositories of the spirit of God. How we seek to actualize this truth for women will vary from one society to another.

Approaches to the Text and to Revelation

The sociohistorical and linguistic milieu of the qur'anic revelation is reflected in the contents, style, objectives, and language of the Qur'an. Revelation is always a commentary on a particular society. Muslims, like others, believe that a reality, which transcends history, has communicated with them. This communication took place within history and was conditioned by it. Even a casual perusal of the Qur'an will indicate that, notwithstanding its claim to be "a guide for humankind" (Q. 2:175) revealed by "the Sustainer of the universe" (Q. 1:1), it is generally addressed to the people of the Hijaz who lived during the period of its revelation.

The picture that the Qur'an portrays of the transcendent is one of God actively engaged in the affairs of this world and of humanity. This constant concern for all of creation is also shown by the sending of prophets as instruments of his progressive revelation. The principle of *tadrij*, whereby injunctions are understood to have been revealed gradually, best reflects the creative interaction between the will of God, realities on the ground, and the needs of the community being spoken to. The Qur'an, despite its inner coherence, was never formulated as a connected whole, but was revealed in response to the demands of concrete social situations.

It is understandable that gender activists who continue to locate themselves within the religious community of Muslims (as distinct from the faith community of Islam) find it difficult to confront the inherent difficulties that notions of an ahistorical text present. However, those who place gender justice at the core of their concerns—rather than Scripture—cannot but be cognizant of the severe limitations that such ahistorical notions place on them.

Approaches to Interpretation

The principle of progressive revelation reflects the notion of the presence of a Divine Entity who manifests his will in terms of the circumstances of his people, who speaks to them in terms of their given reality, and whose word is shaped by those realities. This word of God thus remains alive because its universality is recognized in the middle of an ongoing struggle to rediscover its meaning. The challenge for every generation of believers is to discover their own moment of revelation, their own intermission in revelation, their own frustrations with God, joy with his consoling grace, and their own being guided by the principle of progressive revelation.

The meaning assigned to a text by any exegete cannot exist independently of his or her personality and environment. There is therefore no plausible reason why any particular generation should be the intellectual hostage of another, for even the classical exegetes did not consider themselves irrevocably tied to the work of their previous generation. Interpreters are people who carry the inescapable baggage and conviviality of the human condition. Indeed, each and every generation of Muslims since the time of Muhammad, carrying its peculiar synthesis of the human condition, has produced its own commentaries of the Qur'an. The present generation of Muslims, like the many preceding ones, faces the option of reproducing meaning intended for earlier generations or of critically and selectively appropriating traditional understandings in order to reinterpret the Qur'an as a part of the task of reconstructing society.

The inevitable, active participation of the interpreter in producing meaning actually implies that receiving a text and extracting meaning from it do not exist on their own. Reception and interpretation and, therefore meaning, are thus always partial. Every interpreter enters the process of interpretation with some preunderstanding of the questions addressed by the text—even of its silences—and brings with him or her certain conceptions as the presuppositions of his or her exegesis. Meaning, wherever else it may be located, is also in the remarkable structure of understanding itself. "There is no innocent interpretation, no innocent interpreter, no innocent text" (Tracy 1987, 79).

CONCLUSION

All of us, whether in our offices, bedrooms, kitchens, mosques, or boardrooms participate in the shaping of the images and assumptions that oppress or liberate the other, and thus ourselves. Our view of what we owe to women, is really a view of what we owe to ourselves. The kind of theology that we develop in thinking through this is as much a statement of our deepest selves as it is about the God whose presence we seek in a broken world desperate for wholeness and justice.

NOTES

1. This is not confined to Muslims. A number of papers such as those of Ze'ev W. Falk and Tavivat Puntarigvivat (chaps. 5 and 8 in this vol., respectively) reflect a similar position that suggests that "pure religion will sort out the problems."

2. Sa'diyya Shaikh, for example, in an analysis of classical exegesis of the *nushuz* verses, notes that it is "apparent in the language of all three *mufasireen* [Tabari, Zamakhshari, and Razi] who address the male as "you" while women are referred to as "they," "the third party," and "the other." She, however, fails to draw attention to the more fundamental problem that this poses in the case

of the Qur'an. Amina Wadud-Muhsin deals with this problem insofar as it relates to the question of the Arabic language structure and the absence of a neuter. While she makes a convincing case for the inclusion of women in the apparently masculine form of the personal pronoun and even ordinary nouns, she does not address the question of the essentially male audience of the Qur'an (1992, 4–7).

3. Wadud-Muhsin has an interesting rendition of the meaning of this text.

> *Faddala* cannot be unconditional because verse 4:34 does not read "they (masculine plural) are preferred over them (feminine plural)." It reads *"ba'd* (some) of them over *ba'd* (other)." The use of *ba'd* relates to what obviously has been observed in the human context. All men do not excel over all women in all matters. Some men excel over some women in some manners. Likewise, some women excel over some men in some manners. So whatever Allah has preferred, it is still not absolute. (1992, 71)

The question of God's preference though, and its implications for gender equality as an inherent right, remains unaddressed.

4. Fatima Mernissi has dealt with the notion of *nushuz* and its proximity to that of *bid'ah* (deviation/innovation) and their use as tools to suppress human creativity "in terms of multiple, unforeseeable potentialities . . . which must be liquidated in order to bring about the triumph of the sacred, the triumph of the divine, the non-human" (Mernissi, 1986, 89). She argues that Muslim societies reject demands for gender justice "not simply because these societies fear women but because they fear individualism" (ibid.).

5. The way in which Wadud-Muhsin presents this gradation of essentially male prerogatives in dealing with a recalcitrant wife illustrates the manner in which gender sensitive Muslims have struggled to "swallow" this text after much sugar coating. "In case of [marital] disorder," she asks 'what suggestions does the Qur'an give as possible solutions?' 'There is 1. A verbal solution. . . . If open discussion fails, then a more drastic solution: 2. Separation is indicated. Only in extreme cases, a final measure: 3. the scourge is permitted.' " (Wadud-Muhsin 1992, 77). The inadequacy of this kind of approach is evident from the following questions: Are these really tentative and heuristic "suggestions" and "possible solutions" that the Qur'an offers or divine directives? Is the issue here one of marital order versus disorder, or one of disobedience to the husband? Is a "verbal solution" or "open discussion" really the equivalent of "warn" or "reproach" them (women), the wording that the Qur'an employs? Although Wadud-Muhsin wants to see a two-way conversation, nothing in the text suggests this. Who defines "extreme cases" and for whom is a case an extreme one? Why are the first two measures described as "suggestions" but the final one—scourging—merely "permitted?" (75).

6. Two *hadith* are usually invoked in the quest for a positive gloss to this text: "Could any of you beat his wife as he would beat a slave, and then lie with

her in the evening?" (Bukhari and Muslim) and "Never beat God's handmaidens (Abu Dawud, Nasa'i, Ibn Majah, Ibn Hanbal). In the farewell sermon, the Prophet stipulated that beating should be resorted to only if the wife "has become guilty, in an obvious manner, of immoral conduct" and that this should be done "in such a way as not to cause pain." The mode of beating ranges from using "a toothbrush or some such thing" (Tabari 1992: Vol. 4:70) to "a folded handkerchief" (Razi 1990: Vol. 10:93). The conclusion to this discussion by the modernist translator Muhammad Ali is also illustrative of this desperation to see gentleness. "Thus very slight chastisement was allowed only in extreme cases" (Ali 1973, 200). Similarly, translators have been at pains to add a veneer of gentleness to the suggestion/prescription "Beat them" with many inserting "lightly" in brackets after "beat them" *(Hilali)* and some even adding "if it is useful" *(Hilali)* or "if it is necessary" (Irving).

7. Razi cites an incident of the women of Medina coming to the Prophet's home complaining that their husbands were beating them. The Prophet said about these men: "You do not find them among your better ones" (1990: Vol. 10:91).

REFERENCES

Asad, Muhammad. 1980. *The Message of the Qur'an.* Gibraltar, Spain: Dar al-Andalus.

Coulsen, N. J. 1974. *A History of Islamic Law.* Edinburgh, Scotland: University Press.

Engineer, Asghar Ali. 1995. *Muslim Women, Veil, and Qur'an.* Bombay: Institute of Islamic Studies.

———. 1994. *The Qur'an, Male Ego, and Wife Beating.* Bombay: Institute of Islamic Studies.

Hassan, Riffat. 1996. "Rights of Women within Islamic Communities." In *Religious Human Rights in Global Perspective,* John Witte, Jr. and Johan van der Vyver, eds. The Hague: Martinus Nijhoff Publishers, 361–386.

Ibn Manzur, Muhammad ibn Mukarram. n.d. *Lisan al-`Arab.* 3 vols. Cairo: Dar al-Ma`arif.

Mernissi, Fatima. 1986. "Femininity as Subversion: Reflections on the Muslim Concept of Nushuz." In *Speaking of Faith: Cross Cultural Perspectives on Women, Religion, and Social Change,* Diana L. Eck, and Devaki Jain, eds. New Delhi: Women's Press, 88–100.

Proezesky, Martin. 1989. "Is the Concept of Human Rights Logically Permissible in Theistic Religion?" In *Journal for the Study of Religion,* 2(2): September.

Rahman, Fazlur. 1989. *Major Themes of the Qur'an.* Minneapolis: Bibliotheeca Islamica.

Rajavi, Maryam. 1995. *Islam and Women's Equality.* Paris: Foreign Affairs Committee of the National Council of Resistance of Iran.

Razi, Fakhr al-Din al-. 1990. *Tafsir al-Fakhr al-Razi*. 32 vols. Mecca, Saudi Arabia: al-Maktabah al-Tijariyyah.

Tabari, Abu Ja`far Muhammad ibn Jarir, al-. 1992. *Jami` al-Bayan `an Ta'wil Ay al-Qur'an*. Beirut: Dar al-Kutub al-'ilmiyyah.

Shaikh, Sa'diyya. 1997. "Battered Women in Muslim Communities in the Western Cape: Religious Constructions of Gender, Marriage, Sexuality, and Violence." M.A. thesis, University of Cape Town.

Shari`ati, `Ali. 1980. *Marxism and Other Western Fallacies: An Islamic Critique*. Trans. by R. Cambell. Berkeley: Mizan Press.

Siddiqi, Mohammed Mazheruddin. 1972. *Women in Islam*. Lahore, Pakistan: Institute of Islamic Culture.

Tracy, David. 1987. *Plurality and Ambiguity: Hermeneutics, Religion, Hope*. San Francisco: Harper & Row.

Wadud-Muhsin, Amina. 1992. *Qur'an and Woman*. Kuala Lumpur, Malaysia: Penerbit Fajar Bakti Sdn. Bhd.

Zamakhshari, Abu al-Qayyim Mahmud ibn `Umar, al-. n.d. *Al-Kashshaf `an haqa'iq ghawamid al-tanzil*. Beirut: Dar al-Kutub al-`Arabi.

8

A Thai Buddhist Perspective

TAVIVAT PUNTARIGVIVAT

WOMEN IN ALMOST EVERY culture and society have been exploited or oppressed in one form or another, to a greater or lesser degree, throughout the long history of humanity. A Social Darwinist may explain that it is because women are physically weaker than men. If this is the case, then men everywhere are still in the savage stage and act according to the rule of the wild. But men and women in every society claim that they have a culture or civilization, so this kind of Social Darwinist attitude must be rejected. A patriarchalist, on the other hand, may not recognize the exploitation of men over women. This is even a more dangerous view. Some feminists may request that women are equal to men in every aspect of life—including physical and biologic. This view reflects the incomplete understanding of the biologic differences between men and women. Women are biologically different from men, but difference does not mean unequal. This difference has long been exploited by the male bias. So the issue is not calling for women's rights on the basis of a biologic sameness, but for women's rights on the basis of a nonbiased interpretation of biologic differences. Once we find a more just way of this interpretation, it is easier to define the cultural roles of men and women in a given society. In any case, the political, economic, social, and legal rights of women must be equal to those of men.

The doctrinal teachings of the world's religions usually provide the groundwork for the equal rights of men and women. In Buddhism, for example, women and men possess the same Buddha-nature and women, as well as men, can attain Enlightenment—the highest spirituality. Due to male bias, however, religions at the institutional level have

long and continuously oppressed women. In Thailand, the Bhikkhuni
Sangha (Order of Nuns) has never been given a chance to exist. There
are only *mae ji* (head-shaven women in white robes), but the status of
mae ji is so low that it is practically even lower than that of laywomen.
The widespread phenomenon of prostitution and women's poverty in
Thailand is partly due to this lack of a sound female religious institution—the one like Bhikkhuni Sangha—to support women spiritually
and to provide them socially with an alternative for a better life.

WOMEN FROM A RELIGIOUS PERSPECTIVE

During the time of Siddhattha Gotama the Buddha some two thousand
five hundred years ago, the status of women in India, like in the rest of
the "civilized" world that extended from China to Greece, was servile,
degraded, and miserable. The Indian caste system was also strong and
deep-rooted. As a spiritual leader and social reformer, the Buddha
brought remarkable changes to human society regarding the annihila-
tion of the caste system and the emancipation of women within the
Buddhist world.

Status and Role of Women in Buddhism

Before the time of the Buddha, Brahmin hegemony had long reduced
women to a position of menials or chattels. According to *Manusmrti* (the
laws of Manu), a woman became fettered to a man for life—she was
confined to her home, being a servant to her father and brothers, and
eventually to her husband. Under Manu women have no right to study
the Vedas. Faithful allegiance and submissiveness to her husband was
the only way to celestial bliss. Nayaka Thera Piyadassi, a Sri Lankan
Buddhist monk, reports:

> Such wifely fidelity was not confined only to the duration of her
> husband's lifetime. It had to be pursued even to the funeral pyre of
> her husband. It was expected of an Indian wife that she should fol-
> low her husband to the next world by immolating her body by
> flinging herself in to the burning flames of her husband's pyre. Al-
> though these barbaric practices had once been completely abol-
> ished and exterminated . . . [they are] a clear pointer to the debased
> position that women held in society in the days of long ago, and
> may still be held to some degree. (Piyadassi 1991, 281)

The birth of a daughter was considered a misfortune. When King Kosala was having a conversation with the Buddha, the news was brought to him that his queen, Mallika, had borne him a daughter. Noticing that the king was distressed, the Buddha remarked:

> Do not be perturbed O, King,
> A female child may prove
> Even a better offspring than a male,
> For she may grow up wise and virtuous. (Kindred Sayings, 1:111)

The Buddha assured him that a female child may prove even better than a boy, becoming virtuous, wise, reverent, and respectful. He recommended to his disciple to look upon every woman as if she were "your own mother or sister," and he taught laypeople that "to respect one's mother and one's wife is to be blessed" (Kabilsingh 1991, 33). The Buddha pointed out that a woman is the mother of man, and that no person is worthy of greater reverence and veneration than one's mother. It is impossible for a child to pay off the debt that he or she owes to a mother. In the Buddhist texts sometimes woman is referred to, out of respect, as a society of mothers *(matugama)*. The Buddha taught men to protect their sisters, to treat their wives as equals and friends, and to allow their daughters the same opportunities in life as they give their sons.

The Buddha declares that a woman was equal to a man in respect of her capacity to attain *Nibbana*.[1] Each woman, like each man, had in her Buddha-nature, the potentiality of becoming a Buddha. Referring to the path leading to the Enlightenment, the Buddha compares it to a chariot and observes:

> And be it woman, be it man for whom
> Such chariot does wait, by that same car
> Into Nibbana's presence shall they come. (Kindred Sayings, 1:45)

In Buddhism differences in sex do not obstruct the attainment of the highest spirituality. All progress and achievement, both mundane and supramundane, are also within the reach of women.

Bhikkhuni Sangha: The World's First Order of Nuns

The establishment of the Bhikkhuni Sangha (Order of Nuns) by the Buddha over two thousand five hundred years ago was an innovation.

It conceded to women a nobility of nature, a strength of morality, and a capacity for wisdom, equal to that of men. According to Piyadassi, this event marks two historical importances. First, the Buddha permitted the establishment of the Bhikkhuni Sangha at a time and place in history when women had been relegated to an inferior and discredited place in society. Second, although several other religious systems have flourished and blossomed in India from that time up to now, none of these other religions have established an Order of Nuns.[2]

The *Anguttara Nikaya* gives a comprehensive record of Buddhist women, *bhikkhuni* (nuns), and *upasika* (laywomen), who did splendid work not only as followers, but as preachers of the Dhamma. The life and history of Maha Pajapati Gotami, and her ordination and the establishment of the Bhikkhuni Sangha, is an illuminating story. It reveals what power and impact the determination and courage of a single woman could produce on the society of her time. It is the history of the emancipation of women in Buddhism. Gotami stands out as a figure among the women who influenced the course of feminine emancipation.

King Suddhodana, who ruled the Sakyans at Kapilavattu, married both Maha Maya and her sister Gotami. Such a marriage was quite in conformity with the social traditions of the day. When Queen Maya died seven days after the birth of Prince Siddhattha, Gotami took the responsibility of raising the child. In so doing, she not only earned the gratitude of the Buddhist world but also put Siddhattha in a position of obligation to her. On the death of Suddhodana, Gotami decided to renounce the world. After a long and difficult journey on foot to see the Buddha, Gotami asked the Buddha for ordination, but it was not granted. Affected with pity at this painful sight, Ananda, the faithful disciple of the Buddha, requested the Buddha for Gotami's ordination three times without success. Then he thought of a different approach and had the following conversation with the Buddha:

> "Lord, are women capable, after going forth from the home unto the homeless life under the Norm-Discipline set forth by the Tathagata,—are they capable of realizing the Fruit of Stream-winning, of Once-returning, of Never-returning, of Arahantship?"[3]

> "Women are capable . . . of doing so, Ananda."

> "Then, Lord, if women are capable . . . of so doing, inasmuch as Maha-Pajapati, the Gotamid, was of great service to the Exalted One,—for she was aunt, nourisher, and milk-giver, on the death of his mother she suckled the Exalted One,—well were it, Lord, if women were permitted to go forth from home unto the homeless life under the Norm-Discipline set forth by the Tathagata." (Woodward and Hare 1979, 80-81)

Facing such a strong appeal by Ananda, the Buddha then granted full ordination to Gotami under the condition that she kept the Eight Important Rules *(gurudharma)*. Those rules are as follows:

> A sister, even if she be a hundred years in the robes, shall salute, shall rise up before, shall bow down before, shall perform all duties of respect unto a brother, even if that brother has only just taken the robes. Let this rule never be broken, but be honored, esteemed, reverenced, and observed as long as life doth last.

> Secondly, a sister shall not spend the rainy season in a district where there is no brother residing. Let this rule never be broken. . . .

> Thirdly, at the half-month let a sister await two things from the Order of Brethren, namely, the appointing of the Sabbath and the coming of a brother to preach the sermon. Let this rule never be broken. . . .

> Fourthly, at the end of keeping the rainy season let a sister, in presence of both Orders, of Brethren and of Sisters, invite inquiry in respect of three things, namely, of things seen, heard, and suspected. Let this rule never be broken. . . .

> Fifthly, a sister guilty of serious wrong-doing shall do penance for the half-month to both Orders. Let this rule never be broken. . . .

> Sixthly, when a sister has passed two seasons in the practice of the Six Rules she may ask full ordination from both Orders. Let this rule never be broken. . . .

> Seventhly, a sister shall not in any case abuse or censure a brother. Let this rule never be broken. . . .

> Eighthly, henceforth is forbidden the right of a sister to have speech among brethren, but not forbidden is the speaking of brethren unto sisters. Let this rule never be broken, but be honored, esteemed, reverenced, and observed as long as life doth last. (Woodward 1979, 80–81)

Gotami agreed to the rules, whereupon she was ordained the first *bhikkhuni* in Buddhism. Thus, for the first time in the history of religion an Order of Nuns was established and women were admitted to the monastic life. Then the Buddha replied:

"Ananda, if women had not been permitted to go forth from the home unto the homeless life under the Norm-Discipline set forth by the *Tathagata,* then would the righteous life last long, the Good Norm would last, Ananda, a thousand years. But now, Ananda, since women have been permitted to go forth from the home unto the homeless life . . . not for long will the righteous life prevail; only for five hundred years, Ananda, will the Good Norm stand fast. . . .

"Now just as, Ananda, a man should cautiously build an embank-
ment to a great waterwork, to prevent the water from flowing
out,—even so, Ananda, have I cautiously proclaimed these Eight
Important Rules, not to be broken as long as life shall last." (Woodward 1979, 82)

After the establishment of *Bhikkhuni* institution, a large number of
women were drawn to the Sangha. It was recorded in the *Therigatha*
(Psalms of the Sisters)[4] that thousands of *bhikkhuni* and laywomen attained various levels of spiritual development. Among the *bhikkhuni*,
at least thirteen were praised by the Buddha, including Gotami, foremost in seniority; Patacara, foremost in *Vinaya* (discipline); and Dham-
madinna, foremost in giving dharma talks. (Anguttara Nikaya, 4: 347)
Many laywomen were also praised for their spiritual qualities, including Visakha for generosity, Samavati for compassion, and
Katiyani for unshakable faith. These successes of women represented
the completion of the four groups of Buddhists as instituted by the
Buddha: *bhikkhu* (monk), *bhikkhuni* (nun), *upasaka* (layman), and *upasika* (laywoman).

The question is often asked whether the Buddha's hesitation in
granting permission for women to enter the Sangha was because he regarded women as inferior to men and thought them to be unfit for such
a high vocation. According to Piyadassi, the Buddha's hesitation can be
explained on the basis that he was able to perceive that if women entered monastic institutes, the cardinal quality of celibacy, which was
fundamental to the functioning of a monastic institution, would be influenced and affected. And it is because of this that he proceeded to lay
down the eight important rules or safeguards.

These eight conditions have often been cited by Western scholars as
proof (by current standards) of a negative gender bias in Buddhism.
They range from requiring senior nuns to pay homage to new monks—
a rule that reverses the usual hierarchy of seniority in the Sangha—to
stipulating that a nun must never speak badly of a monk, nor admonish
improper behavior in a monk, although monks retain the right to criticize nuns. Chatsumarn Kabilsingh, a female Buddhist scholar, inter-
prets the imposing of the eight rules as the Buddha's strategy to the
establishment and protection of the Bhikkhuni Sangha. She claims that
in order to facilitate their acceptance into the Sangha, the Buddha
needed to assure the *bhikkhu* that they had nothing to lose by the admission of women. Given the social climate of the time, the *bhikkhuni's*
subordination to *bhikkhu* can be seen as a strategy to insure their protection in the Sangha (Kabilsingh 1991, 28–29).

According to Kabilsingh, it was not intended that *bhikkhuni* were to serve *bhikkhu*. When *bhikkhu* began to take advantage of their superior position and required the *bhikkhuni* to spend their time on chores and services rather than on spiritual practice, the Buddha established rules forbidding this. Although the eighth *gurudharma* forbade *bhikkhuni* from criticizing the behavior of *bhikkhu*, Buddhist laywomen (and men) were allowed and even encouraged to do so. While the Buddha was alive, recurrent abuses of male privilege and power in the Sangha were kept in check (29).

Buddhist Scriptures are believed to be recorded more than four hundred years after the passing away of the Buddha. They are usually regarded as historical records based on memories, beliefs, faiths, and interpretations. They went through several major revisions in various Buddhist councils throughout history, and all those revisions were done solely by males. Therefore some passages could be added later on by male bias—particularly the eight rules and the prediction of the life of Buddhism. The prediction that the life of Buddhism would be a thousand years old without women's ordination, and would be shortened to five hundred years old with women's ordination into the Sangha has been proven wrong historically.

The Bhikkhuni Sangha in India had been continuously passed on until the tenth or eleventh centuries, when Indian Buddhism as a whole was eclipsed by the invasion of Islam. During King Asoka's reign in the third century B.C., Sanghamitta Theri and a group of learned *bhikkhuni* went to Sri Lanka and established a Bhikkhuni Sangha there, which was to last for more than a thousand years. In the eleventh century, political turmoil and the invasion of South India's Chola dynasty brought on the disappearance of the Buddhist Sangha in Sri Lanka. The Sri Lankan Bhikkhu Sangha was later revived by receiving the ordination lineage from Thailand, but the Bhikkhuni Sangha was less fortunate and was never revived in Sri Lanka. The Sri Lankan *bhikkhuni* lineage, however, has survived in China. A group of Sri Lankan nuns were invited to help give ordination to a group of Chinese women in the year 433. This lineage, the Dharmagupta sect of the Theravada tradition, is still active in China, and has been transplanted to Korea, Japan, and Vietnam (30–31).

WOMEN FROM AN ETHICAL PERSPECTIVE

A Buddhist passage states that women are subject to five woes: she must leave her family at marriage; she must suffer the pain of menstruation, pregnancy, and childbirth; and she must always work hard taking care of her husband (Samyutta Nikaya, 18, 297). Three of these "woes"—menstruation, pregnancy, and childbirth—are simply properties of the female body. The Buddhist attitude is that men should have sympathy with women in these regards. Men should particularly share the sufferings—at least mentally—and take care of women during their pregnancy and childbirth since these are the mutual responsibilities of both sexes. The other two "woes" were social conventions concerning roles and behavior that should be changed in contemporary society on the basis of the equal rights of men and women. While the text speaks of the "five woes" of women, it also states that women bring five strengths to a marriage: attractiveness, wealth, virtue, vigor, and the ability to bear children.

Buddhist Ethics toward Marriage

Even though Theravada Buddhists tried to describe love and marriage in the bleakest possible terms, we can find plenty of love stories and examples of happy marriages in the Buddhist literature. For a successful marriage, the Buddha suggests the well matching of a couple in five ways. "This husband and wife are indeed well-matched—well-matched in faith, well-matched in virtue, well-matched in generosity, well-matched in goodness, well-matched in wisdom. A perfect pair and a wonderful example of wedded bliss, surely they will be together for eternity, enjoying great felicity" (Woodward and Hare 1979, 69–70).

So, true love does prevail in Buddhism.

The Duties of Husband and Wife

Instructions to girls about to marry are recorded in *Anguttara Nikaya*. The Buddha advised them to rise early, to work willingly, to order their affairs smoothly, and to cultivate gentle voices. They should honor and respect all persons honored and respected by their future husbands, whether parents or recluses, and on the arrival of these should offer them a seat and water. Other instructions were similar to those given to wives, namely, skill in the various handicrafts, care of servants and sick people, and care of the wealth brought home by the husbands (Saddhatissa 1970, 135).

The *suttanta* gives five ways in which a wife should be ministered to by her husband:

    a. by being courteous to her;
    b. by not despising her;

c. by being faithful to her;

d. by handing over authority to her;

e. by providing her with necessary adornments. (134)

In return, the wife should minister to her husband:

a. by ordering the household well;

b. by showing hospitality to their relatives;

c. by demonstrating fidelity;

d. by taking care of his wealth;

e. by her industry. (Saddhatissa 1970, 134)

Women's Qualities to Win Power

In *Anguttara Nikaya* the Buddha enumerates the four qualities by which woman wins power in this world and has this world in her grasp. These are as follows:

1. She is capable in her work; whatever her husband's home industries, whether in wool or cotton, she is skillful, gifted with an inquiring mind into the work, and able to carry it out.

2. She is able to manage her servants, knowing the duties of each and seeing these are carried out.

3. Furthermore, she knows something of sickness and is able to allot the food suitably.

4. She cultivates the approval of her husband and keeps safe whatever money, corn, silver or gold he brings home. (Saddhatissa 1970, 135)

With these qualities, said the Buddha: "she wins power and this world is within her grasp" (Saddhatissa 1970, 135). The Buddha suggests further that woman may win power in the world beyond by establishing confidence, virtue, charity, and wisdom.

> For confidence she knows the arising of a Tathagata and such and such is so. She is accomplished in virtue by the keeping of the Five Precepts. She is accomplished in charity, living at home with thought free from avarice, delighting in alms-giving. She is wise in the penetration into the rise and fall of things and in the complete destruction of suffering. (Saddhatissa 1970, 135)

It should be noted here that Buddhism arose in the agricultural age within the Indian sociocultural context. As a human being, the Buddha was partly influenced by the culture and society of his time. Some of his ethical teachings, therefore, may seem to be not so relevant to the postindustrial age of today.

Sexual Ethics of Buddhism

One of the most basic teachings of the Buddha is "to refrain from sexual misconduct." Its widely accepted meaning is to have no sex outside of one's marriage. Another text states that one is "to be content with just one wife" (Stevens 1990, 137). So, monogamy is recommended in Buddhism in contrast to Judaism, Christianity, and Islam, in which sexual relations are regulated in detail. Buddhism focused on the essentials. It is the motive, not the act itself, which must be ethical. John Stevens claims that "If the act of sex is consummated selflessly and with compassion, if it is mutually enriching and ennobling, if it deepens one's understanding of Buddhism, promotes integration and spiritual emancipation, and is, above all, beneficial to all the parties involved, it is 'good.' If, on the contrary, sex erupts from animal passion, is based purely on physical pleasure, and originates in the desire to possess, dominate, or degrade, it is 'evil'" (140).

According to Stevens's research, although there may have been superstitious or cultural reasons for avoiding certain kinds of sexual behavior in some Buddhist communities, there are no formal prohibitions against sex acts, conducted between consenting, nonmonastic, heterosexual adult couples (137). There is, however, a special Buddhist hell reserved for adulterers, rapists, and other sex criminals. Divorce is rarely mentioned in Buddhist literature. Since most Buddhist countries have become more modernized, divorce is more and more acceptable among Buddhists. In Thailand, the Sangha hierarchy does not set any rule against divorce.

Since birth control could be interpreted as an interference with the law of karma,[5] there was a tendency in Buddhism to discourage artificial contraception. However, the necessity of birth control in contemporary Buddhist countries has been tacitly recognized. Today most Buddhist countries have an open policy on birth control without any interference from the Sangha.

Abortion was traditionally an abomination—it was viewed as a violation of the precept against killing a living being. But precept in itself cannot be considered outside of a social context. If pregnancy will eventually lead to the mother's death, the earliest stage of abortion is desirable and acceptable among Buddhists. The same may be applied to the case of impregnation by rape, if the woman concerned so desires. In the contemporary social context, therefore, abortion should be reconsidered on the basis of women's rights. A woman has the right to obtain all the necessary information, medically and ethically, regarding her own body including the abortion issue. A well-informed woman is the person who knows what is best for her: to have the baby and socially to take the responsibility for it; or to have an abortion—to release herself from having a child at the time she is not ready—and to take the moral or psychological responsibility for it. A woman as a subject should have the right to make decisions about her own body, because it is she who takes the consequent responsibility. Society as a whole should not make the decision for her and should not pass judgment on her.[6]

According to Kabilsingh, *bhikkhuni* in the West have been doing good work for society. For rape victims and for women who have had abortions, *bhikkhuni* can perform religious rituals that help to reestablish them mentally and spiritually. This has a great psychological effect on women who have experienced trauma and suffering. Ven. Sangye Khadro, an American nun ordained in the Tibetan Buddhist tradition, has suggested purification practices involving four steps, by adopting four mental attitudes: regret, refuge, resolution, and countermeasure. By generating these four states of mind with compassion, women can help to heal the pain and guilt experienced after an abortion (Kabilsingh 1991, 84).

Although homosexuality may have been officially proscribed, Stevens (1990, 139) reports that it in fact flourished in Buddhist monasteries throughout the centuries. Whenever there is a sex scandal in a Buddhist community—and there have been many over the centuries—the primary cause of the trouble is deceit: people deceiving their disciples, families, friends, and communities; and lying to themselves. Therefore, one absolute standard is that no one involved be harmed or deceived in any way. Regarding the ethics of sex, love, and marriage, good Buddhists have always relied on this essential moral standard: "If your heart is pure, all things in your world will be pure" (Stevens 1990, 140–141).

WOMEN FROM A CULTURAL PERSPECTIVE

Like in any society, the family—the most basic social unit—plays an important role in Thai culture. There were many attempts among anthropologists to define the Thai family system, but without a clear structural

explanation. The most influential was John F. Embree's "Loosely Structured" theory. He argued that the Thai family was so loosely structured
that "considerable variation of individual behavior was permitted"
(Embree 1950, 4). It was a social system relatively lacking in social roles
and hence in forms of social organization, so any attempt to elucidate
Thai social structure would prove fruitless. Embree's theory was so influential in the 1950s and 1960s that it obstructed any kind of structural
analysis.

Sulamith Heins Potter's "Female-Centered" theory of the Thai family system was a breakthrough from Embree's theory. Potter points out
that northern Thai family structure can be understood as a system in
which lineality is traced through women, rather than through men, and
authority is passed on from father-in-law to son-in-law by virtue of
their relationships to the line of women. The key factor in understanding the system is the recognition of the structural importance of women.
Without that, the system is unintelligible (Potter 1977, 123).

During seven hundred years of Buddhism in Thailand, there has
never been an official Bhikkhuni Sangha. However, there is a form of religious life for Thai Buddhist women, known as *mae ji*. *Mae ji* shave
their heads, wear white robes, and observe either five or eight precepts.
They follow a form of monastic life without formal ordination or lineage. According to historical records, *mae ji* have existed in Thailand for
at least three hundred years. The Thai female-centered family system,
which places women in an important position, and the *Mae Ji* institution, which places women in a low religious status in Thai society, will
be analyzed in this section as two trends of the indigenous Thai cultural
perspective toward women.

A Female-Centered Family System in Thailand

The Thai family is ordered in a delicate and complex way. It is based on
the dynamic interplay of two factors: the relationships between women
that define the social structure and determine the important relationships between men, and the higher social status and formal authority of
the men. Authority is passed from man to man, but by virtue of relationships to a line of women, that is, it is passed affinally, from father-in-
law to son-in-law. It is a sort of mirror image of patriliny, in which the
important consanguineal links are between mother and daughter rather
than between father and son. Potter says: "I am describing a system in
which the people who are redistributed in affinal groups are men. The
structurally significant people are female, not male. I call this a female-
centered system in contrast to patriliny and matriliny which, as they are

understood currently, would both be male-centered systems" (Potter 1977, 20).

Another important element is the cultural expectation that marriage will be matrilocal for at least a token period. This means that a married man is living with his wife's consanguines, who are his own affines. The important other men with whom he is likely to reside are his wife's father and brother-in-law, all of whom have also married in a similar manner. Kabilsingh explains how this type of family structure was formed.

> Under the system of corvee labor in the Ayudhya period, men would be away from their homes at least every other month, sometimes for as long as three months. During their absence, women took care of the families. Because of this, it was customary for newly married couples to live with the wife's family. This led to a matrilineal social system and also to relative financial independence for women. (Kabilsingh 1991, 18)

According to Potter, social relationships in the northern Thai family are ordered on three important principles. First, formal authority belongs to men rather than to women. Second, juniors must defer to seniors, and seniors take responsibility for the welfare of juniors. Third, family relationships are a lineality traced through women, where men are merely affinal members of matrilineal women consanguineally related to one another at the core (Potter 1977, 99). As far as marriage is concerned, parents may make suggestions and apply pressure, but it is the custom for a man and a woman to choose one another, and marry for love. In a system like this, the wife is in a most important position. Her husband's status in the family is conferred by her. The effect of all this is to give a woman an important voice in the management of family life, a position of power that comes from her place in the structure of the family. However, the rule of respect for seniors tends to reinforce the position of the husband (101).

It is also important that inheritance rules in northern Thailand divide property equally among all children, both male and female, with the house usually going to the youngest daughter. John E. deYoung reports: "Both sons and daughters inherit rice land equally, but the house and house compound frequently are inherited by right of succession by the daughter, who with her husband expects to make her home in the family household. The custom of one married daughter remaining in the house of her parents and inheriting the family house is so widespread throughout the north that it suggests a system of specialized matrilocal residence at an earlier period, although at present the system no longer is consistent" (deYoung 1958, 23).

According to deYoung, the social position of the Thai peasant woman is powerful. She has long had a voice in village governmental affairs. She often represents her household at village meetings. Through their marketing activities Thai farm women produce a sizable portion of the family cash income, and usually act as the family treasurer and hold the purse strings. But deYoung observes that in the commercialized delta area in central Thailand where large amounts of money are earned by the sale of rice, the male seems to keep control of this income himself.

Mae Ji : A Degraded Religious Status of Thai Women

The existence of *mae ji* is not supported in the Buddhist Scriptures or by Thai law. *Mae ji* are usually regarded as *upasika* (laywomen) who live in temples. An abbot is responsible for *mae ji* only on the basis that they are residents of the temple. Yet *mae ji* are denied the right of a civilian, such as the right to vote, as are monks in Thailand, because they are culturally expected to have renounced worldly concerns. Kabilsingh evaluates the status of *mae ji* arguing that, as *mae ji* do not have an official legal position in the Sangha, the laity does not feel obligated to support them. Monks, as fully ordained members of the Sangha, are seen as worthy "fields of merit" for offerings, but *mae ji* are not. *Mae ji'* lack of self-esteem, coupled with negative social attitudes, have resulted in an extremely low social status. Marginalized, undereducated, and economically unsupported, *mae ji* are alienated in present-day Thai society[7] (Kabilsingh 1991, 39).

In 1969, the Sangharaja initiated a national meeting of *mae ji*, and the Institute of Thai Mae Ji was formed with his support. A foundation was also founded in 1972 to support the institute. The institute has attempted to establish administration for registering and organizing *mae ji*, but it has met with only partial success (Kabilsingh 1991, 39–40). Kabilsingh reports that many older *mae ji* have taken up begging in the belief that people would prefer giving money to them rather than to ordinary beggars. Unfortunately, this has contributed to the poor public image of *mae ji*. Members of the Institute of Thai Mae Ji are particularly concerned about this practice and try to discourage it by placing older, destitute *mae ji* in old-age homes. But this does not address the root cause of the problem, which is the poverty of many *mae ji* due to the lack of institutional and societal support.

As part of the Sangha, *mae ji* should be able to offer spiritual guidance to laypeople, but the lack of education limits the possibilities.

Women should be given full support to bring forth their strength in Buddhism. They should receive proper education within the Sangha and should be encouraged to become ordained if they so wish. Kabilsingh points out that in the Buddha's time, one found many successful role models for women in the Sangha. However, through the long history of Buddhism in Thailand, she says, these positive role models have been suppressed; consequently the revival of the Bhikkhuni Sangha would be an important way to elevate the status of women in religious life (Kabilsingh 1999, 42).

The replacement of *mae ji* by a Bhikkhuni institution would greatly raise women's status at the core of Thai culture and would begin to address many of women's problems in Thailand—including poverty, child abuse, and prostitution.

WOMEN FROM A SOCIOPOLITICAL PERSPECTIVE

Third World's underdevelopment and First World's development are not two isolated phenomena. They are organically and functionally interrelated. Underdevelopment is the result of the long history of exploitation, unequal terms of trade, and dependency relationships. The Third World economy is designed to produce only a limited number of commodities demanded by the global market, rather than overall development to meet the needs of local people. The nature of the Third World can be understood only if it is viewed as this set of relationships: the relationships between a controlling First World center and dependent Third World peripheries, whether they are former colonies or the neocolonial independent states of today. This dependency relationship has been one of the major causes of the chronic and massive poverty within the Third World. It is extremely difficult, or in some cases impossible, to overcome the problem of underdevelopment unless there is a structural change in this dependency relationship. As John C. Raines and Donna C. Day-Lower have pointed out, ethics must seek a comprehensive basis for its analysis. What is good for the developed world cannot be at the expense of underdeveloped nations, anymore than what is good for international capital can be at the expense of local communities in the First World (Raines and Day-Lowes 1986, 13).

As Third World people, women in the underdeveloped countries—including Thailand—have been exploited by the global economic structure.[8] As the female sex, women have also been exploited or oppressed by the indigenous male bias. As a result, women in the Third World have been doubly exploited or oppressed by the combination of global economic and traditional gender structures.

Women in the Third World

Since multinational corporations go overseas for cheap labor and for a work force that is docile, easily manipulated, and willing to do boring, repetitive assembly work, Third World women are their natural choice. They use those women's lower social status to pay them less than men by claiming that women are only supplementary income earners for their families. Multinationals prefer single women with no children and no plans to have any. Pregnancy tests are routinely given to potential employees to avoid the issue of maternity benefits. The companies prefer to train a fresh group of teenagers rather than give experienced women higher pay. In their *Women in the Global Factory*, Annette Fuentes and Barbara Ehrenreich have argued that most such women earn subsistence-level incomes, whether working for a multinational or for a locally owned factory (Fuentes and Ehrenreich, 1987, 18). Corporate executives may insist that wages are sufficient in view of the lower standards of living, but the minimum wage in most East Asian countries fails to provide for basic living. Despite this, most women are significant wage earners for their families. Consequently, there is pressure on women from farm and lower-income urban backgrounds to delay marriage and to work to support their families.

Most women work under conditions that can break their health or shatter their nerves within a few years, often before they have worked long enough to earn more than a subsistence wage. Fuentes and Ehrenreich argue that while electronics companies require perfect vision in their new employees, most women will need glasses after only a few years on the job (20). These women look through microscopes up to nine hours each day, attaching thin wires to silicon chips.

Accordingly, women factory workers are in a precarious situation, treated like temporary workers and always under the threat of layoffs. Sick leave, holidays, and vacations are almost unheard-of. A probationary or apprenticeship period of six months or so, during which pay is only three-quarters of the regular wage, is common. By laying off workers just before the end of their probation, companies save the expense of paying full wages. As a result, Fuentes and Ehrenreich report that stress and anxiety permeate the women's work lives, contributing to health problems; for example, they point out that many factories operate several shifts, forcing workers to rotate day and night shifts. Such irregular schedules interfere with sleep patterns, fostering nervous ailments and stomach disorders. Lunch breaks may be very short, and bathroom breaks are treated as a privilege (23).

Women all over the world are becoming a giant reserve army of labor at the disposal of globe-trotting multinationals. No woman can feel job security on the assembly line as long as the profit motive guides multinational activities. Faced with sexual and racial discrimination, women will be further hurt as remaining technical and managerial jobs go mainly to white men. Saralee Hamilton points out that multinational corporations target women for exploitation. As a result, she says, if feminism is going to mean anything to women around the world, it must find new ways to resist corporate power internationally (Fuentes and Ehrenreich 1987, 59). One way to resist that power is to use organized pressure in specific cases of corporate abuse. The boycott of Nestle products to protest their infant formula promotion in Third World countries is a good example of a successful consumer action. Another important strategy is to foster an information exchange between Third World activists and their counterparts in the industrialized countries. Sharing knowledge can empower women workers in their struggle and is a priority in women's solidarity work.

As Fuentes and Ehrenreich conclude, the most difficult but important task in confronting multinational domination is creating direct links between women workers internationally. It could take years before such networking links are powerful enough to challenge multinationals and the governments that support them, but in the process, women's lives will grow closer (1987, 59).

Besides economic exploitations, Third World women, especially in Asia and particularly in Thailand, have been facing gender oppression in its crudest form—prostitution—both at a national scale and increasingly on a global scale.

Prostitution: A Third World Phenomenon

Prostitution in Asia involves the influences of the economy, sex, class, race, military, and imperialism. Although forms of prostitution have existed in Asia for centuries, the growth of mass prostitution was linked to the entrance of Western powers and their armies. By the early twentieth century, Japan had begun to replace Europe as the major power dominating Asia. According to Elizabeth M. Bounds, the Japanese armies at first brought their own women, who were bonded servants purchased from Japanese peasant families. By the 1920s, when the empire was prospering, laws were passed banning Japanese women from prostitution, which meant the substitution of women from Japanese-occupied Asian territories. During World War II, an estimated 50,000 to

70,000 Korean women were sent as "comfort troops" to the Japanese front. Most of these women were killed during the war or by the Japanese at the time of their surrender to the Allied forces (Bounds 1991, 134–135).

After 1945, the United States replaced Japan as the major military presence in Asia and the Pacific. The Korean and Vietnam wars brought thousands of soldiers, not just to Korea and Vietnam but also to the rest and recreation (R and R) centers in Japan, Okinawa, the Philippines, and Thailand.

Bounds points out that military bases created a parasitic culture of bars and hotels; for example, there were at one time during the Vietnam War a half million prostitutes in Saigon. But R and R centers outside Vietnam also had to be offered. Alternative sites of mass prostitution were established in Thailand, where up to 70,000 soldiers visited annually, and around bars in the Phillippines where 100 troop ships docked each year at Subic Bay. In both areas, the U.S. military presence created a new and prosperous domestic industry focused on drinking, dancing, and sex (135).

In Thailand, prostitution was mentioned during King Rama I's reign (1782–1809). There was a tax on prostitutes and brothels called "tax for the road." Prostitution was legalized in 1934 by the Thai government. The "Prevention of Venereal Disease Act B.E. 2477" (1934) requested prostitutes to be registered so that they could receive regular medical care. Thailand remained under this Act until 1960, when the United Nations declared the abolition of prostitution. The Thai government responded to the U.N. policy by replacing the 1934 law with "The Act to Deter Prostitution," making prostitution illegal (Kabilsingh 1991, 71–72).

Nevertheless, Thailand's prostitution escalated dramatically during the 1960s when the United States established military bases here during the Vietnam War. Even after the bases were dismantled, prostitution continued to spread in various guises—bar-girls, singers, partners, and other "cover" occupations—serving foreign tourists as well as local men. Kabilsingh comments that Thailand has sacrificed its women along with social and cultural values for a short-lived economic boom (72–73). Besides imperialism that usually comes together with military power, prostitution has also embodied racism. Bounds points out how racism lies behind the images of exotic, alluring, and docile Asian women. Just as racism lies behind the historical substitution of other Asian women as Japanese army prostitutes, so present-day Asian women serve as prostitutes for Japan's new business army in the clubs of Tokyo and Osaka (Bounds 1991, 139).

Asian countries were seen to have the "comparative advantage" of beautiful beaches and low-wage service workers. Much of the tourist infrastructure—hotels, planes, and tour packages—is foreign-owned and operated, so that between 40 percent and 75 percent of the profits eventually leave the domestic economy. Management jobs often go to foreign workers, leaving indigenous workers to serve the needs of foreigners in the lowest-paid and lowest-skilled jobs. Bounds continues her analysis by arguing that sexuality is sold as a country's natural resource. It is sold through airline advertisements or through the inclusion of sexual services within package tours. The Philippines, Thailand, and Korea supported prostitution while formally outlawing it and using that law only against prostitutes, not against bar and brothel owners. The result is that prostitution has become a significant sector of the economies of these countries, turning the state into an unofficial pimp (Bounds 1991, 136–137).

Asian women feel responsibility for the welfare of their families. For almost all Asian prostitutes, the major reason for working is to send money home. In Thailand, the young women who became prostitutes, usually the eldest daughters, were made to bear a heavy financial burden to see their families through.[9] This is the distorted ethical value of "filial piety" responding to modern economic pressure. As Kabilsingh has argued, girls become prostitutes out of a sense of duty to their parents, to do their share in bearing the family's economic burden. When the family is in deep debt because of agricultural failures, or from the father's gambling losses, eldest daughters are often asked to "sacrifice" for their parents and younger siblings. Cases are recorded where fathers sold their daughters into prostitution simply to buy extra cows for farming. All this is done in the traditional Thai belief that children ought to show "gratitude" to their parents (Kabilsingh 1991, 78).

In its effort to help prostitutes in Thailand, EMPOWER, a nongovernmental organization, believes that the first step must be a recognition of the important role prostitutes already play as economic agents. "They are the major productive force of the state entertainment industry . . . the largest [source of] income of the country" (Bounds 1991, 141). So the organization offers English classes because they believe that knowledge of English will help the women gain more control over their conditions of employment, with the possibility of the eventual creation of a prostitutes' union. But all this assistance might prove to be, tragically, too late. The deadly disease of AIDS has become an overwhelming threat to Thai prostitutes. A more helpful strategy is to find a more effective way to deter women from resorting to prostitution in the first place. The empowerment of women is what is needed, and must be an integral part of the struggle for social justice within the new global context.[10]

WHAT MEN OWE TO WOMEN

We have looked at the issues of women in various aspects—religious, ethical, cultural, and sociopolitical—from a Third World Buddhist perspective and out of the Thai experience. Now we come to the central dilemma of "what men owe to women." As Karl Marx has pointed out: "the criticism of religion is the prerequisite of all criticism" (Marx 1975, 243). Since religion is the root of a culture or a society, the oppression of women's religious rights represents the essential oppression that men have inflicted on women. Other forms of ethical, cultural, and sociopolitical oppression of women can then be simultaneously worked out, both from a societal and a global context.

What men essentially owe to women, in the Thai Buddhist context, is men's refusal of women's religious rights—the rights to ordination— hence men's refusal of women's rights in other cultural aspects. Prostitution is an obvious and systematic gender oppression, especially in the Third World, and particularly in Thailand. Granting women's religious rights—the revival of Bhikkhuni Sangha—is seen as a positive, culturally specific, and structural response to prostitution, sexual, and child abuse in Thailand.

Women's Religious Rights: The Root of All Rights

Buddhism as a religion or doctrine—the teachings of the Buddha—elevated the status of women to equality with men. In the "Buddha-nature" theory, the Buddha points out that all human beings, both male and female, possess the same Buddha nature—the original nature of pureness, calmness, and brightness, the potentiality to become an enlightened person. Both women and men have the same chance to attain Nirvana or Enlightenment, the highest spiritual stage in Buddhism. There are many examples of women's spiritual success in the Buddhist literature. The establishment of Bhikkhuni Sangha was the witness that, for the first time in the world's history, women were given equal religious rights to that of men.

Buddhism as an institution, however, has been oppressing women religiously by taking away (in most Buddhist countries) their rights to ordination granted by the Buddha. At the first Buddhist Council, right after the passing away of the Buddha, women were not represented and

Ananda was charged with the offense of introducing women to the Order. This reflects the male bias toward women in the religious realm. The anxiety that women's ordination would cause decay to religion has proved wrong. In the long history of the Bhikkhuni institution in Buddhist cultures, including India, Sri Lanka, and China (including Taiwan), there was no historical evidence that the Bhikkhuni Sangha has caused Buddhism to be depressed. Instead, it has become a significant educational source for women throughout history. In Taiwan—probably the strongest hold of the Bhikkhuni Sangha nowadays—the Bhikkhuni Sangha has significantly contributed to both religion and society.

The frequent excuse for not allowing the revival of Bhikkhuni Sangha in the Theravada countries is that the Bhikkhuni Sangha no longer exists in the tradition. According to the tradition, a woman needs to be ordained by a *bhikkhuni* preceptor *(Pavattini)* first, and then by a *bhikkhu* preceptor *(upachaya),* and all of this in front of the assembly of at least five *bhikkhu* and five *bhikkhuni*. Since there are no more Theravada *bhikkhuni*, ordination, it is argued, is impossible. The ordination ceremony is, however, a form of rituals created by human beings—a social norm to be applied or not applied by the agreement of society's members. It is not like a biologic species that cannot be revived. The Bhikkhuni Sangha still exists in the Mahayana tradition in China, whose original lineage came from the Dharmagupta subsect of the Theravada tradition in Sri Lanka. There have been several attempts by Thai women to be ordained in the presence of Taiwanese Bhikkhuni Sangha, but these women were persecuted by the Thai authority and by Sangha hierarchy. This refusal to establish the Bhikkhuni Sangha (in the cases of Thailand, Myanmar, Laos, and Cambodia)[11] and the revival of the Bhikkhuni Sangha (in the case of Sri Lanka) represents male religious bias toward women and is to be condemned.

Instead, women's rights to ordination were replaced by the low-status *mae ji* institution in Thailand. Legally, *mae ji* have never been recognized as part of the ordained Sangha. As the ordained, monks enjoy legal privileges such as paying half-fare for all public transportation in Thailand, while *mae ji* do not have the same privilege. Thai laws prohibit ordained people from voting in elections. *Mae ji* are, however, refused the right to vote because they are, ironically, supposed to reject worldly concerns, just as are the monks. *Mae ji* are not allowed to go for alms in the morning for their daily food and are not offered necessities by people as are monks. All they have received are the leftovers (of food and necessities offered by people) from monks. The social status of *mae ji* is so low that they are treated almost like the homeless who live under certain rules in Buddhist monasteries.

Originally, the status of Thai women was probably the highest in Asia, owing to the female-centered family system in Thai society. Exploitation and oppression of women, however, has come, on the one hand, from the more recent class structure within Thai society and, on the other hand, from the dependency relationship between Thailand as the Third World and the United States, Western Europe, and Japan as the First World. The overall result of these impacts has pushed the status of Thai women to the lowest in memory, particularly when it comes to the issue of prostitution.

There is a resemblance between prostitutes and *mae ji* as to their life choices. Kabilsingh argues that due to "gratitude" or obligation, some women become prostitutes to repay their parents materially, while others choose to become *mae ji* to repay their parents spiritually, offering them the merit of their religious activities (Kabilsingh 1991, 78).

Bhikkhuni and Prostitution: A Structural Response

Thailand has worldwide fame, or rather shame for having a well-established sex industry. A great number of young women have been structurally oppressed through prostitution, a form of neoslavery.[12] Although prostitution is illegal, the Thai government, because of its inefficient and corrupt bureaucratic system, cannot solve the problem. Prostitution is, of course, against the teachings of the Buddha. But the Thai Sangha hierarchy basically keeps silent on the issue.

Economic hardship in the rural areas, caused by unjust tenancy, agribusiness, and the lack of governmental interest in improving agriculture, has driven rural young people to migrate to towns and cities in search of jobs. Most of them become cheap laborers in construction, factories, and service businesses.[13] A large number of young women, particularly from northern Thailand, become prostitutes or work in the sex-related service business. They are pressured by structural poverty, consumerism, and the distorted traditional value of "filial piety" that daughters should support their desperate families out of a sense of gratitude. Some of those unfortunate young women from rural areas, however, were deceived and forced into prostitution in Japan and Taiwan by the illegal works of mafia gangs.

Some may argue that those young women could live a simple life at home in the country by working at their traditional jobs in the household and rice fields, without having to resort to prostitution. However, times have changed. Under the development projects from the central government, roads, radios, televisions and popular magazines have reached the villages. With them the religion of consumerism has spread, and people are no longer happy with their traditional values (Sivaraksa 1992, 3–9). Their traditional life has been threatened with desperate poverty by unjust tenancy and agribusiness, while consumerism brought by radios, televisions and popular magazines, increases their felt demand for consumer goods. Today most rural Thai families are torn apart by these two forces. Under these circumstances, it is hard for young men and women to stay home and be happy in the rural areas. Today most rural villages, especially in the northern and northeastern regions, are in effect populated only by those left behind, old people, and children.

Thai prostitutes face not only structural gender oppression but also the deadly disease of AIDS.[14] In Thailand, the proportion of people who are infected with HIV is among the highest in the world. Thai prostitutes are among those groups of people who are the most hard-hit by AIDS. In Thailand, prostitution is basically a by-product of unjust economic and social structures. It is the most obvious form of gender oppression and the most basic violation of women's rights. Prostitution is a well-known fact in my country, but very few Thai people talk about it in public. Thai feminists and Buddhist social activists are beginning to speak up and to defend the rights of their mothers, sisters, and daughters, taking seriously the fact that prostitution represents a distortion of local cultural values caused by modern structural poverty.

The lack of opportunity in providing education by the Thai state has resulted in a large number of uneducated and undereducated children in the country. There is, however, a custom of ordination for boys as *samanera* (novices) and for men as *bhikkhu* (monks) for their religious training and education. Using this ordination channel for education, parents in remote areas have been sending their sons to get ordained and educated at the nearby temple. Most of the monks and novices around the country are from these remote areas. They have gradually moved to a bigger temple, closer to town and to city for higher education and training. When these ordained people disrobe (return to lay life), as the Thai tradition allows, they are turned into educated adults who are usually well accepted in society. For those who continue their ecclesiastical careers, they have become educated monks guiding people spiritually. The Bhikkhu Sangha is, therefore, a necessary institution for those less fortunate boys who want an education and a chance to be incorporated into society.

Poor girls in Thai society, unfortunately, do not have the same chance as boys. If these girls were lucky enough, they would receive support from some private organizations, such as the Children Foundation, for their education and professional training. But most girls are not that lucky. Many of them become laborers in local or transnational factories, working extremely hard for extremely low wages. Pressured by poverty, by the distorted cultural value of "filial piety," and by consumerism, many of them resort to prostitution or to sex-related businesses.

For those "lucky" girls who receive some kind of support from a monk or from a religious organization, they may face sexual abuses from that same authority. The urgent question now is, How can these girls from the countryside receive their education and training safely and securely without being the victims of sexual abuses? In a way, the replacement of *mae ji* by the Bhikkhuni institution would be a solution. The Bhikkhuni Sangha would provide the chance for those less fortunate girls to be ordained and educated in the temples of *bhikkhuni* the same way the boys have already enjoyed the temples of *bhikkhu*.

The revival of Bhikkhuni Sangha would elevate women's religious status to a level equal to that of men. On the one hand, when women have faith in the religion, they could study dharma directly from a female teacher, without having to gather around the monks—avoiding the path from which a lot of sexual abuses and scandals have occurred. On the other hand, a woman could become a preceptor *(pavattini)* who has her own rights to ordain a *samaneri* (female novice) or a *bhikkhuni*. According to the tradition, women who have kept the Six Rules for two years can be ordained first by a female preceptor *(pavattini)* and then by a male preceptor *(upachaya)* in the presence of at least five *bhikkhu* and five *bhikkhuni*.

The Bhikkhuni institution would begin to alleviate the problems of prostitution and child abuse. When those less fortunate girls and women have access to a better life in ordination, the chance that they will resort to prostitution or be subjected to child abuse will be greatly reduced. They can obtain education and training in the *bhikkhuni* monasteries and become educated adults. If they so wish, they can disrobe and have a family. This is allowed in the Thai Buddhist tradition. If they continue to be *bhikkhuni*, they can become spiritual leaders of the community.

Sexual misconduct or abuses in religious institutions may be viewed as misbehavior caused by the greed or lust of an individual monk. But from a structural perspective, the lack of religious institutions for women themselves—the Bhikkhuni Sangha—is the root cause of the problem. When women are refused the rights of having their own proper religious institution, they need to rely on the male religious institution for their spiritual life and their chance in society. The completion of the Four Buddhist Sangha, namely, *bhikkhu* (monks), *bhikkhuni* (nuns), *upasaka* (laymen), and *upasika* (laywomen), is needed in the modern time no less than in the time of the Buddha. In Thailand today, that is "what men owe to women."

Notes

1. *Nibbana* is a Pali word equivalent in meaning with nirvana in Sanskrit. It is the highest stage of Buddhist spirituality.

2. According to Anantanand Rambachan, Jainism—a religion in India established by Mahavira, a contemporary of the Buddha—also has an order of nuns although it is not a world religion within today's context.

3. These are the four stages of achievement of the highest perfection in Theravada Buddhism.

4. These psalms recite the great ecstasy and rapture the nuns obtained by their becoming ordained and thereafter attaining sanctity.

5. Karma means action. The law of karma in Buddhism is, therefore, the "law of action" in such a way that one action is the cause for another action. The effected action is then the cause for still another action. It goes on in this way as the chain of cause-and-effect of one's own activities. There is a belief in popular Buddhism that one's own actions in the previous life were the cause for one's social status in this life; and one's actions in this life affect social status in the next life.

6. It is generally accepted that where abortion was illegal, the number of women who suffered from abortions because of the ill-treatments by nonprofessionals was high. But where abortion was legalized, that number decreased significantly. This social reality should be taken into account in considering the issue of abortion.

7. Field of merit (*na-bun* in Thai) is a metaphor in Buddhism that *bhikkhu* is like a field *(na)* in which a Buddhist could throw seeds of merit *(bun)* and yield the result of the harvest (merit).

8. Forty-five percent of Thai women work, the highest percentage in Asia.

9. Peasant girls in Thailand are sold by their struggling parents into "contracts," or bonds, which means that the girl is at the mercy of the owner until she has earned the contract payment. Some of these bonded women are kept in their room in chains, as was tragically revealed in a club fire at a Thai resort, which killed several women imprisoned in a back room (Bounds 1991, 134).

10. For more details on prostitution and its liberation, see Brock and Thistlethwaite (1996).

11. The Bhikkhuni Sangha has never been given a chance to exist in these four Theravada countries.

12. Although prostitution and the international sex industry exploit adults and children of both sexes, the vast majority of prostitutes and sex workers in Thailand are women and girls.

13. Young women make up about 80 percent of Thailand's low-wage factory work force. The fire on May 10, 1993, at Kader Industrial (Thailand) Co., a factory in the Phuttamonthon area fifteen miles west of Bangkok, which killed at least 213 and injured 500 workers—most of them were young women— revealed what the working conditions and safety standards in factories are like for most rural women. The blaze may have been the deadliest factory fire in history, far surpassing the 146 killed on March 25, 1911, at the Triangle Shirtwaist Co. factory in New York (Philadelphia Inquirer, May 12, 1993).

14. For more details about the AIDS crisis in Thailand, see Bonacci (1992).

REFERENCES

Bonacci, Mark A. 1992. *Senseless Casualties: The AIDS Crisis in Asia*. Washington, DC: Asia Resource Center.

Bounds, Elizabeth M. 1991. "Sexuality and Economic Reality: A First World and Third World Comparison." In *Redefining Sexual Ethics*, Susan E. Davies and Eleanor H. Haney, eds. Cleveland, OH: Pilgrim Press.

Brock, Rita Nakashima and Susan Brooks Thistlethwaite. 1996. *Casting Stones: Prostitution and Liberation in Asia and the United States*. Minneapolis: Fortress Press.

DaGrossa, Pamela S. 1989. "Kamphaengdin: A Study of Prostitution in the All-Thai Brothels of Chiang Mai City." In *Crossroads*, 4(2), Grant A. Olson, ed. DeKalb: Center for Southeast Asian Studies, Northern Illinois University.

deYoung, John E. 1958. *Village Life in Modern Thailand*. Berkeley and Los Angeles: University of California Press.

Elders' Verses II: Therigatha. 1991. Translated with an introduction and notes by K. R. Norman. Pali Text Society Translation Series No. 40. London: Pali Text Society.

Embree, John F. 1950. "Thailand—A Loosely Structured Social System."*American Anthropologist*.

Fuentes, Annette and Barbara Ehrenreich. 1987. *Women in the Global Factory*. Boston: South End Press.

Kabilsingh, Chatsumarn. 1991. *Thai Women in Buddhism*. Berkeley: Parallax Press.

Kindred Sayings (Samyutta-nikaya) or Grouped Suttas. 1989. Part I. Kindred Sayings with Verses (Sagatha-vagga). Translated by Mrs. Rhys Davids. Assisted by Suriyagoda Sumangala Thera. London: Pali Text Society.

Marx, Karl. 1975. *Early Writings*. New York: Vintage Books.

Piyadassi, Nayaka Thera. 1991. *The Spectrum of Buddhism*. Foreword by Bhikkhu Bodhi. Colombo, Sri Lanka: Karunaratne & Son.

Potter, Sulamith Heins. 1977. *Family Life in a Northern Thai Village: A Study in the Structural Significance of Women*. Berkeley, Los Angeles and London: University of California Press.

Raines, John C. and Donna C. Day-Lower. 1986. *Modern Work and Human Meaning*. Philadelphia: Westminster Press.

Saddhatissa, H. 1970. *Buddhist Ethics: Essence of Buddhism.* London: George Allen & Unwin.

Sivaraksa, Sulak. 1992. *Seeds of Peace: A Buddhist Vision for Renewing Society.* Tom Ginsburg, ed., foreword by H. H. The Dalai Lama, prefaced by Thich Nhat Hanh. Berkeley: Parallax Press.

Stevens, John. 1990. *Lust for Enlightenment: Buddhism and Sex.* Boston and London: Shambhala.

Woodward, F. L. 1973. *Some Sayings of the Buddha.* London, Oxford and New York: Oxford University Press.

Woodward, F. L. and E. M. Hare, translators. 1979. *The Book of Gradual Sayings.* London: Pali Text Society.

9

A Taoist Perspective

*Appreciating and
Applying the Principle
of Femininity*

Liu Xiaogan

AMONG WORLD PHILOSOPHIES and religions, Taoism is probably a unique tradition in that it fundamentally advocates the principle of femininity, and uses it to provide practical instructions for how men should treat women fairly. The word *femininity* is here borrowed as a general term to render Chinese words such as *yin, ci, and pin*, which indicate the universal force, attribute, style, or manner in opposition to the masculine. The Chinese words are not easily translated, and I must insist immediately that they do not involve stereotyping women or men since the principle of femininity is not lacking in men. Bear with me as we try to show how this concept can be useful in other cultures to promote gender justice and harmony.

In the first two parts of this chapter, I introduce a new concept, "the principle of femininity" deriving from my study in Laozi's philosophy. The practical aspects of gender harmony and equality in Taoist religious movements will be investigated in the third part. The last part is a further discussion of the significance of the aforementioned theories in the perspective of gender justice.

THE MODEL OF THE PRINCIPLE OF
FEMININITY: TAO OR THE WAY

The name of Taoism itself already indicates the fundamental importance of the concept of the Tao, which is conventionally rendered as the
Way. Laozi, the first thinker of Taoism,[1] believes that Tao is the final
source or the very primitive origin of the world, and myriad things
come from it. Laozi illustrates the function of Tao. "Tao produces the
One, The One produces the two, The two produces the three, And three
produces ten thousand beings" (chap. 42; Chan 1963, 160). The One is
the original state of the universe without any difference in itself, probably just pure *qi*. The Chinese word *qi* literally denotes air, vapor, steam,
and breath. Chinese people generally believe that everything in the universe—plants, animals, and humanity—is formed from *qi* and must return to it. The two signifies heaven and earth, or *yin* and *yang*. The *yin* is
feminine and the *yang* is masculine. The three is heaven, earth, and
man, or *yin*, *yang*, and their combination. What is the One, the two, and
the three, however, is not essential. Instead of giving an astrophysical
report, Laozi just wants to give a formulaic demonstration of the origin
and development of the universe: Tao—One—two—three—myriad beings. The formula indicates that the development of the universe is
from one to many, from simplicity to complexity, from a single primitive element to innumerable and boundless worlds.

Tao is invisible, inaudible, subtle, formless, and infinite; thus no
word is suitable for it. Laozi says that he cannot find a right name for it.
He has to use metaphors to describe it. The metaphor he selects is significant in the perspective of gender issues: he draws an analogy between Tao and mother, instead of father and God. Laozi says: "There
was something nebulous existing, born before heaven and earth, silent,
empty, standing alone, altering in no way. Moving cyclically without becoming exhausted, which may be called the *mother* of all under heaven.
I know not its name, I give its alias, Tao" (chap. 25; Chen 1989, 116).

Obviously, Tao is not personal: it is nebulous, silent, empty, change-
less, and moving cyclically. Neither is Tao God. Laozi clearly declares:
"We don't know whose child Tao is; it seems to have even preceded the
Lord" (chap. 4; Henricks 1991, 56). Laozi doesn't believe a god is the final reason or creator of the world. He thinks there must be something
higher or more radical. Thus, he creates a new concept, Tao, to denote
the origin of all things, including gods.

However, why does Laozi compare Tao to a mother instead of a father? This is certainly not accidental, because Laozi repeatedly uses the

metaphor of mother for Tao and for the origin of the universe, for example: "(Tao) is the *mother* of ten thousand things" (chap. 1). Laozi claims: "The world had a beginning, which can be considered the *mother* of the world. Having attained the mother, in order to understand her children. Having understood the children, if you return and hold on to the *mother*, till the end of your life you'll suffer no harm" (chap. 52; Henricks 1991, 21). Tao resembles the mother and all things in the world are like her children. To understand the essential Tao it is necessary to know concrete beings. Man should not just follow trivial things and forget the general Tao. Thus having understood the children, you should still return and hold onto the mother. Again, *mother* instead of father here represents the cardinal and universal Tao.

In the *Laozi*, the word *mother* is used seven times in five chapters,[2] in comparison with *father*, which appears three times in two chapters,[3] though the word *father* is also used in positive ways. This is just one aspect of Laozi's preference for femininity. Similar to the metaphor of mother, Laozi also draws an analogy between the root of the universe and the mysterious femininity *(xuan pin, or hsiüan-pin)*. "The spirit of the valley never dies. This is called the mysterious femininity. The gateway of the mysterious femininity, is called the root of heaven and earth. It continues on as if ever present. And in its use, it is inexhaustible" (chap. 6; Schwartz 1985, 200).

Although the function of Tao is infinite and majestic, it is always low-keyed and demands nothing, which also reminds us of the traditional stereotype of a female feature. "Tao gives birth to them and Te (virtue) nourishes them; substance gives them form and their unique capacities complete them. Therefore the ten thousand things venerate Tao and honor Te. As for their veneration of the Way and their honoring of Te, no one rewards them for it; it constantly is on its own. (Tao) gives birth to all beings but doesn't try to own them, It acts on all beings but doesn't make them dependent, it matures them but doesn't rule them" (Henricks 1991, 20). The attitude of Tao toward all beings it produces is more female than male. Borrowing Fromm's theory, Ellen M. Chen has illustrated that Tao embodies mother love more than father love (Chen 1969, 402).

In demonstrating the motherly or the feminine feature of Tao, again, what does Laozi intend to suggest? There are two aspects of the question, metaphysical and axiological or ontological and ethical. Metaphysically, Laozi believes the origin of the universe is natural and spontaneous, not caused by any person or god according to any plan or purpose. All characteristics of Tao, naturalness, quietness, generosity, tolerance, and amiability, are often attributed to femininity. On the contrary, ambition, courage, aggressiveness, competitiveness, and possessiveness, are sometimes related to masculinity, in the popular stereotype. Laozi is using this stereotyping without saying that only men have certain qualities and that only women have others. In the concrete, men and women would be assumed to have both. It is in this way that Laozi uses mother instead of father as the metaphor of Tao.

The image of the female that illustrates Laozi's conception of the origin of the universe runs counter to the traditional belief that God or heaven created and ruled over the natural world and human activities. Laozi's cosmology is a reaction to the theories prevailing in the Shang dynasty (sixteenth–eleventh century B.C.E.) and the early Zhou dynasty (eleventh–sixth century B.C.E.). Laozi builds a metaphysical hypothesis diametrically opposed to monotheism, which attributes the origin of the universe to God, who has a strong will and blueprint in mind. Different from Tao, God is mostly portrayed in the image of the father and the husband and is seen as a derivative category, not as the primary source.

The concept of Tao concerns not only a cosmological theme, but also one that concerns human life and the social order and has a normative import. Unlike some of his Western counterparts, Laozi is not a philosopher interested in pure metaphysics and theoretical speculation. Tao is the cardinal root of the universe, but also and just as importantly, the model and standard of human behavior and activity. Thus, the metaphor of the mother and the female also serves as a behavioral exemplar. This is the axiological or ethical aspect of Laozi's female preference, and to that we turn next.

THE PRACTICE OF THE PRINCIPLE OF FEMININITY: *Ziran & Wuwei*

The reason why Laozi emphasizes the femininity of Tao is to advocate its value as a moral principle in the human world. The core value of his philosophy is *ziran (tzu-jan)*, or "itself-so." *Ziran* (in this context) is by no means simply biologic nature or the natural world (Liu 1998, 212–213). The essential importance of naturalness is clarified in the text. "Human persons model themselves on the Earth; The Earth models itself on Heaven, Heaven models itself on Tao; And Tao models itself on *Naturalness*" (chap. 25; Chen, 1989). Tao is the highest concept of the universe, as the origin or mother of the universe. However, it follows the principle of naturalness. Thus, naturalness is endowed by Tao with the position of the pivotal value. The last sentence: "Tao models itself on

Naturalness" reveals the radical feature of Tao and the importance of naturalness. But this is not the main message of the passage. In order to discern the true message, we should omit the middle parts in the chain of "Human beings—Earth—Heaven—Tao—Naturalness." When we do, we find out that in the final analysis it is humans who should practice naturalness. Again, the sentence: "Human beings should model themselves on naturalness" doesn't refer directly to environmental protection, but to pursuing the natural order of harmony in all contexts of human life.

This point is clearly presented in the following: "The best rulers are those whose existence is merely known by the people; the next best are those who are loved and praised. The next are those who are feared. And the next are those who are reviled. . . . (The great ruler) values his words highly. He accomplishes his task; he completes his work. Thus his people all say that he is natural" (chap. 17; Chan 1963, 148). Among the gradation of the qualities of rulership, best of all is the ideal king of Taoism who just reigns without ruling. People know of his existence but do not feel his interference, so they praise him for "being natural." Obviously "being natural" is highly valued. Second comes the perfect ruler who, according to traditional or Confucian standards, bestows favors upon people and receives love and praise from them. He seems optimal for average people. But not in the perspective of Taoism, because even good rulers interrupt the people's natural activities. Rulers of the third group are crude, and thus the people dread to meet or even to mention them. The worst, finally, are the cruel tyrants who make people hate and insult them.

Laozi praises sage rulers who practice the principle of naturalness because they bring people and societies natural life, marked by peace and harmony. According to Eric Fromm, the natural manner is related more to the mother instead of the father (Chen 1969, 402). Indeed, the female may be easier, more patient, and tolerant with their children. A sage ruler who exercises natural management and protects the natural social order embodies, in a sense, the principle of femininity though he is a man. Thus you can see that "femininity" has a normative meaning. It relates to qualities that women may in fact often have, but it says they are normative for all, especially for rulers. In other words, empirically these noble traits may be found more often in women, but the normative truth is that this should not be so, since men, especially rulers should have these qualities. They befit humanity as such and not just women.

Obviously, the ideal rulership, reigning without ruling, demands one to take as little action as possible. This spirit is summarized in another of Laozi's concepts, *wuwei*. Although *wuwei* literally means "no action," its essential meaning is taking no action to interrupt natural harmony and balance. About nonaction and its relation to naturalness: "He who takes actions fails. He who grasps things loses them. For this reason the sage takes no action (*wuwei*) and therefore does not fail. He grasps nothing and therefore he does not lose anything" (chap. 64). This stanza states the reason why sages take no action. This aspect is the passive side, and it prevents failure.

The following is the positive side: to maintain naturalness, the core value. "Therefore, the sage desires to have no desire. He does not value rare treasures. He learns to be unlearned, and returns to what the multitude has missed. Thus, he supports all things in their natural state, but dares not take any action" (Chan 1963, 170). Sages neither seek to be rich nor fight for objects the multitude are fascinated with, let alone preying on others or taking from them. They are prudent and dare not take any action. All of these are the manifestation of the spirit of *wuwei*, which works in turn to protect the naturalness of all beings. Thus, we see that naturalness is a core moral value, while *wuwei* is the methodological principle to actualize and sustain it. Dramatically enough, both *ziran* and *wuwei* are easily associated with femininity: they usually suggest an easy and tolerant attitude, a quiet and low-keyed nature, a moderate and generous mind.

In addition, softness and weakness are presented as positive traits and are manifestations of *ziran* and *wuwei*. They also are apparently female features according to conventional stereotypes, even though we may not agree with those stereotypes today. In his five-thousand-character text, Laozi mentions softness eleven times and weakness ten times.[4] In most situations, Laozi argues about their benefits and advantages; for example, he says: "In the whole world, nothing is softer and weaker than water. And yet for attacking the hard and strong, nothing is better. There is nothing you can use to replace it. That the weak can overcome the strong—that the soft can overcome the hard— there is no one in the whole world who doesn't know it, and yet there is no one who puts it into practice" (chap. 78, Henricks 1991, 182). This claim that weakness and gentleness can overcome strength, and that softness can overcome hardness, is quite distinctive, if not unique in comparative religion. This derives from Laozi's experience and from his description of many social and historical facts, but it also comes from his belief and advocacy of the principle of Tao. "Weakness is the function of Tao" (chap. 40). We see the systematic coherence in Laozi's philosophy between the metaphysical concept and human moral values and principles.

One can and should overcome the formidable by applying to it the way of the soft and weak and the meaning Laozi gives to them, a meaning that comes close to gentleness. Laozi repeatedly emphasizes this elementary preposition. "The weak and the tender overcome the hard and the strong" (chap. 36; Chan 1963, 157). Or again: "Keeping to weakness is called strength" (chap. 52; Chan 1963, 164). Finally: "The still and the hard are companions of death, the tender and the weak are companions of life" (chap. 76; Chan 1963, 174).

Furthermore, Laozi directly uses the metaphor of the female and the male to reinforce his argument. "A big country may be compared to the lower part of a river. It is the converging point of the world; it is the *female* of the world. The *female* always conquers the male by stillness, and in stillness she occupies the low position" (chap. 61; Chan 1963, 168). Traditionally, some people devalue the low position, as they do tranquillity and femininity. Laozi, however, finds the opposite to be true, specifically their substantive superiority.

About the advantage of female attributes in their relationship to the concept of *wuwei*, Benjamin I. Schwartz comments that in the sex act the female role is seemingly passive. Yet, as Laozi notes, the "female conquers the male by stillness; in stillness she occupies the lower position." She acts "by not acting" not only in the sex act but in generation. Thus, as Schwartz argues, the female is the epitome of *wuwei*. He also points out that Laozi's exaltation of the feminine symbolizes the principles of *wuwei* and spontaneity *(ziran)* (Schwartz 1985, 200). Such an analysis dramatically reveals the association of Taoist thought and female attributes. However, he overstates in a sense the sexual significance of femininity in Taoism. The *Laozi* doesn't mean to discuss the issue of sexuality. All words related to female or male in the *Laozi* are used only in the sense of a metaphor or a symbol and imply more fundamental and more radically normative meanings for human social and political life. It is in this sense that they find their significance for gender justice and harmony in a way that is not at all superficial.

Application to Men's Obligations to Women

It is logical that Laozi advocates the application of this principle of femininity when he judges the role and function of the female as a social model. He claims: "When you know masculine yet hold on to femininity, you'll be the ravine of the country. When you're the ravine of the country, your constant virtue will not leave. And when your constant virtue doesn't leave, you'll return to the state of the infant" (chap. 28; Henricks 1991, 80). In this stanza, the first line is Laozi's advocacy that one should apply the principle of femininity even though one knows the strength of the masculine. The rest of the stanza demonstrates its benefits and advantages. The noteworthy point is that Laozi wants to apply the principle of femininity not because one cannot exercise a male role as it is often perceived. Neither is it that he doesn't know the stereotype of masculine strength. By urging femininity, he thus actually opposes the common discrimination and bias against women from the point of view of the fundamental or ontological level.

While Laozi appreciates and applies the principle of femininity, he is by no means a one-sided advocate of the traditional female role. He promotes the principle of femininity in order to criticize and correct the dominant principle of behavior, such as aggression, oppression, stealing, and greed. At bottom, his philosophy is grounded upon the principle of the harmony of the *yin* and *yang*. Although the *yin* could sometimes indicate female, feminine, and femininity, while the *yang* could indicate male, masculine, and masculinity, the meaning of *yin* and *yang* are much more general and broad than any one of their English language counterparts. Laozi claims: "Ten thousand beings carry femininity (*yin*) on their backs, and embrace masculinity (*yang*) in their front, through the blending of the material force (*qi*), harmony is achieved" (chap. 42; Chen 1989, 157). The theory that Laozi demonstrates here is commonly shared by most Chinese schools. It is common sense for Chinese people that everything in the universe comprises elements or aspects of *yin* and *yang*, and simultaneously belongs to either *yin* or *yang*; for example, the sun is *yang*, the moon is *yin*, and both are attributed to heaven, typically a symbol of *yang*. The earth is typically *yin*. But on the earth, the side toward sunshine or a mountain or the bank of a river is *yang*, while the opposite side is *yin*. Similarly, women are *yin*, and men are *yang*. Abdomens, however, either of women or of men, are *yin*, and backs are *yang*; a tendon is *yin*, and skin is *yang*; kidneys are *yin*, and bladders are *yang*. The *yin-yang* theory believes that everything contains both *yin* and *yang*, and nothing belongs exclusively to either *yin* or *yang*. A double-fish-circle perfectly reflects this idea:

In the figure, the black fish represents *yin* with a white eye as *yang*, while the white fish represents *yang* with a black eye as *yin*. Between the white and the black is a curve instead of a straight line, which suggests that there is no clear division of *yin* and *yang*. Both are dynamic. Thus, the figure denotes the dynamic balance between *yin* and *yang*, and the unity in multiplicity that pervades the whole universe.

GENDER EQUALITY: HARMONY OF YIN AND YANG

The *yin-yang* theory is fully adopted by Taoist religion and becomes a part of its theoretical foundation, which exerts great influence upon its view of women and men in society. In Taoist tradition, women have a more equal position than in other religious traditions. It is obvious to the Taoist that in the universe, both mortal and immortal worlds, there cannot be only *yang* without *yin*, nor too much *yang* and too little *yin*. Thus in the Taoist pantheon there are more goddesses than in other religions. Here *goddess* is a general term including female immortals. The word *immortal* is a specific term rendering the Chinese word *xian* (*hsien*), which features physical immortality and the possibility for a mortal to ascend to the immortal.

Along with the enlargement of the pantheon, the number of goddesses in Taoist hagiographies increased. It is understandable that the absolute number of goddesses is less than that of gods because it has developed in patriarchal societies and mirrored those historical facts. However, through the paralleling of the functions and the numerical increase of gods and goddesses, we see in a sense the idea of equity between the feminine and the masculine in the Taoist tradition.

The earliest intention to collect literature of both male and female immortals is found in the first Biography of Immortals (*Lie Xian Zhuan,* or *Lie Hsien Chuan*) edited in the Eastern Han dynasty (25–220 C.E.), which includes stories of female immortals available at the time. Ge Hong (Ko Hung, 283–263?), the first Taoist theologian and the author of *Biographies of Gods and Immortals,* assigned his seventh volume mostly to goddesses and female immortals.

In the Tang dynasty (618–907), the first and most important of Taoist female hagiographies, *Records of the Collection of Immortals in the Immortal City,* authored by Du Guangting (Tu Kuang-t'ing, 850–933), originally gathered 109 biographies of female immortals. However, the extant version contains only 38 immortal women, many of them being people of the Tang, who became Taoist saints.[5] In addition to the divine kinship of female immortals, the book presented the biography of The Nine Heaven Mysterious Maiden (Jiu Tian Xuan Nü). She was the master of the Yellow Emperor, the legendary ancestor and leader of the

Chinese peoples, and she bestowed on him books of esoteric military arts that helped him win a critical war. In the Taoist tradition, many goddesses and female immortals are the masters of male rulers and are worshiped by those rulers. We see, in short, little gender discrimination in Taoist hagiographies.

Taoism enjoyed periods of royal patronage in the Tang and Song dynasties (960–1279), and hence developed rapidly in those periods. Thus in the Yuan dynasty (1271–1368) a Taoist priest Zhao Daoyi (Chao Tao-i) collected 121 biographies of female immortals in his book.[6] After the Yuan dynasty, neo-Confucianism became the official ideology, and women's social positions and activities became very restricted. Taoism suffered for a long time without royal support in the Ming dynasty (1368–1662) and in the Qing dynasty (1644–1901). However, *A History of Immortals of All Dynasties* completed in the Qing dynasty still has a special volume for 133 female immortals.[7]

The position of female immortals in Taoist hagiographies is partially determined by Taoist theories and by the role of liturgy; for example, the early celestial movement was organized on the basis of an absolute equality between men and women who, as Libationers, shared in equal numbers the leadership of the liturgical organization. The celestial masters themselves shared their duties with their wives. In the dioceses there were as many female as male masters. This balance was fundamental. Only a man and a woman together, as a couple, are qualified for the high position in the practice of perfection. The parity of men and women in Taoist organizations and practices suggests in fact a certain ascendancy, in the organization as well as in religious practice, on the part of women. This is worth noting because the general situation of women in society was far below that of men (Schipper 1993, 128–129). Certainly, this is not the whole picture of Taoism; for example, in the later Quanzhen movement, under the influence of Buddhism after the twelfth century, celibacy was practiced.

The importance of goddesses in Taoist literature is also based on the historical activities of female Taoist leaders; for example, the wife of the second Celestial Master and the mother of the third one, Madam Lu, was an important and influential leader in the Five Peck Rice movement in Later Han (Zhan 1990, 49; Schipper 1993, 129). Another example is Wei Huacun (251–334), a married woman, mother of two, who is the main initiator and first "patriarch" of the Shangqing (supreme purity) movement. She had been a Libationer, which implied membership in the hierarchical organization of the Celestial Masters. She is considered to be the founder of the movement and is the source for a ritual that she revealed to Yang Xi, the actual organizer, part of which is preserved in the Taoist Canon as one of the most ancient written records of the Celestial Masters' liturgy (Schipper 1993, 129; Robinet 1997, 115–116).

Thus, the females in the Taoist historical development and polytheist system by no means play only supporting roles to men. Many goddesses have their own positions and function independently of any god. It seems that there is a sense of gender equity in the Taoist tradition. The interesting example is the Queen Mother of the West, the highest and most powerful goddess. Her name in Chinese is literally "Western-King-Female," which is parallel and contrary to "Eastern-King-Male," or King Father of the East. Interestingly, her male counterpart is far less famous and popular in Taoism and folklore.

The duty and role of the Queen Mother of the West is comprehensive. As Suzanne Cahill points out, immortality and the means for attaining this status are under her control. It is she who authenticates both divine and worldly power. Because she transmits the word of the Taoist texts, she reveals the path from the human to the celestial realms. She also passes on talismans, arts, and ritual practices associated with the Shangqing Taoist techniques of achieving transcendence. It is she who sanctions the various ascents to transcendence, and then registers these new immortals. (Cahill 1986, 157).

As a goddess, representing ultimate *yin*, she was certainly the leader and protector of female transcendents, and also had a special relationship with all women. "She appears as teacher, judge, registrar, and guardian of female believers." She nurtures all women in Taoism, but is the special patron of women outside the normal world of family. She protects Taoist nuns, as well as female artists and prostitutes. In sum, her role both symbolized and ritually represented Taoist concerns about, and sympathy for, women (Cahill 1993, 213–214).

In the Taoist Canon and in modern China, many Scriptures were edited and written for women and specified that in their titles. In addition, there are many physical and spiritual cultivation techniques and rules designed for female practitioners. Most authors of the Scriptures were male priests according to our knowledge. However, male authors seem to be adept in female physiology, and help females to study immortal arts. Because of physiological differences, physical cultivation techniques for women are distinct from those for men; for example, men should focus their meditation on the cinnabar field (*dantian*, or *tantien*) two inches below the navel, while women should focus on the sea of vital force (*danzhong*, or *tan-chong*) between the breasts. The details of the techniques are varied according to a woman's age, marital status, and menstruation condition. According to Taoist masters, it may be easier for women than for men to make progress toward the immortal ideal because of their concentration and modesty (Schipper 1993, 239; Hong 1991, 245).

THE ART OF THE BEDCHAMBER

Another important aspect of Taoism concerning gender issues is the *art of the bedchamber*. The term itself began much earlier than the institutionalized religious movement. Most texts were lost long ago, but some extant text fragments of the art of the bedchamber are kept in the Taoist Canon and are found in a Japanese collection. The historic and significant discovery in this aspect is the silk and bamboo manuscripts about sexual arts in a tomb from Han China (burial dated 168 B.C.E.) that were unearthed in 1973. Scholars have identified them with later Taoist documents dealing with the art of the bedchamber (Li Ling 1993, 400–401). What is special about the Taoist art of the bedchamber is its purpose: it takes the art of sexual activities primarily as a way to increase vitality and to realize longevity and immortality, rather than merely pursuing sexual enjoyment.[8]

The earlier art of the bedchamber was adopted and practiced by the first Taoist movements and discussed in their classics.[9] Ge Hong, the most important theologian in early Taoist religion, argued for the necessity of the art of sexual intercourse to achieve longevity and immortality. Even if one were to take all the famous medicines, Hong says, without knowledge of how to save the essence of life in sexual activities, it would be impossible to attain health, let alone longevity. People should not give up sexual intercourse entirely. Otherwise they will contract melancholia through inactivity, and die prematurely from the many illnesses resulting from depression and celibacy. On the other hand, overindulgence diminishes one's life, and it is only by harmonizing the two extremes that damage can be avoided. The art of the bedchamber is easily misunderstood as a guide to enjoying sex, and has sometimes led to obscenity and promiscuousness.

The so-called *art of the bedchamber* is a very broad term, which embraces many theories and techniques from different sects and authors, and is related to sexology, medicine, hygiene, psychology, biophysics, and mysticism. Some Taoist sects use the metaphorical terminology of alchemy to describe and instruct the exercises of the sexual art, while some later Taoist schools wanted to purify their sects by excluding sexual arts from their doctrines.

The art of the bedchamber is multifarious. Here are some general ideas: the essential concept in the art of the bedchamber is *jing (Ching)*, a word meaning "vital essence" and "semen." Ancient Chinese believed that sperm is a kind of life essence, thus the principle of the art of the bedchamber is to save and preserve *jing*, the essence of vital force, in sexual intercourse. Consequently, men should try to postpone and to avoid ejaculation in sexual intercourse in order to save and accumulate the essence of vital force. Foreplay and slow and complete arousal are important for healthy intercourse. Men should pay attention to women's reflexes step by step, and delay climax to adjust for the differential in arousal time between him and her to ensure the woman's full satisfaction. To benefit both men and women, the yoga of sex, a system of techniques, is also necessary for simultaneously stimulating and conserving sexual energy. There are a lot of trivial details and instructions about the action and posture; for example, intercourse at different times, or facing different directions—north, south, east, or west—would cause corresponding effects on health.

Women play an important role in the manuals of sexual hygiene. Kristofer Schipper says that what has been clearly demonstrated is the fact that in every period women have been the initiators in the techniques of the body. In some of the ancient literature concerning the art of the bedchamber, it is goddesses who instruct the Yellow Emperor, the founder of civilization, in the arts of love, healing, and in the begetting of many children. The same goddesses also teach the emperor strategy, which is a closely related science. Schipper also claims that Chinese sex manuals are the only ancient books in the world on this subject that do not present sexuality solely from the male point of view. They reflect a rather impressive knowledge of female anatomy and reflexes (Schipper 1993, 125–126).

Furthermore, according to Douglas Wile, in many texts of the art of the bedchamber, although men are unmistakably both authors and audience, women nevertheless play a highly visible if not equal role. A woman's pleasure is a precondition for releasing her essence to her partner, but recognition of her rights in the bedroom goes beyond simply milking her for sexual secretions. The detailed analysis of women's sexual response bespeaks at least a partial accounting of women's sensibilities and health requirements, in addition to the emphasis on emotional harmonization between partners (Wile 1992, 44). To sum up, although the art of the bedchamber is generally male-centered, and some aspects should be criticized, it has clearly showed knowledge of and concern for women's feeling and happiness, which is noteworthy for men even today.

DISCUSSION: POSITIVE RESOURCES IN TAOISM

How should one understand and interpret the usage of the metaphors related to femininity in Laozi's philosophy? How can we evaluate and appropriate the ideas of equity and harmony of *yin* and *yang* in Taoist religion? These are fundamental in uncovering the positive resources in Taoism for a modern discussion of gender justice. Thus, to discuss these questions is not only an academic investigation, but also is required for the practical application of Taoist positive resources in modern societies. Remember that these richly symbolic traditions house poetic insights of peoples passed down to questions that are always with us.

There are two opposite points of view regarding the female symbol in Taoism. One is represented by Needham, who insists that Taoism derived from the matriarchal society and reflected the worship of the female.

In effect, Joseph Needham claimed that ancient Taoist societies were matriarchal, which is the reason why the symbol of the feminine is so dear to Taoists (Needham 1956, 105). He was followed in turn by Ellen M. Chen, who strongly suspects that the Tao Te Ching as a thought form traces its original inspiration to the existence of a matriarchal society (Chen 1969, 401, 403). This kind of argument is disputed by Schipper, who claims that theories concerning matriarchy in ancient China are far from proven (Schipper 1993, 125).

Even if there were so-called matriarchal societies in ancient China, it was unlikely that Laozi could draw inspiration from them, because the hypothetical matriarchy preceded him by thousands of years. It was too remote for Laozi to recover anything about matriarchy, and there was not yet any literature for his referral. In fact, Laozi doesn't discuss any gender issues. He never even mentions the terms *nan* (man) and *nü* (women). All terms concerning gender, such as *ci* (*ts'u*, "femininity"), *pin* (p'in, "femininity"), and *mother* are repeatedly mentioned only in a metaphorical sense. Female dominance and worship of the female are certainly not of his concern.

Thus, we don't have any evidence to say that Laozi's philosophy is a reflection of a matriarchal tradition and the worship of the mother and the female. The same holds for the Taoist religious tradition. In Taoist belief and practice, there is apparently worship of goddesses, but it is not necessarily worship of the female or worship of her procreative power, although scholars are divided on this (Zhan 1990).

If Taoist doctrines were mainly reflections of a matriarchal tradition and female worship, its positive elements for today's gender discussion would be very limited. We cannot return to or build today new matri-archal societies.

The other extreme of opinion about the feminine characteristics in Laozi's philosophy is proposed by Roger I. Ames. He contends that Laozi's philosophy pursues the androgynous ideal instead of a one-sided exaltation of female characteristics. He argues that the original and originating person in the Taoist tradition is androgynous, rather than either masculine or feminine. Very provocative is the notion that Taoism seems to identify individual, social, and political problems as the result of masculine dominance. The logical implications of this, Ames claims, is that social progress seems to entail integration of the masculine/feminine dichotomy (Ames 1981, 43).

I appreciate Ames's discernment of a Taoist ideal that entails an in-tegration of the masculine and the feminine. Solid textual and concep-tual evidence to support his argument is easy to find. It is not necessary, however, for him to avoid or deny the feminine principle or the femi-nine characteristics in Laozi's thought. It is entirely logical and reason-able for Laozi to emphasize the feminine principle when he sees individual, social, and political problems directly resulting from mas-culine dominance, which is what Ames correctly claimed.

The feminine feature is clearly demonstrated in the Taoist text, which is even more distinct when we compare Laozi with Confucian-ism in China and Christianity in the West. Needham has stressed this contrast between Taoism and Confucianism. He claims that Confucian knowledge was both "masculine and managing" (Needham 1956, 33). The Taoists condemned it and sought a more feminine and receptive knowledge, one that was the fruit of a more passive and yielding atti-tude toward nature.

So also, Chen compares Taoism with Christianity. In Christianity, there is an active asceticism in its stress on work and on the need to battle the flesh for the sake of salvation. Only this way can one accu-mulate merits on earth to gain heaven. And all this aims at winning the favor and love of a father, as in "Our Father in Heaven." Taoism, on the other hand, teaches nonaction, the need to relinquish efforts, to simply abide by the mother and to celebrate the love of the mother (Chen 1969, 403).

Indeed, in comparison with the other religious traditions, Taoism is more feminine than Confucianism, which is in turn more feminine than Christianity. However, both the so-called feminine Taoism and mascu-line Christianity are androgynous in the final analysis from a Taoist per-spective because nothing in the world is pure *yang* or pure *yin*. If we identify Taoism with androgyny, we forfeit the unique feature of Taoism and, in turn, have much less to contribute to issues of gender justice from the Taoist point of view. Still, Ames's work is significant in that he emphasizes the androgynous ideal in Laozi's philosophy as a central symbol for rethinking and rebuilding the relation of the male and the female in the modern world.

Most authors of Taoist texts seem to be male. Is this an advantage or disadvantage for the discussion about gender fairness? Taoist theories of balance and harmony of *yin* and *yang* are different from the female protests against, and resistance to, the empirically historic dominance of the male. Taoist male authors have presented positive ideas and suggestions for modern men about how we should treat women. They do not simply stress what we should not do to them but rather what positively we should do. This is an important resource.

In addition, Taoism metaphysically believes that the balance and harmony of *yin* and *yang* is a universal rule. That is why people should reflect this harmony and balance in their lives. Taoism also believes that the balance and harmony of the feminine and the masculine in the life of an individual and in the practices of society benefit both females and males. Neither the absolute domination of female nor that of male is normal or natural. These theories imply that men should be more active in remedying the injustices of gender relationships, not simply for the sake of women, but also for men themselves.

To sum up, Taoist philosophy presents as ontologically and ethically fundamental the principle of femininity. This offers rich insights for gender harmony and justice. Taoist religion also provides practical instructions for men in how to treat women more fairly. The equality and harmony of *yin-yang* provides an overarching symbol of justice for gender relationships. All this relates creatively to male privilege in the world today and female struggles for justice in relation to that privilege, a struggle that Taoism claims men should join for their own ontological healing.

NOTES

The author wishes to thank all participants of the project for their valuable comments and suggestions, especially the feminist scholars Christine Gudorf, Riffat Hassan, Eva Neumaier-Dargyay, and Laurie Zoloth-Dorfman. The author has learned a lot from their questions and criticisms, and has tried to modify this essay in response to their insight. However, not all their points could be included, partially because of the limitation of the length of the work. Almost one-third of the original draft has been cut. Thus, some general information of Taoism, which is helpful for nonspecialist audiences had to be omitted. For a brief introduction to Taoism, please refer to Liu (1993), or Robinet (1997).

1. After a long and careful textual analysis, I am convinced that the main body of the *Laozi* was probably formed in the sixth or fifth century B.C.E. (Liu 1997, 7–65; Chen 1989, 4–10). For different opinions, see Graham (1990); and Baxter (1998).

2. There are four in chapters 1, 20, 25, and 59, and three in chapter 2.

3. See chapters 21 and 42.

4. Softness appears in chapters 10, 36, 43, 52, 55, 116(x4), and 78(x2). Weakness appears in chapters 3, 36(x2), 40, 55, 76(x3), and 78(x2).

5. The Chinese title of the book is *Yongcheng ji xian lu (Yong-chleng chihsien lu)*. Cahill says that the book contains twenty-eight immortal women; however, Zhan Shichuang says thirty-eight. See Cahill (1993, 214) and Zhan, (1990, 32).

6. *The Sequel to True Immortals Embodying the Way and Discerning the Mirror in All Dynasties (Lishi Zhenxian Tidao Tongjian Houji)*; see Zhan, 34.

7. *Lidai Xianshi*, see Zhan, 35.

8. It is difficult to distinguish the Taoist *art of the bedchamber* from general sexual instructions and techniques because of the ambiguity of the term itself and the diversity of theories concerning sexual arts among Taoist priests and Scriptures. I use two points as standards to identify the Taoist texts concerning the art of bedchamber: first, those that take sexual intercourse as an exercise for the purpose of longevity and immortality, and second, those mentioned by great Taoist theologians and priests in the documents of the Taoist Canon. Schipper proposes a more strict distinction. He insists that the ultimate goal of the Taoist adept was to use intercourse as one way of creating within himself a divine embryo from which the transcendent spirit would emerge. In this act of sexual transformation, the Taoist male identified with the generative aspect of feminine sexuality—not a role assumed by the male in general sex manuals. Cited in Harper (1987, 541 n. 4).

9. For example, see the Five Peck Rice movement, *Laozi Xiang'er Zhu, Taiping Jing*.

REFERENCES

Ames, Roger T. 1981. "Taoism and the Androgynous Ideal." In *Women in China*, Rochard W. Guisso and Stanley Johannesen, eds. Youngstown, NY: Philo Press.

Baxter, William H. 1998. "Situating the Language of the Lao-tzu: The Probable Date of the Tao-te-Ching." In *Lao-tzu and the Tao-te-ching*, Livia Kohn and Michael LaFargue, eds. Albany: State University of New York Press. 231–254.

Cahill, Suzanne. 1986. "Performers and Female Taoist Adepts: Hsi Wang Mu as the Patron Deity of Women in Medieval China." *Journal of the American Oriental Society* 106(1): 155–68.

———. 1993. *Transcendence and Divine Passion: The Queen Mother of the West in Medieval China*. Stanford, CA: Stanford University Press.

Chan, Wing-tsit. 1963. *A Source Book in Chinese Philosophy*. Princeton, NJ: Princeton University Press.

Chen, Ellen M. 1969. "Nothingness and the Mother Principle in Early Chinese Taoism." *International Philosophy Quarterly* 9: 391–405.

———. 1974. "Tao as the Great Mother and the Influence of Motherly-Love in the Shaping of Chinese Philosophy." *History of Religions*, 14 (August): 51–64.

———. 1989. *The Tao Te Ching: A New Translation with Commentary*. New York: Paragon House.

Graham, A. C. 1990. "The Origins of the Legend of Lao Tan." In *Studies in Chinese Philosophy and Philosophical Literature*. Albany: State University of New York Press, 111–124. Reprint in *Lao-tzu and the Tao-te-ching*. Livia Kohn and Michael LaFargue, eds. Albany: State University of New York Press, 1998, 23–40.

Jingmen Musium, 1998. *Guodian Chumu Zhujian (Bamboo slips from Guodian tomb of the Chu)*. Beijing: Wenwu Chubanshe.

Harper, Donald. 1987. "The Sexual Arts of Ancient China as Described in a Manuscript of the Second Century B.C." *Harvard Journal of Asiatic Studies* 47(2):539–593.

Henricks, Robert G. 1991. *Lao-Tzu Te-Tao Ching*. London: Rider, an imprint of Random Century Group.

Hong, Jianlin. 1991, ed. *Daojia Yangsheng Miku*, (Secret collection of Taoist art of nourishing life). Beijing: Dalian Chubanshe.

Lau, D. C. 1987, trans. *Lao Tzu: Tao Te Ching*. Middlesex, England: Penguin Books.

Li Ling, 1993. Zhongguo Fangshu Kao (An investigation into Chinese prescription and exorcism). Beijing: Renmin Zhongguo Chubanshe.

Liu, Xiaogan. 1993. *Taoism. In Our Religions*, Arvind Sharma, ed. San Francisco: Harper San Francisco, 229–289.

———. 1994. *Classifying the Zhuangzi Chapters*, with a foreword by Donald J. Munro. Michigan Monographs in Chinese Studies, no. 65. Ann Arbor: Center for Chinese Studies, University of Michigan.

———. 1997. *Laozi: Niandai Xinkao yu Sixiang Xinquan* (A new investigation of the date and thought of Laozi). Taiwan: Great East Book Co.

———. 1998. "Naturalness (Tzu-jan), the Core Value in Taoism." In *Lao-tzu and the Tab-te-ching*, 211–228.

Kohn, Livia and Michael LaFargue. 1998, eds. *Lao-tzu and the Tao-te-ching*. Albany: State University of New York Press.

Needham, Joseph. 1956. *Science and Civilization in China, Vol. 2*. London: Cambridge University Press.

Ren Jiyu and Zhong Zhaopeng. 1991. Daozang Tiyao (Abstracts of Taoist canon). Zhongguo Shehui Kexue Chubanshe (China social science press).

Robinet, Isabelle. 1997. *Taoism: Growth of a Religion.* Trans. by Phyllis Brooks. Stanford, CA: Stanford University Press.

Schipper, Kristofer. 1993. *The Taoist Body.* Trans. by Karen C. Duval. Berkeley: University of California Press.

Schwartz, Benjamin I. 1985. *The World of Thought in Ancient China.* Cambridge: Harvard University Press.

Wile, Douglas. 1992. *Art of the Bedchamber: The Chinese Sexual Yoga Classics including Women's Solo Meditation Texts.* Albany: State University of New York Press.

Zhan, ShiChuang. 1990. *Taojiao yu nüxing* (Taoism and the female). Shanghai: Shanghai Guji Chubanshe.

10

A Native North American Perspective

To Protect the Ground We Walk On

Christopher Ronwanièn:te Jocks

Prologue

THE MOHAWK PEOPLE ARE ONE of the six Iroquois nations whose original homelands stretch across what is now upstate New York. It is an inland region of richly wooded hills and mountains, bordered on the north by Lake Ontario and the St. Lawrence River, and divided elsewhere by numerous streams, rivers, and lakes. The other Iroquois nations are the Oneidas, the Onondagas, the Cayugas, the Senecas, and after 1722, the Tuscaroras. The traditional languages and cultures of each are distinct yet closely related. The Mohawk people call themselves "Kanien'kehá:ka," which means "People of the Flint Place," referring to their longtime home in what is now called the "Mohawk River Valley," west of Albany. The Mohawks are still understood to inhabit and to guard the eastern door of the Iroquois lands. Today there are eight Mohawk territories, only the most recent and smallest of which is located in the Mohawk Valley. The others are scattered to the north, in an area that includes northern New York, southern Quebec, and the province of Ontario.

259

For almost four hundred years Mohawks have fought to protect their political and cultural sovereignty despite the overrunning of their territory by British, French, and American citizens. Today many Mohawks live in urban centers for at least some parts of their lives, often (though not always) because of employment in high-steel construction, a traditional Mohawk occupation since the late nineteenth century (Hill 1987; Blanchard 1983). Still, most maintain close ties with relatives back home, and return whenever possible. While they are away, some conduct themselves as citizens of either the United States or Canada, but in their own territories most Mohawks consider themselves neither Americans nor Canadians, but members of the Iroquois Confederacy. Some are practicing Christians, predominately Catholic, and some of these profess a traditionally Mohawk understanding of their Catholic identity and commitments. But a significant and growing core devote themselves to the Longhouse, a religious, political, and social way of life whose roots go back in Iroquois country long before the European invasion.

It is impossible to convey in a few words the essence of any cultural or religious tradition, but in its practice as well as in the narratives born of its oral traditions, Iroquois tradition today emphasizes:

a. a strong sense of gratitude for one another and the gifts of creation, manifested in the yearly cycle of ceremonies;

b. the importance of women as the vital, distinct, and indispensable bearers of culture, supported by men;

c. the interrelationship of those areas known in the West as religion, politics, social life, economics, and ecology, as exemplified in the Creation story, the clan system, the tradition known today as the "Great Law," and in some communities, the nineteenth-century teachings of the Seneca visionary, Handsome Lake.

Mohawk people may not embrace U.S. or Canadian citizenship, but they have lived in or near Euramerican civilization from its first introduction to this continent. Their exposure to modernity was not filtered by geographic isolation as was the case with many of the more western and northern indigenous peoples in North America. From the late seventeenth century on, Mohawks and other Iroquois people traveled widely in North America as well as in Europe, and were no strangers to urban life. Today this gives them a unique vantage point from which to reflect and to comment upon the postmodern world and its peculiar predicaments.

The following is an instance of this reflection and commentary. It is not an official nor even a representative statement of Mohawk "theology" or traditional thought on the theme of men's obligations to women. Rather, it is the response of a scholar of religion who happens to be of Mohawk descent, who maintains ties of kinship and descent in Mohawk country, and who has devoted his academic life to the study of Longhouse thought and action.

Living in rural or urban enclaves in the midst of the most technically advanced, ravenously consuming human society in earth's history, Native North American people live their lives almost invisible to the world at large. Either that, or they are associated only with Hollywood images of epic bravery or savagery, purity or promiscuity, or just sad victimization. Even so, five hundred years after the European invasion and its increasingly well-documented legacy of attempted genocide and forced acculturation, key members of these communities still maintain long-standing ties of culture, knowledge, language, and love, with the ground they walk on, this Turtle Island, as well as with their human and more-than-human predecessors. They are painfully aware of history; they believe that human understanding of, and participation in, these ties has been severely damaged and weakened over the past five hundred years. Yet they devote themselves, often passionately and tirelessly, to protecting what is left.

Today the assault on traditional thought and practice is not diminishing but is accelerating, thanks to the same global economic and social forces against which religious people struggle everywhere. Family violence, crime, and other expressions of social pathology, including violence directed at women, are serious problems in virtually every Native community today. Some Native leaders, like political leaders everywhere, take a modern, materialistic approach to these problems. They see poverty as the root cause, and economic development as the most hopeful antidote. But traditionalists often see mainstream economics itself as the problem. For them, traditional relationship structures remain the premises, the sources, the foundations, of all that is worthwhile, meaningful, and enjoyable in collective and individual life.

Within these communities today, "what men owe to women" has to do with repairing the damage done to these ways of thinking and doing: restoring, strengthening, sometimes adapting and updating them so they make sense and function now; so they promote the life and livelihood of "all our relations" at the beginning of the twenty-first century. But that is not the story I will tell here. Rather, I will air my views as to what *other* women and men might take into consideration when considering the dilemma of "what men owe to women," having considered something of the historical and recent experiences of one specific indigenous North American people, the Mohawk Nation, of the

Iroquois group of nations.[1] I build my response around the notion of protection: physical protection of communities, of the doings of women that are at the heart of those communities, and protection of the more-than-human world and all its inhabitants, perceived by Mohawks as the groundwork and source of all life. I hope that feminist readers will not be offended by the designation of "protection" as an obligation of men, because in a traditional Mohawk context this is not in the least correlated with notions of women's weakness, but instead, with an acknowledgment that certain physical and emotional qualities more commonly found and cultivated among men are useful for the actual defense of communities from physical attack.[2] In fact, in many cases this protection has been directed by women, both historically and in recent times. The more important aspect of my thesis is that in the Mohawk world as in most, perhaps all, of Native North America, it is not possible to separate the obligations of men to women, and the obligations of women and men to the ground on which we walk.

GIVING THANKS

The word *longhouse* refers to the matrilineal clan-administered, multi-family physical living structures in which Mohawk and other Iroquois people lived until the middle eighteenth century. By extension, the word now refers to a well-developed social, ceremonial and, in some cases, political tradition with strong roots in that past. It also refers to the people who follow those ways, and to the physical structures where they now meet for social, political, and ceremonial gatherings. Any such gathering, no matter what its function, begins with a ritual known in the Mohawk language as *ohén:ton karihwatéhkwen*, the "Opening," sometimes called the "Thanksgiving Address."[3] In it the speaker draws the minds of the listeners into a journey through all of creation, proceeding in a gradual upward direction from the earth we stand on to the powerful Beings who are understood to inhabit the Sky World. As each entity is named, the speaker describes its role in the maintenance of life, according to gathered and maintained Longhouse thought. "And we see that even today," the speaker will say, for example, "the grasses and medicinal plants are present and continue to fulfill their duty. For this we express our thanks, and so our minds are together."[4]

  The Iroquois manner of giving thanks is profound, complex, and central to Longhouse practice. More than just a sentiment of personal or collective gratitude, it expresses and embodies the vision of an animate cosmos maintained and energized through reciprocal relationships of responsibility and enjoyment that involve all living beings, not only humanity. In fact, human beings are exceptional not for their superior intellect or their eternal "soul." Instead, of all creation they are the weakest, the most prone to moral failure. So the thanksgiving ritual urges them (us) to reflect on how all of creation continues to do its part, and thus, how we need to rededicate ourselves to assisting in the support of life. This is our highest calling, what some modern Longhouse speakers have called our "Original Instructions."[5] Yet in doing all this, the ritual instills not just an intellectual awareness, nor simply a sense of obligation or urged assent. It generates an emotion of palpable happiness, as speaker and listeners consider together this beautiful universe, of which we are all integral parts. The work of culture demands an expenditure of time and effort. But look what it makes possible! This emotional response is not incidental, but essential, to the work of *ohén:ton karihwatéhkwen*. When the ritual is done well, when the minds of the people are brought together and filled with warmth and respect, it is said that "the Good Mind" *(ka'nikonhrí:io)* has been joined. Then the "doings" can begin.

Just as this ritual begins most gatherings, whether for ceremonial purposes, for political or decision-making purposes, or for enjoying an evening of visiting and traditional social dances, so too it begins my reflection on men's obligations to women. From the publication of Lewis Henry Morgan's *League of the Hau-de-no-sau-nee* in 1851, outside commentators have noted the distinctive, important place of women in the Iroquois world.[6] Some, like Morgan, have gone so far as to designate Iroquois societies as "matriarchal." Longhouse commentators today reject this label, preferring to speak of the balance between genders, with neither in a position of dominance. My observations support this response, but whether our reference is Morgan in 1851 or *Ms.* magazine in 1991, my point is that the status of Iroquois women is firmly grounded in *ohén:ton karihwatéhkwen*. To the extent that human society subjugates or diminishes women, it will damage, through that behavior toward them, the relationships that bind humanity with its own more-than-human relatives (so-called nature). As this happens, the values of generosity, reciprocity, and long-term responsibility become increasingly vulnerable to the impulses of exploitation, violence, and short-term gain. If the most fundamental imperative of human culture is to celebrate and maintain the interrelationships between humans and other entities—the synchronic patterns and diachronic cycles that provide the basis for all—then how can it but honor and respect and listen to women, who are closer than men to some of its most mysterious regenerative powers?

On the other hand, from the perspective of the modern democratic ethos, any reference to the biology of gender difference, even positive reference, is suspect. Abstract notions of an absolute equality of choice appear to be undermined when women are associated with motherhood, nurturing, or the care and guidance and teaching of children. From the perspective of traditional Iroquois women and men, however, such associations are sources of honor and respect. In fact, it seems to be a disturbing indicator of cultural pathology in the broader society that occupations concerned with the raising of children are generally considered less important, and are paid at much lower levels, than careers associated with the buying and selling of things. Besides, in its association of women with the nurturing, generative mysteries of earth, Iroquois tradition does not value women simply because it is they who have babies and nurse them. Just as a man may fulfill the traditional roles of protector or provider or vision seeker through many kinds of occupations, so there are many ways of "mothering" for modern Iroquois women. Women are respected because they nurture the spirit of the people and remind them of their responsibilities, their kinship with all life. So can men. But somehow women are understood to have a greater aptitude for these things; they are likely to understand these kinds of concerns more dependably and more often than men. The experience of biologic motherhood is only one means of embodying this capacity. In actual fact, childless women are sometimes chosen to be clan mothers.[7] Audrey Shenandoah, a contemporary Iroquois clan mother from the Onondaga people, puts it like this:

> The women within our own society have a special place of honor. We have the ability to bring forth life to this earth. We are given, further, the sacred responsibility of nurturing that life from the beginning, from the most necessary and important time in a human's life; from the time that they are infants and learning their first things about living, teaching them, first ways, that they must treat one another as humans, that they are to survive.

> All through a person's life, from the time they are conceived, from the time they are born, until the time they leave this earth, their care is truly in the hands of the women, the mothers of our nations, and that is a sacred trust. (Shenandoah 1991, 22)

Therefore, if men everywhere are to consider their obligations to women, these thoughts suggest that Longhouse traditions might begin by urging the following: First, men could recover their sense of deep, transforming gratitude for the gifts of creation, and commit themselves to supporting and protecting those gifts. From the Iroquois Longhouse perspective, this will lead naturally to respect for women, since the centrality of female powers and qualities in all communities of beings seems obvious upon even the most cursory observation. Second, men could follow the lead of *ohén:ton karihwatéhkwen* further, and cultivate strong communities of reciprocal relations; communities that include *all* the beings with whom we share place. Many Native traditions would agree that close and respectful observation of the more-than-human members of these communities will reveal who among them are the senior, charter members. Third, men will then want to work these discoveries into their storytelling traditions, reviving their love of language and other forms of creative expression.

MINDFULNESS, IROQUOIS STYLE

The distinction between reason and emotion, thinking and feeling, or cognition and affect, has long been a cornerstone of Western philosophical and religious reflection. It also has deep roots in everyday life and usage, and is an important aspect of mainstream methods in education. Could we imagine a worldview, a way of life, a philosophical system in which nothing similar to this basic distinction existed?—A system not rooted in the vision of 'o λόγɑ(reason) As it turns out, the Mohawk language is part of such a system. In it there is no way to distinguish between the two—reason and emotion—as broad and contrasting categories; for instance, the same noun-root that is used to form the basic noun *o'nikón:hra*, usually translated as "mind," or the verb *wake'nikonhraiénta's*, "I understand it," is also used to build expressions translated as, "I am discouraged," "I tempt him," "I am pleased about it," "be careful!" or "her or his mind is stuck on it," this last referring to any kind of mental/emotional attachment. Here is one linguist's morphological analysis of these and a couple of related compositions:

wake'nikonhró:kten	*se'nikòn:rarak*
I-mind-lack-[suffix]	you-mind-watch/guard
"I became discouraged, gave up"	"be careful!"
take'nikonhrahní:rat	*ri'nikonhratákwas*
you to me-mind-tight-[suffix]	I to him-mind-take out-[suffix]
"give me courage!"	"I tempt him"

iako'nikonhra'nontá:kon

her-mind-stuck to it

"her mind is stuck on it,
   attached to it" [e.g., to property]

ionte'nikonhrahawíhta'

she-[ ]-mind-[ ]-slide, move-[suffix]

"she moves her mind" [physically]

wake'nikonhraiénta's

I-mind-receive-[suffix]

"I understand it"

iako'nikonhranòn:waks

she-mind-hurt-[suffix]

"her mind is hurting,
   she's suffering mentally"

(Druke 1980)

While these translations employ the standard gloss of "mind" for the basic meaning of the noun root -*'nikonhr-*, it is clear that its meanings extend far beyond the usual meaning of "mind" in English. They include what in that language would be regarded as emotional and psychological states and qualities of volition. These are only tentative suggestions at this point. Corroboration would require extensive investigation not only in terms of morphology and lexicography, but structures at the sentence, and at the discourse-level as well. But as yet I have found nothing that points toward either "pure reason," or unbridled emotion, as concepts that are even specified or defined in Iroquois language or culture. That a human being might be able to think and act on the basis of an abstract rationality devoid of emotion, unconnected to the personal valences and colors of the situation and context; that such a rationality could even be conceived of I suspect would seem to be almost unthinkable, especially before the invasion of European ideologies.

This is but a theory, but there is more to it. It should not be read to imply that there are no distinctions in Iroquois thought or language between qualities of mind reflected in action. Rather, it seems that a different distinction takes the place at the thinking/feeling polarity, one that is revealed in the basic grammar of Mohawk verbs. It concerns whether the person being spoken of is the determining *agent* in relation to the emotion-thoughts with which they are being associated, or whether they are a receiving *patient* thereof.[8] Some of these distinctions are straightforward in relation to English; for example, *kkwítha* (I move it), *kató:rats* (I hunt it), *ké:saks* (I look for it), and *kón:ni*, (I make it). These are all verbs that take the agent form, while *wakí:ta's* (I sleep), *wakotá:se* (I receive it), *wakáhta's*, (I have my fill), and *waké:ka's* (I find it tasty) take the patient, receptive form.

Others, however, don't seem to correspond as well; for example, *kí:tenhre* (I have pity on it) is constructed as an agent form, as is *kentórha*

(I am lazy), while *wakeniténhton* (I am humble) and *wakiéhson* (I smile or laugh), are patient or passive forms. Feeling pity is something a person does actively, while humility is something that happens to that person. Being lazy is a deliberate act; smiling is not. Some verbs can use either agent or patient and passive constructions, in which case the distinctions can be revealing; for instance, the agent form in *ie'nikonhráksen* ("she [agent]-mind-is bad") leads to the gloss, "she is evil-minded"; while the patient form in *iako'nikonhráksen* ("she [patient]-mind-is bad") is glossed as "she is sad; she is crying over sadness."[9]

The words that most surprise an English speaker with regard to being agent or patient and passive, seem to describe emotional or habitual states. This suggests that speakers of the Mohawk language may not understand these states in the same way that English speakers do. At the very least, the nature and origins of some aspects of personality, identity, or subjective experience may be understood differently. Western imagination easily associates reason with male gender and emotion with female, producing such cultural images as the emotional homemaker swept away by a romantic novel or soap opera, versus the shrewd, calculating, successful male as military planner or as business executive. For anyone who finds such stereotypes disturbing, there could be some utility in considering a system of thought, not only in which men and women are not so typed, but in which the abstraction behind the typology *does not even exist*. "What men owe to women," then, might include, for each act of theorizing, each abstraction, every policy-making initiative and its implementation, the obligation to more actively take into account its emotional underpinning and consequences. It might include, as well, an obligation to more actively seek to understand the logic of emotions, the choices we make when we name emotions, and the implicit statements they make for us about the nature and structure of consciousness, experience, and relationships.

In Longhouse discourse the concept of "the good mind," *ka'nikonhrí:io,* is a cornerstone. Cultivating it is one of the prime obligations of being human. Its signs are at once affective and cognitive. Under its influence, we feel warmth and gratitude toward all our relatives, human and otherwise, and we feel a sense of responsibility to continue to provide the best conditions possible for all to thrive. But at the same time, the Good Mind is manifested in clear thinking and in clear, persuasive speaking. The most highly regarded speakers in the Longhouse are not the loudest or the most passionate, but those who speak clearly and calmly, whose words are well-organized and well-considered, who listen closely and patiently, and who are able to put immediate, pressing issues into a longer perspective for the good of all. There is an alternative model to Western modes of leadership at work here, and it is worthy of thought as we consider "what men owe to women."

THE HOLDERS OF TITLES

Most readers will have had most of their experience grounded in cultures of patriarchy, or at least, strongly influenced by it. As a result, when we read that in Iroquois tradition: "women are respected because they nurture the spirit of the people and remind them of their responsibilities, their kinship with all life," we may assume that this respect is something granted or conceded to women *by men*, because again, we expect the work of culture to be primarily the work of men. Such a statement might well lead us to investigate whether or to what extent this respect is real, as opposed to merely symbolic; that is, how *real* women—wives, daughters, sisters, co-workers, and neighbors—are understood and treated by men in relation to mythical female entities. But in the Iroquois case, emphatically it is both women and men who make culture. Women's authority comes not only from their abstract relationships with natural forces and with culture as cultivation, as construed by Longhouse tradition. More concretely, women are also understood to be the keepers or holders of three kinds of titles that make organized human life possible. These are:

1. title to land;
2. clan names or titles that link every individual to the land, to the community, and to their shared history;
3. fifty chiefs' titles that form the basis of the traditional Iroquois system of government.

These are titles in an Iroquois sense. They convey responsibility for the care of others, both human and otherwise: not freedom to command others or to profit by their efforts. All these titles are held by the clans, membership in which is matrilineal. According to the teachings I have heard, the Iroquois clan system was instituted by an inspired male because human beings needed structure to remind them of their dependence on each other, and their dependence on the rest of creation. Yet it was women elders who discovered the names and identities of the clans, and so became the original Clan Mothers. They did this by closely observing the world around them as they gave their thanks to the Creator. Thomas Porter (Sakokwenienkwas) translates the original instruction.

> He told the people that they should be very observant of anything
> that seemed unusual, especially in the early morning hours of the
> day. He specifically told the women, who were the eldest of each
> family, to be especially watchful. He also told them that they must
> give thanks (prayer) to the Creator who in fact is the maker of the
> whole universe and all its life. (Porter n.d., 3)[10]

Out of this symbolic priority, tremendous concrete responsibilities
developed. Before the European invasion it was the clans that organized and supervised all of the people's activity on cleared land, including the division of tilled fields. (In this sense, they are sometimes said in
English to have "owned" the land, although again, this is not land own-
ership in the sense of having authority to *sell* the land.) The clans
"owned" the living structures as well, and they distributed not only the
vegetable crops grown in the village fields, but the meat that men
brought in from hunting in the forests. Finally, the clans maintain and
assign names. This is still done ritually, twice a year. Clan names convey
membership in the Longhouse, and relate an individual to those that
have gone before, since the names are "recycled" from former, deceased
holders within the clan. An intense effort has been underway in all Iroquois communities during the last thirty years to revive people's understanding of traditional naming, and to promote and facilitate more
rigorous application of these procedures, where they had in recent
times become lax.

Thus in the traditional vision, in many different ways, it is the
women, through the clan system, who maintain and care for the very
heart of the community's *culture*—in the radical sense of the fertile
ground, made up of the living and the dead, from which shared community grows. These important roles became even more pronounced
under the system of all-Iroquois, intervillage governance known in English as the "Great Law" (in Mohawk, the *Kaianeren'kó:wa*).[11] In that system, clan mothers were given the responsibility of maintaining and
assigning the clan's chiefly titles, which are carried by men, theoretically
for life. Yet I say "theoretically," because the clan mothers give, but they
can also remove a chief's name and authority if he is deemed to have
abused the office and has refused for the traditional three times to correct his behavior. Furthermore, separate councils of women have always
existed, whose assent to all significant decisions is required. As Shenandoah remarks:

> The clan mother's duties have to do with the community affairs, the
> nation affairs, but they also have another role and that has to do
> with the spiritual side. They set ceremonial times and watch the

moon for our people. We . . . still have those people who must watch
the phases of the moon, who know when it is time to call the faith
keepers and the women together to sit, and to set time for the ceremonies which are held at various times throughout the year. . . .
(Shenandoah 1991, 22)

In addition to these political and ceremonial duties, clan mothers
have social and personal responsibilities as well. Shenandoah recounts
the responsibility this way:

[The clan mother] must be ready to call her clan people together if
a person from another clan has suffered sickness, some kind of
tragedy or emergency. Any time a family needs help, the duty of
the clan mother is to tell her people and to designate people in her
clan to go over and help that family, for it is our way that we do not
leave a family alone in time of trouble, we must be there to help
them. (Shenandoah 1991, 22)

This prominence, which in Iroquois context is a prominence of responsibilities rather than of privilege, is emphasized in the traditional
narrative of the Great Law's origin, which is considered and treated as an
integral part of the tradition.[12] In that narrative it is often said that a
woman, *Tsikonhsáhsen* ("Her face is new;" sometimes "Lynx," or "Her
face is fat"), is the first to accept this new inspiration, this new way of life,
which turns out to be a revitalization and extension of very old notions of
community, communication, and responsibility. Later in the story, in several versions at least, the efforts of the Peacemaker to heal and convert the
cannibal Atotárho, the last holdout against the League, are unsuccessful
until he adds *Tsikonhsáhsen* to the ones who "shall together form a circle,
standing alongside your body." Here is one version of the Peacemaker's
(*Tekanawita's*) speech at this point as translated by John Arthur Gibson:

"Now, moreover, it is accomplished;
now she has arrived,
our mother, the Great Matron whose name is Tsikonhsahsen;
now she has accepted the Good Message,
and this moreover is what you should confirm and adopt,
the Great Law,
so that she may place antlers on you, our mother,
and they shall together form a circle, standing alongside your body."
Thereupon the man [Atotárho] looked at Tekaihoken and Hayenhwatha' and
    Tsha'tekaihwate' and Ho'tatshehte' and Kanonhkwen'yoton' and Tioha'kwente'
    and Haka'enyonk and Tsi'nontawenhe' and Skanyataiyo' and Tsha'tekaenhyes.

Thereupon Tekanawita said,
"Now you are looking at all of the ones who will be standing with you."
Thereupon the man bowed his head.
Thereupon his hair stopped writhing and all of his fingers became quiet.
Thereupon Tekanawita said,
"Now, indeed, it is functioning, the Peace." (Gibson 1993, 221–239)

MODERN TIMES

Today, the authority and respect claimed by Iroquois women continues to distinguish not only political and ceremonial life but everyday life as well, in Kahnawake as in other communities. If a woman chooses to speak up, she can expect to be listened to. She follows a long tradition. A poignant example occurred in 1912, when most of the able-bodied young men of Kahnawake, already famous as high-steel construction workers, were working on a single job, an ambitiously designed bridge over the St. Lawrence River at Quebec. On August 29, 1907, the center span collapsed, killing ninety-six men, including thirty-three Mohawks. Only five Mohawks survived; it was a serious tragedy for the small community. But the women of the village met while they grieved, and dictated that henceforth the Mohawk men would split up, and never again all work at the same site. At the insistence of their women and their sense of the long-term safety of the community, the men agreed to sacrifice, in the short-term, some measure of ease, efficiency, and camaraderie (Hill 1987, 22).

More recently, women were prominent on the front lines, as well as behind-the-scenes, during the so-called Oka Crisis of 1990, in which military and police forces of Quebec and Canada blockaded and invaded Mohawk communities at Kanehsatake and Kahnawake. Their purpose was to destroy Native resistance to a land development scheme that involved a golf course expansion and luxury home development on a tract of land known as "the Pines." The land had been used exclusively by Mohawks since the mid-eighteenth century, and they insisted that it had been taken from them illegally. The quiet, wooded grounds were important to the Indian community, in no small part because of the dead buried there.[13]

Documentary accounts of the conflict leave no doubt that women were key leaders of the Mohawk resistance. But women were just as important in the less political work of assisting people not directly involved in the confrontation through what became a very difficult summer.[14] When a complete government blockade was enforced around Kahnawake, women there quickly organized a food bank, and traveled around the village to ensure that no family or individual was left alone or without food.

Another incident is perhaps even more emblematic of the respect commanded by Mohawk women. On September 18, Canadian army troops landed by helicopter on Tekakwitha Island and attempted to invade Kahnawake in an illegal search for weapons. They did not expect significant resistance, and so were surprised when an angry crowd of Mohawk people blocked their way into town, determined to stop them. A fight broke out, and there is video footage of a Mohawk hospital administrator steering her wheelchair directly through the melee of tear gas, screaming and throwing rocks in order to make the soldiers stop. The tear gas, she said, was drifting onto the nearby hospital grounds, causing breathing difficulties for some of the elderly patients. Mohawk women are not known for passivity, nor for waiting around in a crisis for their menfolk to decide it is time to take action. (The attempted invasion failed. Fortunately for all, the soldiers were ordered not to fire their weapons. Eventually they were ordered to retreat.)

Yet it is not only in times of crisis that the distinctive nature of gender relations in Mohawk/Iroquois life is evident. At Kahnawake, the matrilineal clan system was considerably weakened by the patrilineal laws and policies of British Canada and French Quebec, as well as by the influence and customs of the Catholic Church. From the late nineteenth until the mid-twentieth century, Canadian law attempted to enforce patrilineal rules of divorce, property inheritance, and even community membership. Even so, women in all of the Mohawk communities never relinquished or were deprived of their everyday authority and respect in local matters. In some cases, notably in efforts over the last thirty years to revive the clan system and other important aspects of traditional life, women have been visibly in the fore. Women have led and predominately staffed Kahnawake's vital social service organizations as well as its education system, with its strong emphasis on Mohawk language immersion and cultural education. Men have supported them in this work, whether in the context of Longhouse Men's and Women's councils, or in more informal modes of collaboration. Even in families with no connection to Longhouse traditionalism, one finds that it is considered traditional not just for women to be listened to or consulted, but to take the lead in matters concerning community welfare and the future. It is considered traditional for men to contribute to these deliberations and to support the decisions that result from the women's initiative.

The lesson for men elsewhere, from Mohawk experience, is that the practical as well as symbolic authority of women must be recognized. Once again, the modern democratic ideal is to erase (read, "forget") gender and other cultural distinctions. But if women choose to organize politically, culturally, socially, or in any other way, *as women*, can men learn to accept this, and to actually heed their voices, in other words, accord them real power, *as women?* How many men in business or community organizations would accept veto power over major political or economic decisions to be held by women's groups? How many would install procedures to regularly elicit agenda items from such groups? How different might our government and business organizations be if such things took place? It is perhaps in comparison with a tradition such as that of the Iroquois Longhouse, that we men might begin to see more clearly how deeply embedded patriarchy is in our social and political structures.

CONCLUSION: CONSUMING OUR MOTHER

The Mohawk word *onwnéntsia* is translated as "nation," or "people." The Iroquois Confederacy, for example, can be called *wisk nihonwentsiá:ke* (Five Nations). However, the root of this word conveys a profoundly Iroquois concept of nationhood with important implications. Its fundamental meaning is of something in the ground—basement, cultivation, and excavation are all translated into Mohawk with this root. Nationhood is thus something that is rooted in the ground, rooted in the land where a people lives, and to their relationship to that land. For this reason, a frequent ritual oration speaks of our concern for the future by pointing out our care for the generations yet unborn and describing them as "those whose faces are looking up to us from the ground."

This relationship of people to their ground is not only the subject of religious reflection or ceremonial enactment; it is the basic "stuff" of any economy. Ultimately, even in the twenty-first century, it is from the ground that we will continue to keep ourselves alive. How we do this, in a Mohawk or Iroquois view, says as much about our underlying nationhood *and religion* as our pieties and ceremonial gestures, maybe more. I would suggest that it also determines, in large part, the limits of our ability as men to accord the women of our communities the love and respect that some of us, at least, feel they are due. The marketplace, indeed, eats away our humanity, and leaves us with less than adequate resources to effect the changes we yearn for, even as it eats away at the vitality of our real, physical "culture"—our soil, our ground, our Mother.

The global technological economic engine is the most powerful force of our times. Yet it is scarcely possible to imagine anything more completely alien to traditional economies in most Native communities. These economies were powered not by accumulation or development or expansion or profit, but by *giveaway*. An individual or a community gained respect and admiration by giving away time, giving away goods, attention, and care. In some contexts, ceremonies became extravagant exercises in giving away, effecting not only social or economic vitality and stability, but transformation and renewal of the entire physical/natural world with all its inhabitants. But giveaway worked in everyday scenes as well, in countless small gestures and exchanges. It was a way of life, and in damaged form, still is. In his cowritten autobiography, John (Fire) Lame Deer, a Lakota, tells about a man who lost a leg in an industrial accident, only to blow the entire insurance payout, some fifteen thousand dollars, on entertaining friends and relatives for weeks on end. The man had no regrets, as Lame Deer recalls. Rather, he said he wished he might lose his other leg so that he could start the gift-giving all over again. Such a man became quite a hero, even to other tribes, and he was, Lame Deer claims, welcome everywhere (Lame Deer and Erdoes 1972, 45–46). Now here, from a Native point of view, was a *man*. The various, more-than-human members of the cosmic community continue to give of themselves for the continuation of all life; the highest religious calling of a human being, from this perspective, is to do likewise.

Thus it seems to me that the inroads of technology and economy have done more to subvert traditional life than Christian missionaries or even soldiers ever could have done. Even where Native people have resisted conquest intellectually, we have all been colonized, to one extent or another, whatever our race, by the marketplace. If exploitation of the earth we live on, and exploitation of the customers we persuade to buy our products stand noisily behind our every transactions, how then can we men hope to relate more equitably with women? Or, how can we hope to improve our relations with women enough to make any significant difference? These are the large forces, and against them we find ourselves capable of only small, corrective moves.

As an American Indian man, it is easy for me to become discouraged as I see First Nations' languages eroding, and the economic values of global exploitation landing like weeds and setting everywhere deep roots in Native soil. The cultures of First Nations do not have magic answers for these times. Most Native people are too busy with their own economic, political, and psychological survival to have much heart left for teaching others about giveaway. What some of us can offer, though, is a little history and perhaps a few ideas. Human societies have existed, and have thrived, and have built their worlds differently. Individuals with strong memories and vital strands of that knowledge remain. Our soils are poorer now; our stock of traditional seeds much weakened. But we continue to plant, to grow perhaps some tougher varieties that can withstand this dry season.

We Indian men have a special obligation, inherited from previous generations of warriors and hunters and keepers of knowledge. The sacrifices and protection they fashioned made it possible for us to grow up and survive; to know something of the paths and the knowledge that brought our people, or our relatives, or our communities to where we stand now. Now we owe the same to our children, and to their children, all those whose faces look up to us from the ground. We must continue to protect the seeds that remain, and the ground where those seeds must be planted. We must continue to protect and assist and comfort the women as they plant these seeds and care for them. We can nourish seeds too, with our love, with our labor, and with the songs and stories we men strive to learn. We will feel the pain and the shame of what has been lost, perhaps forever. But we need to find, as well, the hope of what can still return to us.

EPILOGUE

Native North American traditionalists whom I have met, whether Mohawk or Ojibwe, Pueblo or Apache, always express far more interest in how people live, and what they've learned about the world around them, than what they say they believe in. The "walk" is more telling than the "talk." For this reason, a textually based study of gender relations, of what men might be thought and said to owe women in these wordy traditions, cannot be very fruitful. Texts there are, but they are stories—events, really, meant to maintain and deepen certain culturally prioritized perceptions and abilities, to strengthen people's bonds with each other, and with their place and past, and to gain thereby a maturity to choose what is helpful to preserve their future dominance from the constant offerings of what remains, nevertheless an essentially alien and colonizing civilization. Arguments in Indian discourses over the "correct" interpretation of doctrine regarding gender, or anything else, are not customary or helpful.

For these and for other reasons I have found less than completely satisfying this attempt to present a North American First Nations perspective on the issue of "what men owe to women." For First Nations people this is not a matter of doctrine, not a matter of correcting misogynistic religious texts or interpretations of texts. Answers can only come from the contexts of specific lives, as they are found in specific places, connected to particular pasts and to the lives of particular communities of human and more-than-human beings.

Perhaps there is something to the suggestion that monotheism might somehow be inherently patriarchal, or at least, might be said to create conditions favorable to patriarchy. Is it an accident that the most severely monotheistic religious traditions seem to be associated with the most severely patriarchal cultures? Mohawk/Iroquois tradition actually has a monotheistic strain today, thanks to the influence of the teachings of the Seneca visionary, Handsome Lake, in the early nineteenth century, and of other cultural leaders who were unavoidably influenced to one degree or another by Christianity. Yet the more decentralized and diversified of religious observances embedded in Longhouse practice, those posited on a complex universe composed of many sources of power, of life, and of destruction, seem to be undergoing the strongest revival in recent years. Part of the import of these developments is an increasing seriousness of regard, of study, of reverence, for the multicentered natural world. Corollary to this is an increasing commitment to the clan system, under the leadership of the clan mothers, as the basis for twenty-first century traditional life and survival. I think it is safe to say that the Mohawk response to the issue of "what men owe to women" will only gain in vitality from these religious recoveries of past but not lost wisdom.

Members of other Native nations in North America might respond differently.[15] Not all of them base their traditional lives on matrilineal clans. Not all have clear formal authority vested in women as Iroquois tradition has. In many cases informal practice more than makes up for the absence of formal authority. But there are places in Indian country today where abuse of women has become a critical problem; in fact it is not unheard-of in Mohawk communities. In the face of the tremendous odds against which any Native person or community battles to secure a traditional way of life, identity, and web of relationships; in the midst of modernity and postmodernity, can one wonder why despair and rage sometimes win out. But I see in the earnest work of Mohawk traditionalists to understand, to revive, to deepen, and to expand their inherited knowledge and way of life, an important and instructive ideal for all men and women to consider regarding, "what men owe to women."

NOTES

1. Most of the examples I will cite derive from Mohawk traditions and experience, or from the larger Iroquois Longhouse world of which they are a part. I have attempted to avoid the publication of any knowledge that is protected by traditional restrictions. I apologize in advance for any errors I may have made, on this or on any other account.

2. To think of defense in this way may seem like a vestige of a long-distant barbaric past to privileged men and women in the world today, but it has been a fact of life in Mohawk country as recently as 1990, when in a series of confrontations armed and armored state and provincial law enforcement personnel, as well as federal army troops, invaded Mohawk territories at Kanehsatake, Akwesasne, and Kahnawake.

3. The authoritative scholarly texts on *ohén:ton karihwatéhkwen* are Chafe (1961) and Foster (1974). For obvious reasons, the one type of gathering where *ohén:ton karihwatéhkwen* does not take place consists of mourning rituals.

4. *Ohén:ton karihwatéhkwen* is normally spoken in Mohawk (or in one of the other Iroquois languages), although it is sometimes done in English, depending on who is attending. This is my own English gloss of the kind of statement one hears.

5. This idea appears frequently in discussions of Longhouse tradition found in the pages of *Akwesasne Notes*, published since the late 1960s from the Mohawk Nation at Akwesasne, whose mailing address is via Rooseveltown, NY. This journal is now the official publication of the Mohawk traditional council of chiefs. Another good example can be found in a July 1991 PBS interview with Oren Lyons, Onondaga, faithkeeper for the traditional council at Onondaga, by Bill Moyers ("Oren Lyons: The Faithkeeper").

6. This classic of early anthropology is read in numerous subsequent editions. It should not go unnoted that Morgan, in the same chapter in which he outlines some of the significant authority over traditional daily life vested in Iroquois women, feels compelled, nonetheless, to interject the well-worn stereotype that "The Indian regarded woman as the inferior, the dependent, and the servant of man, and from nurture and habit, she actually considered herself to be so" (Morgan 1854/1901, 324). A full discussion of this seeming contradiction would need to address at least three sets of issues: the sources and possible biases employed by the author, Morgan; the differences between ideals and actual personal attitudes and actions about women by Iroquois men; and the effects of Iroquois exposure to Euramerican gender mores, particularly through Christianization.

7. I am not in a position to answer the question as to whether women who have never married, perhaps women who might be regarded in the mainstream as lesbians, could be or have been clan mothers. If it is some kind of inward sense or aptitude that is idealized and sought after when choosing clan mothers rather than the outward experience of motherhood, then it would stand to reason that the outward experience of marriage or of heterosexual relations, would not be required either. On the other hand, there is a kind of social conservatism about the Longhouse that does emphasize a standard version of family life, however extended. This was a strong emphasis in the teachings of Handsome Lake, the early-nineteenth-century Longhouse reformer and traditionalist.

8. The distinction is roughly analogous to the English distinction between active and passive forms, but not identical. This relates deeply to Liu Xiaogan's reflections on Taoism.

9. Again, Druke (1980) is the source of these glosses.

10. The same account can be found in a narrative published by the anthropologist Hewitt, in which this inspired man, described as "a male human being, one with the body of a youth, who ever had very little to say, who was an upright and good person," declares: "So then, thus it shall come to pass; just before the daylight will have fully dawned, she, the most elderly one in each uterine family (*ohwachira*) shall go to fetch fresh water to be used when she will prepare food; so then when she dips up the water she must notice carefully what kind of thing she will see, so then, she must by no means forget it" (Hewitt 1928, 594, 598–599).

11. *Kaianeren'kó:wa* is easily translated. It describes a way of doing things that results in great peace, great benefit, the way human society was intended to be; in other words, which promotes the "Original Instructions." The *Kaianeren'kó:wa* was thought by scholars to have arisen as recently as the early sixteenth century C.E. But Longhouse elders have generally thought it much older. Mann and Fields (1997) argue for a specific founding date of 1142.

12. In the Longhouse, the tradition of the *Kaianeren'kó:wa* is maintained not by reference to any of the written versions of its "text," but by periodic live recitations. In these recitations the rules or procedures by which the traditional Iroquois Confederacy is to operate are never recited until the narrative of their origin is told. The narrative is not an entertaining add-on. I see this as indicating an important tenet of Iroquois epistemology: that human knowledge is always contextual; one cannot know anything without knowing the story of its origins and its travels, including the story of how one has learned it oneself.

13. An interesting matter of semantics and cultural politics: One may note how the generally sympathetic liberal anglophone press tended to prefer the term *burial ground*, with its popular aura of primitive, earthy reverence, to the more modern, utilitarian *cemetery*, in its descriptions of this aspect of the conflict.

14. The most comprehensive publication is probably York and Pindera 1992, which is generally sympathetic in its description of the Warrior Society's role in the conflict. The neotraditionalist Warrior Society headed the military defense of Kahnawake and Kanehsatake, but was in conflict with the Confederacy chiefs at Onondaga and Akwesasne. Johansen (1993, chap. 6), presents the latter's point of view.

15. The literature on gender issues in Native North American societies has grown considerably in the last fifteen years. Woodsum (1995) is an excellent bibliography of both historical and contemporary sources, arranged topically. Several recent sources on women's lives and roles, symbolic and real, deserve particular note. General or comparative sources include Green (1980), Bonvillain (1989), Medicine (1993), Shoemaker (1995), and Klein and Ackerman (1995).

Important studies of women in specific First Nations contexts would have to include two classics of anthropology: Reichard (1934) and Landes (1938/1997). More recent specific studies would include Powers (1986), Spittal (1990), Stockel (1990), and Perdue (1998).

REFERENCES

Blanchard, David. 1983. "High Steel: Kahnawake Mohawk and the High Construction Trade." *Journal of Ethnic Studies* 11, 41–60.

Bonvillain, Nancy. 1989. "Gender Relations in Native North America." American Indian Culture and Research Journal 13(2): 1–28.

Chafe, Wallace L. 1961. *Seneca Thanksgiving Rituals.* Bureau of American Ethnology Bulletin 183. Washington, DC: U.S. Government Printing Office.

Druke, Mary A. 1980. "The Concept of Personhood in Seventeenth and Eighteenth Century Iroquois Ethnopersonality." In *Studies on Iroquoian Culture,* Nancy Bonvillain, ed. Occasional papers in Northeastern Anthropology 6. Rindge, NH: Dept. of Anthropology, Franklin Pierce College, 59-70.

Foster, Michael F. 1974. *From the Earth to Beyond the Sky: An Ethnographic Approach to Four Longhouse Iroquois Speech Events.* National Museum of Man Mercury Series, Canadian Ethnology Service Paper no. 20. Ottawa: National Museums of Canada.

Gibson, John Arthur. 1993. *Concerning the League: The Iroquois Tradition as Dictated in Onondaga,* newly elicited and translated by Hanni Woodbury in collaboration with Reg Henry and Harry Webster on the basis of A. A. Goldenweiser's Manuscript. Memoir 9, Algonquian and Iroquoian Linguistics. Syracuse: Syracuse University Press.

Green, Rayna. 1980. "Native American Women." *Signs: Journal of Women in Culture and Society* 6(2): 248–267.

Hewitt, J. N. B. 1928. *Iroquoian Cosmology, Part 2.* Forty-third annual report of the Bureau of American Ethnology, 1925–1926. Washington, DC: U.S. Government Printing Office.

Hill, Richard. 1987. *Skywalkers: A History of Indian Ironworkers.* Brantford, Ontario: Woodland Indian Cultural Education Centre.

Johansen, Bruce E. 1993. *Life and Death in Mohawk Country.* Golden, CO: North American Press.

Klein, Laura F. and Lillian A. Ackerman. 1995. *Women and Power in Native North America.* Norman: University of Oklahoma Press.

Lame Deer, John (Fire) and Richard Erdoes. 1972. *Lame Deer Seeker of Visions: The Life of a Sioux Medicine Man.* New York: Simon & Schuster.

Landes, Ruth. 1938/1997. *The Ojibwa Woman.* New York: Columbia University Press; reprinted by University of Nebraska Press.

Mann, Barbara and Jerry Fields. 1997. "Dating the Iroquois League." *American Indian Culture and Research Journal* 21(2): 105–149.

Medicine, Bea. 1993. "North American Indigenous Women and Cultural Domi-
    nation." *American Indian Culture and Research Journal* 17(3): 121–130.
Morgan, Lewis Henry. 1854/1901. *League of the Ho-de-no-sau-nee or Iroquois*. New
    York: Dodd.
Ms. 1991. "Mohawk Women, Kanienkehaka." *Ms*. (May/June): 18–21.
Perdue, Theda. 1998. *Cherokee Women: Gender and Culture Change, 1700–1835*.
    Lincoln: University of Nebraska Press.
Porter, Thomas (Sakokwenienkwas). n.d. *Clanology: Clan System of the Iroquois*.
    Cornwall, Ontario: North American Indian Traveling College.
Powers, Marla N. 1986. *Oglala Women: Myth, Ritual, and Reality*. Chicago: Uni-
    versity of Chicago Press.
Reichard, Gladys A. 1934. *Spider Woman: A Story of Navajo Weavers and Chanters*.
    New York: Macmillan.
Shenandoah, Audrey. 1991. "Everything Has to Be in Balance." In *Knowledge of
    the Elders: The Iroquois Condolence Cane Tradition*, José Barreiro and Carol
    Cornelius, eds. Ithaca, NY: Northeast Indian Quarterly.
Shoemaker, Nancy, ed. 1995. *Negotiators of Change: Historical Perspectives on Na-
    tive American Women*. New York: Routledge.
Spittal, W. G., ed. 1990. *Iroquois Women: An Anthology*. Ohsweken, Ontario: Iro-
    qrafts.
Stockel, H. Henrietta. 1990. *Women of the Apache Nation: Voices of Truth*. Reno:
    University of Nevada Press.
Woodsum, Joanne. 1995. "Gender and Sexuality in Native American Societies:
    A Bibliography." *American Indian Quarterly* 19(4): 527–554.
York, Geoffrey and Loreen Pindera. 1992. *People of the Pines: The Warriors and the
    Legacy of Oka*. Toronto: Little, Brown, Canada.

Conclusion

Daniel C. Maguire

T HIS VOLUME IS A PRODUCT of the Religious Consultation on Population, Reproductive Health, and Ethics. With significant help from
the Ford, John D. and Catherine T. MacArthur, and David and
Lucile Packard foundations we have been able to assemble an international collegium of scholars from the world's religions and to bring
them together to work on projects such as this one on sexism and on
men's obligations to women.

The Consultation has a bias and is up-front about it. All our scholars are recruited from the feminist, progressive zones of their religions.
All are aware of the downside and debits of their traditions regarding
our issues. As one of our Buddhist scholars, Rita M. Gross, asks of her
religion: "Can a religion founded by a man who abandoned his wife
and newborn infant because he was convinced that they were an obstacle to his salvation possibly serve women's interests and needs?" (Gross
1991, 65). Similar indictments are in order for all the religions. The male-
dominated religions of the world are reservoirs of sexism. Although acknowledging this wholeheartedly, our scholars remain convinced that
there are renewable moral energies in those same traditions awaiting
creative application to the human alienations and terracidal threats that
confront us. The results of this shared vision and shared passion are remarkable. Though we inhabit diverse parts of the globe and different
symbol systems of religious imagination, our common quest has
bonded us into an *universitas* of scholars.

Some universities have been able to achieve a common framework
for study in a particular area and to arrive at an agreed upon vision of
the field. Maybe Tubingen could once lay claim to such a shared and distinctive vision in theology. Most schools do not. There is no Harvard
school of thought in religious studies, nor a Princeton school, nor a Marquette or Temple "school" of religious thought. But there is a budding
school called "The Religious Consultation on Population, Reproductive
Health, and Ethics." This volume illustrates it, as will all of our others.

The seven themes that bind the Consultation scholars are these:

1. In the manner of realistic psychotherapy, we take full account of the negatives in these largely male-ruled religious traditions, but then we move on to stress the *positives* as a cure. We give some warranty to the Buddhist saying that all belief systems are illnesses waiting to be cured, but none of them is pure pathology. We ground our creative work in the foundational texts and authorities of the religions, fully aware of the fact that religions contain, in orthodox Jewish theologian Pinchas Lapide's term, *theopolitical dynamite*. We set out to use that dynamite to bring down the patriarchal walls.

2. Our definition of religion is *normative*. It is not the *descriptive* definition used in the social sciences that must treat as religion whatever phenomenon calls itself "religion." *We see religion as a positive response to the sacred that issues into advocacy and commitment.* The religions out of which we speak, some theistic, some not, are struggling classics of the art of cherishing. None is a perfect success story and there is much to be rejected in each. Yet beneath the inevitable debris that accumulates in any march through the turbulence that we call "history," there flows an heroic reenvisioning of our affective and moral capacities. This positive and normative definition of religion undergirds our assumption that the moral experiences of all religions are complementary and shareable. Each of them touches down to the deepest predicates of human existence. This allows many religions, staying faithful to their own discoveries, to address single problems in fruitful collaboration.

   We see religion as an appreciative, enhancing response to the preciousness of life, a preciousness that merits our supreme linguistic encomium *sacred*. This separates religion from the weird explosions of superstition and magic that fill our human history, which may and should be studied under a different rubric.

   We resist the shallow sophistication of much of Western culture that does not see religion as a culture shaper. We insist that religions are powerful. John Henry Cardinal Newman said that people will die for a dogma who will not stir for a conclusion. In parallel insights, Camus noted that people will not die for scientific truth, and the poet Alexander Pope, reaching to the nether side of religion, said that the worst of madmen is a saint gone mad. All three gentlemen are onto the same point. The tincture of the sacred yields power and effaces limit, for good or for ill.

   Realistic social analysis should recognize that two-thirds of the world's peoples affiliate with some religion and the other third is affected by the gravitational pull generated by these symbol-filled cultural powerhouses. We admit that. And we call that admission "realism."

3. Our common assumption in the Consultation "school" is that the religions we study all have elements of a rich sense of *justice* that becomes our normative rubric for assessing, embracing, or dismissing ideas and practices that have arisen in the traditions. This justice stress militates against individualism and libertarianism, with the weakened sense of the common good and of human rights that these views entail. Thanks largely to the persistence of the United Nations, the concept of *human rights* (necessarily grounded in some theory of justice) has become the key category in the vernacular of international ethics.

4. In all of our projects, the *empowerment of women* is seen as the key to progress on every one of our issues. This moves on to an identification with all of the disempowered, all of the *anawim*, including indigenous peoples, gays and lesbians, economic and environmental refugees, and the environment itself.

5. In all of our projects we recognize the *market economy* not just as a pattern of global business, but as a *surrogate religion* generating visions and value judgments and permeating and transforming cultures throughout the world in ways that are usually noxious.

6. In all of our projects, we have a distinctly Buddhist stress on *interdependency*, and not just human interdependency. We and the stars and all of nature are kith and kin. When the sun completes its parental mission and this orderly moment in the history of the universe unfolds and dissolves back into chaos, we will return to the dust from which we proceeded. To transpose the Catholic Ash Wednesday mantra: stardust we are and unto stardust we shall return. We, being many, are one body more than Paul the Christian Apostle could imagine.

7. Finally, this budding school holds that critical theory requires *conversation* in the deep Latin sense of *conversari*, literally *being with*. (The English "conversation" could mean nothing more than a chat.) Conversation in this epistemological usage is extended social intercourse where emotion and affect can anchor our logical flights of fancy, where disagreements can function like lightning to cleanse the air. All value judgments are rooted in affectivity. Moral and religious intelligence is born in the heart. The heart keeps us in touch with flesh and dirt where all value is ultimately rooted. Solitary, isolated scholarship is tendentially disembodied and *disaffected* and more liable to fall under Sartre's indicting insight that the worst of evils is to treat as abstract that which is concrete.

The scholars-authors of this volume were able to physically meet three times for hardworking and enjoyable sessions. We broke bread together and some of us shared the fruit of the vine. The results were something that e-mail or post could not of themselves produce. *Presence* admits of degrees, as does *meeting*. We are present to those in the airport waiting with us at the gate, but only dimly so. We are more present when we take off. But presence and togetherness take a qualitative leap when the pilot announces mechanical trouble and a need to return to the airport. When the plane lands safely after a struggle, there are no strangers aboard. Affectivity, shared hope, and needs that are *felt* are the sinews of community.

Scholars who meet as we meet become more present, more trustfully candid with each session and in each of our projects, as in this one, we found parting to be filled with "sweet sorrow." We will not wholly part, however, since we will continue as a permanent Task Force of the Religious Consultation on Population, Reproductive Health, and Ethics. We will seek out opportunities to speak in international contexts when the voices of men sensitive to gender justice claims are needed in other conversations.

These are the moral insights that bind us and give us a spirit of collegiality that few find in university departments.

As this project was aborning, our first concern was about having only men as the authors. We did build in critique from outstanding women feminist scholars but we decided on the male authorship for multiple reasons. For one thing, as John Raines noted, the sexism that assaults women is at root a male problem. Men should stop and think about it. Groups of whites talking about racism among themselves while open to critique by persons of color is not unuseful. Self-criticism by separate groupings of men and women, whites and blacks, homosexuals and heterosexuals is healthy. To sit together and compare the way in which sexism has advantaged men and oppressed women in the various traditions was for us illuminating and medicinal. Similar advantage could be found by other groups meeting by themselves. This is not the only way, but it is not an unprofitable process and it can be followed by and coupled with other processes.

Also, our approach to the evil of sexism is not filed under *Internecine*. As the distinguished scholar of Hinduism Katherine K. Young says: "there is one striking omission in most Western feminist discussions of religion. There is virtually no opening to men. . . . Whether deliberately or not, some feminists have demonized men as a class and most in the name of solidarity have not launched an ethical critique in the public square against this" (Sharma and Young 1999, 298–300). Gynocentrism is no better than androcentrism. *Macha* is not superior to *macho*. The goal is dialogue, not conquest. Male anatomy, anymore than female anatomy, is not destiny. Professor Young proposes Gandhi as the model for intergender conversation. "Far from seeing the British as moral cretins, Gandhi respected them as people with moral sensibilities that would eventually support Indian independence. And he was correct" (303). Maybe we men working together—and not at all shrinking from women's critique—wanted to show that men could be something more than moral cretins. Maybe we somewhat succeeded. Let the reader judge.

REFERENCES

Gross, Rita M. 1991. "Buddhism After Patriarchy?", in *After Patriarchy: Feminist Transformations of the World Religions*, Paula Cooey, William Eakin, and Jay McDaniel, eds. Maryknoll, NY: Orbis Books.

Sharma, Arvind and Katherine K. Young, eds. 1999. *Feminism and World Religions*, Albany: State University of New York Press.

Contributors

DR. MARVIN M. ELLISON teaches at Bangor Theological Seminary in Portland, Maine. He is a prominent Christian ethicist and an ordained minister in the Presbyterian Church (USA). He is the author of *Erotic Justice: A Liberating Ethics of Sexuality*.

ASGHAR ALI ENGINEER is one of the leading Muslim liberation theologians who heads a center for Islamic studies in Bombay, India. He is a recipient of the prestigious Indian New Leaders Award for Communal Harmony and has written *Islam Women and Modernity*.

FARID ESACK is a distinguished Muslim scholar and Commissioner for Gender Equality in the government of South Africa. He has written *Qur'an, Liberation and Pluralism* and is an expert on Qur'anic hermeneutics.

DR. ZE'EV W. FALK died in Israel after finishing his contribution to this book and the volume is dedicated to his blessed memory. His voluminous publications include "Gender Differentiation and Spirituality" and "Non-Judicial Conflict Resolution."

DANIEL C. MAGUIRE is a professor of religious ethics at Marquette University and is president of the Religious Consultation on Population, Reproductive Health, and Ethics, which sponsored this volume. His books include *The Moral Core of Judaism and Christianity* and *Ethics for a Small Planet*, coauthored with Larry Rasmussen.

MUTOMBO NKULU-N'SENGHA, a citizen of the Republic of the Congo, is completing his doctoral studies at Temple University and has already won a reputation as an expert on native African religions.

TAVIVAT PUNTARIGVIVAT teaches in the graduate program of Comparative Religion at Mhidol University in Thailand. His expertise is in Buddhism. His books include *The Way of Mahayana Buddhism* and *Sages and Buddhadasa Bhikka*.

JOHN C. RAINES teaches in the Department of Religion at Temple University and has done extensive work on interreligious dialogue. He has written *Islam and the West: A Coming Clash of Civilizations* and *Modern Work and Human Meaning*.

DR. ANANTANAND RAMBACHAN, a native of India, teaches at St. Olaf's College in Minnesota. His writings include *Accomplished the Accomplished: The Vedas as a Source of Valid Knowledge in Shankara* and *The Limits of Scripture*. Dr. Rambachan has lectured extensively and has done a television series on Hinduism for the BBC.

CHRISTOPHER RONWANIÈN:TE JOCKS is a member of the Society for the Study of Native American Religious Traditions. His writings include: "Spirituality for Sale: Sacred Knowledge in the Consumer Age" and "Defending Their People and Their Land: Native American Men and the Construction of Masculinity."

DR. GERARD S. SLOYAN is a Catholic priest, who chaired the Religious Studies Department at the Catholic University of America and at Temple University. His many publications include *The Crucifixion of Jesus: History, Myth, Faith* and *Jesus on Trial: Development of the Passion Narratives*.

LIU XIAOGAN, an expert in Taoism, has published extensively in Chinese, Korean, and in English. His English publications include *Classifying the Chuang Tzu Chapters* and *Our Religions*, which he coauthored with Arvind Sharma.

Index